THE

C

PROGRAMMING LANGUAGE

Second Edition

THE

C

PROGRAMMING
LANGUAGE

Second Edition

Brian W. Kernighan • **Dennis M. Ritchie**

AT&T Bell Laboratories
Murray Hill, New Jersey

Prentice Hall PTR, Englewood Cliffs, New Jersey 07632

Library of Congress Cataloging-in-Publication Data

```
Kernighan, Brian W.
   The C programming language.

   Includes index.
   1. C (Computer program language)  I. Ritchie,
Dennis M.           II. Title.
QA76.73.C15K47  1988      005.13'3          88-5934
ISBN 0-13-110370-9
ISBN 0-13-110362-8 (pbk.)
```

© Published by Prentice Hall P T R
Prentice-Hall, Inc.
A Simon & Schuster Company
Englewood Cliffs, New Jersey 07632

UNIX is a registered trademark of AT&T.

This book was typeset (pic¦tbl¦eqn¦troff -ms) in Times Roman and Courier by the authors, using an Autologic APS-5 phototypesetter and a DEC VAX 8550 running the 9th Edition of the UNIX® operating system.

Prentice Hall Software Series
Brian Kernighan, Advisor

Printed in the United States of America

20 19 18 17 16 15 14 13 12

ISBN 0-13-110362-8 {PBK}
ISBN 0-13-110370-9

Prentice-Hall International (UK) Limited, *London*
Prentice-Hall of Australia Pty. Limited, *Sydney*
Prentice-Hall Canada Inc., *Toronto*
Prentice-Hall Hispanoamericana, S.A., *Mexico*
Prentice-Hall of India Private Limited, *New Delhi*
Prentice-Hall of Japan, Inc., *Tokyo*
Simon & Schuster Asia Pte. Ltd., *Singapore*
Editora Prentice-Hall do Brasil, Ltda., *Rio de Janeiro*

Contents

Preface

The computing world has undergone a revolution since the publication of *The C Programming Language* in 1978. Big computers are much bigger, and personal computers have capabilities that rival the mainframes of a decade ago. During this time, C has changed too, although only modestly, and it has spread far beyond its origins as the language of the UNIX operating system.

The growing popularity of C, the changes in the language over the years, and the creation of compilers by groups not involved in its design, combined to demonstrate a need for a more precise and more contemporary definition of the language than the first edition of this book provided. In 1983, the American National Standards Institute (ANSI) established a committee whose goal was to produce "an unambiguous and machine-independent definition of the language C," while still retaining its spirit. The result is the ANSI standard for C.

The standard formalizes constructions that were hinted at but not described in the first edition, particularly structure assignment and enumerations. It provides a new form of function declaration that permits cross-checking of definition with use. It specifies a standard library, with an extensive set of functions for performing input and output, memory management, string manipulation, and similar tasks. It makes precise the behavior of features that were not spelled out in the original definition, and at the same time states explicitly which aspects of the language remain machine-dependent.

This second edition of *The C Programming Language* describes C as defined by the ANSI standard. Although we have noted the places where the language has evolved, we have chosen to write exclusively in the new form. For the most part, this makes no significant difference; the most visible change is the new form of function declaration and definition. Modern compilers already support most features of the standard.

We have tried to retain the brevity of the first edition. C is not a big language, and it is not well served by a big book. We have improved the exposition of critical features, such as pointers, that are central to C programming. We have refined the original examples, and have added new examples in several chapters. For instance, the treatment of complicated declarations is augmented by programs that convert declarations into words and vice versa. As before, all examples have been tested directly from the text, which is in machine-readable form.

Appendix A, the reference manual, is not the standard, but our attempt to convey the essentials of the standard in a smaller space. It is meant for easy comprehension by programmers, but not as a definition for compiler writers— that role properly belongs to the standard itself. Appendix B is a summary of the facilities of the standard library. It too is meant for reference by programmers, not implementers. Appendix C is a concise summary of the changes from the original version.

As we said in the preface to the first edition, C "wears well as one's experience with it grows." With a decade more experience, we still feel that way. We hope that this book will help you to learn C and to use it well.

We are deeply indebted to friends who helped us to produce this second edition. Jon Bentley, Doug Gwyn, Doug McIlroy, Peter Nelson, and Rob Pike gave us perceptive comments on almost every page of draft manuscripts. We are grateful for careful reading by Al Aho, Dennis Allison, Joe Campbell, G. R. Emlin, Karen Fortgang, Allen Holub, Andrew Hume, Dave Kristol, John Linderman, Dave Prosser, Gene Spafford, and Chris Van Wyk. We also received helpful suggestions from Bill Cheswick, Mark Kernighan, Andy Koenig, Robin Lake, Tom London, Jim Reeds, Clovis Tondo, and Peter Weinberger. Dave Prosser answered many detailed questions about the ANSI standard. We used Bjarne Stroustrup's C++ translator extensively for local testing of our programs, and Dave Kristol provided us with an ANSI C compiler for final testing. Rich Drechsler helped greatly with typesetting.

Our sincere thanks to all.

Brian W. Kernighan
Dennis M. Ritchie

Preface to the First Edition

C is a general-purpose programming language which features economy of expression, modern control flow and data structures, and a rich set of operators. C is not a "very high level" language, nor a "big" one, and is not specialized to any particular area of application. But its absence of restrictions and its generality make it more convenient and effective for many tasks than supposedly more powerful languages.

C was originally designed for and implemented on the UNIX operating system on the DEC PDP-11, by Dennis Ritchie. The operating system, the C compiler, and essentially all UNIX applications programs (including all of the software used to prepare this book) are written in C. Production compilers also exist for several other machines, including the IBM System/370, the Honeywell 6000, and the Interdata 8/32. C is not tied to any particular hardware or system, however, and it is easy to write programs that will run without change on any machine that supports C.

This book is meant to help the reader learn how to program in C. It contains a tutorial introduction to get new users started as soon as possible, separate chapters on each major feature, and a reference manual. Most of the treatment is based on reading, writing and revising examples, rather than on mere statements of rules. For the most part, the examples are complete, real programs, rather than isolated fragments. All examples have been tested directly from the text, which is in machine-readable form. Besides showing how to make effective use of the language, we have also tried where possible to illustrate useful algorithms and principles of good style and sound design.

The book is not an introductory programming manual; it assumes some familiarity with basic programming concepts like variables, assignment statements, loops, and functions. Nonetheless, a novice programmer should be able to read along and pick up the language, although access to a more knowledgeable colleague will help.

In our experience, C has proven to be a pleasant, expressive, and versatile language for a wide variety of programs. It is easy to learn, and it wears well as one's experience with it grows. We hope that this book will help you to use it well.

The thoughtful criticisms and suggestions of many friends and colleagues have added greatly to this book and to our pleasure in writing it. In particular, Mike Bianchi, Jim Blue, Stu Feldman, Doug McIlroy, Bill Roome, Bob Rosin, and Larry Rosler all read multiple versions with care. We are also indebted to Al Aho, Steve Bourne, Dan Dvorak, Chuck Haley, Debbie Haley, Marion Harris, Rick Holt, Steve Johnson, John Mashey, Bob Mitze, Ralph Muha, Peter Nelson, Elliot Pinson, Bill Plauger, Jerry Spivack, Ken Thompson, and Peter Weinberger for helpful comments at various stages, and to Mike Lesk and Joe Ossanna for invaluable assistance with typesetting.

Brian W. Kernighan
Dennis M. Ritchie

Introduction

C is a general-purpose programming language. It has been closely associated with the UNIX system where it was developed, since both the system and most of the programs that run on it are written in C. The language, however, is not tied to any one operating system or machine; and although it has been called a "system programming language" because it is useful for writing compilers and operating systems, it has been used equally well to write major programs in many different domains.

Many of the important ideas of C stem from the language BCPL, developed by Martin Richards. The influence of BCPL on C proceeded indirectly through the language B, which was written by Ken Thompson in 1970 for the first UNIX system on the DEC PDP-7.

BCPL and B are "typeless" languages. By contrast, C provides a variety of data types. The fundamental types are characters, and integers and floating-point numbers of several sizes. In addition, there is a hierarchy of derived data types created with pointers, arrays, structures, and unions. Expressions are formed from operators and operands; any expression, including an assignment or a function call, can be a statement. Pointers provide for machine-independent address arithmetic.

C provides the fundamental control-flow constructions required for well-structured programs: statement grouping, decision making (if-else), selecting one of a set of possible cases (switch), looping with the termination test at the top (while, for) or at the bottom (do), and early loop exit (break).

Functions may return values of basic types, structures, unions, or pointers. Any function may be called recursively. Local variables are typically "automatic," or created anew with each invocation. Function definitions may not be nested but variables may be declared in a block-structured fashion. The functions of a C program may exist in separate source files that are compiled separately. Variables may be internal to a function, external but known only within a single source file, or visible to the entire program.

A preprocessing step performs macro substitution on program text, inclusion of other source files, and conditional compilation.

C is a relatively "low level" language. This characterization is not

1

pejorative; it simply means that C deals with the same sort of objects that most computers do, namely characters, numbers, and addresses. These may be combined and moved about with the arithmetic and logical operators implemented by real machines.

C provides no operations to deal directly with composite objects such as character strings, sets, lists, or arrays. There are no operations that manipulate an entire array or string, although structures may be copied as a unit. The language does not define any storage allocation facility other than static definition and the stack discipline provided by the local variables of functions; there is no heap or garbage collection. Finally, C itself provides no input/output facilities; there are no READ or WRITE statements, and no built-in file access methods. All of these higher-level mechanisms must be provided by explicitly-called functions. Most C implementations have included a reasonably standard collection of such functions.

Similarly, C offers only straightforward, single-thread control flow: tests, loops, grouping, and subprograms, but not multiprogramming, parallel operations, synchronization, or coroutines.

Although the absence of some of these features may seem like a grave deficiency ("You mean I have to call a function to compare two character strings?"), keeping the language down to modest size has real benefits. Since C is relatively small, it can be described in a small space, and learned quickly. A programmer can reasonably expect to know and understand and indeed regularly use the entire language.

For many years, the definition of C was the reference manual in the first edition of *The C Programming Language*. In 1983, the American National Standards Institute (ANSI) established a committee to provide a modern, comprehensive definition of C. The resulting definition, the ANSI standard, or "ANSI C," was completed late in 1988. Most of the features of the standard are already supported by modern compilers.

The standard is based on the original reference manual. The language is relatively little changed; one of the goals of the standard was to make sure that most existing programs would remain valid, or, failing that, that compilers could produce warnings of new behavior.

For most programmers, the most important change is a new syntax for declaring and defining functions. A function declaration can now include a description of the arguments of the function; the definition syntax changes to match. This extra information makes it much easier for compilers to detect errors caused by mismatched arguments; in our experience, it is a very useful addition to the language.

There are other small-scale language changes. Structure assignment and enumerations, which had been widely available, are now officially part of the language. Floating-point computations may now be done in single precision. The properties of arithmetic, especially for unsigned types, are clarified. The preprocessor is more elaborate. Most of these changes will have only minor effects on most programmers.

A second significant contribution of the standard is the definition of a library to accompany C. It specifies functions for accessing the operating system (for instance, to read and write files), formatted input and output, memory allocation, string manipulation, and the like. A collection of standard headers provides uniform access to declarations of functions and data types. Programs that use this library to interact with a host system are assured of compatible behavior. Most of the library is closely modeled on the "standard I/O library" of the UNIX system. This library was described in the first edition, and has been widely used on other systems as well. Again, most programmers will not see much change.

Because the data types and control structures provided by C are supported directly by most computers, the run-time library required to implement self-contained programs is tiny. The standard library functions are only called explicitly, so they can be avoided if they are not needed. Most can be written in C, and except for the operating system details they conceal, are themselves portable.

Although C matches the capabilities of many computers, it is independent of any particular machine architecture. With a little care it is easy to write portable programs, that is, programs that can be run without change on a variety of hardware. The standard makes portability issues explicit, and prescribes a set of constants that characterize the machine on which the program is run.

C is not a strongly-typed language, but as it has evolved, its type-checking has been strengthened. The original definition of C frowned on, but permitted, the interchange of pointers and integers; this has long since been eliminated, and the standard now requires the proper declarations and explicit conversions that had already been enforced by good compilers. The new function declarations are another step in this direction. Compilers will warn of most type errors, and there is no automatic conversion of incompatible data types. Nevertheless, C retains the basic philosophy that programmers know what they are doing; it only requires that they state their intentions explicitly.

C, like any other language, has its blemishes. Some of the operators have the wrong precedence; some parts of the syntax could be better. Nonetheless, C has proven to be an extremely effective and expressive language for a wide variety of programming applications.

The book is organized as follows. Chapter 1 is a tutorial on the central part of C. The purpose is to get the reader started as quickly as possible, since we believe strongly that the way to learn a new language is to write programs in it. The tutorial does assume a working knowledge of the basic elements of programming; there is no explanation of computers, of compilation, nor of the meaning of an expression like n=n+1. Although we have tried where possible to show useful programming techniques, the book is not intended to be a reference work on data structures and algorithms; when forced to make a choice, we have concentrated on the language.

Chapters 2 through 6 discuss various aspects of C in more detail, and rather more formally, than does Chapter 1, although the emphasis is still on examples of complete programs, rather than isolated fragments. Chapter 2 deals with the basic data types, operators and expressions. Chapter 3 treats control flow: `if-else`, `switch`, `while`, `for`, etc. Chapter 4 covers functions and program structure—external variables, scope rules, multiple source files, and so on—and also touches on the preprocessor. Chapter 5 discusses pointers and address arithmetic. Chapter 6 covers structures and unions.

Chapter 7 describes the standard library, which provides a common interface to the operating system. This library is defined by the ANSI standard and is meant to be supported on all machines that support C, so programs that use it for input, output, and other operating system access can be moved from one system to another without change.

Chapter 8 describes an interface between C programs and the UNIX operating system, concentrating on input/output, the file system, and storage allocation. Although some of this chapter is specific to UNIX systems, programmers who use other systems should still find useful material here, including some insight into how one version of the standard library is implemented, and suggestions on portability.

Appendix A contains a language reference manual. The official statement of the syntax and semantics of C is the ANSI standard itself. That document, however, is intended foremost for compiler writers. The reference manual here conveys the definition of the language more concisely and without the same legalistic style. Appendix B is a summary of the standard library, again for users rather than implementers. Appendix C is a short summary of changes from the original language. In cases of doubt, however, the standard and one's own compiler remain the final authorities on the language.

CHAPTER 1: **A Tutorial Introduction**

Let us begin with a quick introduction to C. Our aim is to show the essential elements of the language in real programs, but without getting bogged down in details, rules, and exceptions. At this point, we are not trying to be complete or even precise (save that the examples are meant to be correct). We want to get you as quickly as possible to the point where you can write useful programs, and to do that we have to concentrate on the basics: variables and constants, arithmetic, control flow, functions, and the rudiments of input and output. We are intentionally leaving out of this chapter features of C that are important for writing bigger programs. These include pointers, structures, most of C's rich set of operators, several control-flow statements, and the standard library.

This approach has its drawbacks. Most notable is that the complete story on any particular language feature is not found here, and the tutorial, by being brief, may also be misleading. And because the examples do not use the full power of C, they are not as concise and elegant as they might be. We have tried to minimize these effects, but be warned. Another drawback is that later chapters will necessarily repeat some of this chapter. We hope that the repetition will help you more than it annoys.

In any case, experienced programmers should be able to extrapolate from the material in this chapter to their own programming needs. Beginners should supplement it by writing small, similar programs of their own. Both groups can use it as a framework on which to hang the more detailed descriptions that begin in Chapter 2.

1.1 Getting Started

The only way to learn a new programming language is by writing programs in it. The first program to write is the same for all languages:

Print the words
```
        hello, world
```

This is the big hurdle; to leap over it you have to be able to create the program text somewhere, compile it successfully, load it, run it, and find out where your output went. With these mechanical details mastered, everything else is comparatively easy.

In C, the program to print "hello, world" is

```
#include <stdio.h>

main()
{
    printf("hello, world\n");
}
```

Just how to run this program depends on the system you are using. As a specific example, on the UNIX operating system you must create the program in a file whose name ends in ".c", such as hello.c, then compile it with the command

```
cc hello.c
```

If you haven't botched anything, such as omitting a character or misspelling something, the compilation will proceed silently, and make an executable file called a.out. If you run a.out by typing the command

```
a.out
```

it will print

```
hello, world
```

On other systems, the rules will be different; check with a local expert.

Now for some explanations about the program itself. A C program, whatever its size, consists of *functions* and *variables*. A function contains *statements* that specify the computing operations to be done, and variables store values used during the computation. C functions are like the subroutines and functions of Fortran or the procedures and functions of Pascal. Our example is a function named main. Normally you are at liberty to give functions whatever names you like, but "main" is special—your program begins executing at the beginning of main. This means that every program must have a main somewhere.

main will usually call other functions to help perform its job, some that you wrote, and others from libraries that are provided for you. The first line of the program,

```
#include <stdio.h>
```

tells the compiler to include information about the standard input/output library; this line appears at the beginning of many C source files. The standard library is described in Chapter 7 and Appendix B.

One method of communicating data between functions is for the calling function to provide a list of values, called *arguments*, to the function it calls. The parentheses after the function name surround the argument list. In this

```
#include <stdio.h>              include information about standard library

main()                          define a function named main
                                that receives no argument values
{                               statements of main are enclosed in braces
    printf("hello, world\n");   main calls library function printf
                                to print this sequence of characters;
}                               \n represents the newline character
```

The first C program.

example, `main` is defined to be a function that expects no arguments, which is indicated by the empty list ( ).

The statements of a function are enclosed in braces { }. The function `main` contains only one statement,

```
    printf("hello, world\n");
```

A function is called by naming it, followed by a parenthesized list of arguments, so this calls the function `printf` with the argument `"hello, world\n"`. `printf` is a library function that prints output, in this case the string of characters between the quotes.

A sequence of characters in double quotes, like `"hello, world\n"`, is called a *character string* or *string constant*. For the moment our only use of character strings will be as arguments for `printf` and other functions.

The sequence `\n` in the string is C notation for the *newline character*, which when printed advances the output to the left margin on the next line. If you leave out the `\n` (a worthwhile experiment), you will find that there is no line advance after the output is printed. You must use `\n` to include a newline character in the `printf` argument; if you try something like

```
    printf("hello, world
    ");
```

the C compiler will produce an error message.

`printf` never supplies a newline automatically, so several calls may be used to build up an output line in stages. Our first program could just as well have been written

```
#include <stdio.h>

main()
{
    printf("hello, ");
    printf("world");
    printf("\n");
}
```

to produce identical output.

Notice that \n represents only a single character. An *escape sequence* like \n provides a general and extensible mechanism for representing hard-to-type or invisible characters. Among the others that C provides are \t for tab, \b for backspace, \" for the double quote, and \\ for the backslash itself. There is a complete list in Section 2.3.

Exercise 1-1. Run the "hello, world" program on your system. Experiment with leaving out parts of the program, to see what error messages you get. □

Exercise 1-2. Experiment to find out what happens when printf's argument string contains \c, where c is some character not listed above. □

1.2 Variables and Arithmetic Expressions

The next program uses the formula $°C = (5/9)(°F-32)$ to print the following table of Fahrenheit temperatures and their centigrade or Celsius equivalents:

```
  0   -17
 20   -6
 40    4
 60   15
 80   26
100   37
120   48
140   60
160   71
180   82
200   93
220  104
240  115
260  126
280  137
300  148
```

The program itself still consists of the definition of a single function named main. It is longer than the one that printed "hello, world", but not complicated. It introduces several new ideas, including comments, declarations, variables, arithmetic expressions, loops, and formatted output.

```
#include <stdio.h>

/* print Fahrenheit-Celsius table
   for fahr = 0, 20, ..., 300 */
main()
{
    int fahr, celsius;
    int lower, upper, step;

    lower = 0;      /* lower limit of temperature table */
    upper = 300;    /* upper limit */
    step = 20;      /* step size */

    fahr = lower;
    while (fahr <= upper) {
        celsius = 5 * (fahr-32) / 9;
        printf("%d\t%d\n", fahr, celsius);
        fahr = fahr + step;
    }
}
```

The two lines

```
/* print Fahrenheit-Celsius table
   for fahr = 0, 20, ..., 300 */
```

are a *comment*, which in this case explains briefly what the program does. Any characters between /* and */ are ignored by the compiler; they may be used freely to make a program easier to understand. Comments may appear anywhere a blank or tab or newline can.

In C, all variables must be declared before they are used, usually at the beginning of the function before any executable statements. A *declaration* announces the properties of variables; it consists of a type name and a list of variables, such as

```
int fahr, celsius;
int lower, upper, step;
```

The type `int` means that the variables listed are integers, by contrast with `float`, which means floating point, i.e., numbers that may have a fractional part. The range of both `int` and `float` depends on the machine you are using; 16-bit `int`s, which lie between -32768 and $+32767$, are common, as are 32-bit `int`s. A `float` number is typically a 32-bit quantity, with at least six significant digits and magnitude generally between about 10^{-38} and 10^{+38}.

C provides several other basic data types besides `int` and `float`, including:

`char`	character—a single byte
`short`	short integer
`long`	long integer
`double`	double-precision floating point

The sizes of these objects are also machine-dependent. There are also *arrays*, *structures* and *unions* of these basic types, *pointers* to them, and *functions* that return them, all of which we will meet in due course.

Computation in the temperature conversion program begins with the *assignment statements*

```
lower = 0;
upper = 300;
step = 20;
fahr = lower;
```

which set the variables to their initial values. Individual statements are terminated by semicolons.

Each line of the table is computed the same way, so we use a loop that repeats once per output line; this is the purpose of the `while` loop

```
while (fahr <= upper) {
    ...
}
```

The `while` loop operates as follows: The condition in parentheses is tested. If it is true (`fahr` is less than or equal to `upper`), the body of the loop (the three statements enclosed in braces) is executed. Then the condition is re-tested, and if true, the body is executed again. When the test becomes false (`fahr` exceeds `upper`) the loop ends, and execution continues at the statement that follows the loop. There are no further statements in this program, so it terminates.

The body of a `while` can be one or more statements enclosed in braces, as in the temperature converter, or a single statement without braces, as in

```
while (i < j)
    i = 2 * i;
```

In either case, we will always indent the statements controlled by the `while` by one tab stop (which we have shown as four spaces) so you can see at a glance which statements are inside the loop. The indentation emphasizes the logical structure of the program. Although C compilers do not care about how a program looks, proper indentation and spacing are critical in making programs easy for people to read. We recommend writing only one statement per line, and using blanks around operators to clarify grouping. The position of braces is less important, although people hold passionate beliefs. We have chosen one of several popular styles. Pick a style that suits you, then use it consistently.

Most of the work gets done in the body of the loop. The Celsius temperature is computed and assigned to the variable `celsius` by the statement

```
celsius = 5 * (fahr-32) / 9;
```

The reason for multiplying by 5 and then dividing by 9 instead of just multiplying by 5/9 is that in C, as in many other languages, integer division *truncates*: any fractional part is discarded. Since 5 and 9 are integers, 5/9 would be truncated to zero and so all the Celsius temperatures would be reported as zero.

This example also shows a bit more of how `printf` works. `printf` is a general-purpose output formatting function, which we will describe in detail in Chapter 7. Its first argument is a string of characters to be printed, with each % indicating where one of the other (second, third, ...) arguments is to be substituted, and in what form it is to be printed. For instance, %d specifies an integer argument, so the statement

```
printf("%d\t%d\n", fahr, celsius);
```

causes the values of the two integers `fahr` and `celsius` to be printed, with a tab (\t) between them.

Each % construction in the first argument of `printf` is paired with the corresponding second argument, third argument, etc.; they must match up properly by number and type, or you'll get wrong answers.

By the way, `printf` is not part of the C language; there is no input or output defined in C itself. `printf` is just a useful function from the standard library of functions that are normally accessible to C programs. The behavior of `printf` is defined in the ANSI standard, however, so its properties should be the same with any compiler and library that conforms to the standard.

In order to concentrate on C itself, we won't talk much about input and output until Chapter 7. In particular, we will defer formatted input until then. If you have to input numbers, read the discussion of the function `scanf` in Section 7.4. `scanf` is like `printf`, except that it reads input instead of writing output.

There are a couple of problems with the temperature conversion program. The simpler one is that the output isn't very pretty because the numbers are not right-justified. That's easy to fix; if we augment each %d in the `printf` statement with a width, the numbers printed will be right-justified in their fields. For instance, we might say

```
printf("%3d %6d\n", fahr, celsius);
```

to print the first number of each line in a field three digits wide, and the second in a field six digits wide, like this:

```
  0      -17
 20       -6
 40        4
 60       15
 80       26
100       37
 ...
```

The more serious problem is that because we have used integer arithmetic, the Celsius temperatures are not very accurate; for instance, 0°F is actually about −17.8°C, not −17. To get more accurate answers, we should use floating-point arithmetic instead of integer. This requires some changes in the program. Here is a second version:

```
#include <stdio.h>

/* print Fahrenheit-Celsius table
    for fahr = 0, 20, ..., 300; floating-point version */
main()
{
    float fahr, celsius;
    int lower, upper, step;

    lower = 0;      /* lower limit of temperature table */
    upper = 300;    /* upper limit */
    step = 20;      /* step size */

    fahr = lower;
    while (fahr <= upper) {
        celsius = (5.0/9.0) * (fahr-32.0);
        printf("%3.0f %6.1f\n", fahr, celsius);
        fahr = fahr + step;
    }
}
```

This is much the same as before, except that `fahr` and `celsius` are declared to be `float`, and the formula for conversion is written in a more natural way. We were unable to use 5/9 in the previous version because integer division would truncate it to zero. A decimal point in a constant indicates that it is floating point, however, so 5.0/9.0 is not truncated because it is the ratio of two floating-point values.

If an arithmetic operator has integer operands, an integer operation is performed. If an arithmetic operator has one floating-point operand and one integer operand, however, the integer will be converted to floating point before the operation is done. If we had written `fahr-32`, the 32 would be automatically converted to floating point. Nevertheless, writing floating-point constants with explicit decimal points even when they have integral values emphasizes their floating-point nature for human readers.

The detailed rules for when integers are converted to floating point are in Chapter 2. For now, notice that the assignment

```
    fahr = lower;
```

and the test

```
    while (fahr <= upper)
```

also work in the natural way—the `int` is converted to `float` before the operation is done.

The `printf` conversion specification `%3.0f` says that a floating-point number (here `fahr`) is to be printed at least three characters wide, with no decimal point and no fraction digits. `%6.1f` describes another number (`celsius`) that is to be printed at least six characters wide, with 1 digit after the decimal point. The output looks like this:

```
   0   -17.8
  20    -6.7
  40     4.4
  ...
```

Width and precision may be omitted from a specification: %6f says that the number is to be at least six characters wide; %.2f specifies two characters after the decimal point, but the width is not constrained; and %f merely says to print the number as floating point.

%d	print as decimal integer
%6d	print as decimal integer, at least 6 characters wide
%f	print as floating point
%6f	print as floating point, at least 6 characters wide
%.2f	print as floating point, 2 characters after decimal point
%6.2f	print as floating point, at least 6 wide and 2 after decimal point

Among others, printf also recognizes %o for octal, %x for hexadecimal, %c for character, %s for character string, and %% for % itself.

Exercise 1-3. Modify the temperature conversion program to print a heading above the table. □

Exercise 1-4. Write a program to print the corresponding Celsius to Fahrenheit table. □

1.3   The For Statement

There are plenty of different ways to write a program for a particular task. Let's try a variation on the temperature converter.

```
#include <stdio.h>

/* print Fahrenheit-Celsius table */
main()
{
    int fahr;

    for (fahr = 0; fahr <= 300; fahr = fahr + 20)
        printf("%3d %6.1f\n", fahr, (5.0/9.0)*(fahr-32));
}
```

This produces the same answers, but it certainly looks different. One major change is the elimination of most of the variables; only fahr remains, and we have made it an int. The lower and upper limits and the step size appear only as constants in the for statement, itself a new construction, and the expression that computes the Celsius temperature now appears as the third argument of printf instead of as a separate assignment statement.

This last change is an instance of a general rule—in any context where it is

permissible to use the value of a variable of some type, you can use a more complicated expression of that type. Since the third argument of `printf` must be
a floating-point value to match the `%6.1f`, any floating-point expression can
occur there.

The `for` statement is a loop, a generalization of the `while`. If you compare
it to the earlier `while`, its operation should be clear. Within the parentheses,
there are three parts, separated by semicolons. The first part, the initialization

```
fahr = 0
```

is done once, before the loop proper is entered. The second part is the test or
condition that controls the loop:

```
fahr <= 300
```

This condition is evaluated; if it is true, the body of the loop (here a single
`printf`) is executed. Then the increment step

```
fahr = fahr + 20
```

is executed, and the condition re-evaluated. The loop terminates if the condition
has become false. As with the `while`, the body of the loop can be a single
statement, or a group of statements enclosed in braces. The initialization, condition, and increment can be any expressions.

The choice between `while` and `for` is arbitrary, based on which seems
clearer. The `for` is usually appropriate for loops in which the initialization and
increment are single statements and logically related, since it is more compact
than `while` and it keeps the loop control statements together in one place.

Exercise 1-5. Modify the temperature conversion program to print the table in
reverse order, that is, from 300 degrees to 0. □

1.4 Symbolic Constants

A final observation before we leave temperature conversion forever. It's bad
practice to bury "magic numbers" like 300 and 20 in a program; they convey
little information to someone who might have to read the program later, and
they are hard to change in a systematic way. One way to deal with magic
numbers is to give them meaningful names. A `#define` line defines a *symbolic name* or *symbolic constant* to be a particular string of characters:

```
#define    name    replacement text
```

Thereafter, any occurrence of *name* (not in quotes and not part of another
name) will be replaced by the corresponding *replacement text*. The *name* has
the same form as a variable name: a sequence of letters and digits that begins
with a letter. The *replacement text* can be any sequence of characters; it is not
limited to numbers.

```
#include <stdio.h>

#define    LOWER  0       /* lower limit of table */
#define    UPPER  300     /* upper limit */
#define    STEP   20      /* step size */

/* print Fahrenheit-Celsius table */
main( )
{
    int fahr;

    for (fahr = LOWER; fahr <= UPPER; fahr = fahr + STEP)
        printf("%3d %6.1f\n", fahr, (5.0/9.0)*(fahr-32));
}
```

The quantities LOWER, UPPER and STEP are symbolic constants, not variables, so they do not appear in declarations. Symbolic constant names are conventionally written in upper case so they can be readily distinguished from lower case variable names. Notice that there is no semicolon at the end of a #define line.

1.5   Character Input and Output

We are now going to consider a family of related programs for processing character data. You will find that many programs are just expanded versions of the prototypes that we discuss here.

The model of input and output supported by the standard library is very simple. Text input or output, regardless of where it originates or where it goes to, is dealt with as streams of characters. A *text stream* is a sequence of characters divided into lines; each line consists of zero or more characters followed by a newline character. It is the responsibility of the library to make each input or output stream conform to this model; the C programmer using the library need not worry about how lines are represented outside the program.

The standard library provides several functions for reading or writing one character at a time, of which getchar and putchar are the simplest. Each time it is called, getchar reads the *next input character* from a text stream and returns that as its value. That is, after

```
c = getchar( )
```

the variable c contains the next character of input. The characters normally come from the keyboard; input from files is discussed in Chapter 7.

The function putchar prints a character each time it is called:

```
putchar(c)
```

prints the contents of the integer variable c as a character, usually on the screen. Calls to putchar and printf may be interleaved; the output will appear in the order in which the calls are made.

1.5.1 File Copying

Given `getchar` and `putchar`, you can write a surprising amount of useful code without knowing anything more about input and output. The simplest example is a program that copies its input to its output one character at a time:

```
read a character
while (character is not end-of-file indicator)
      output the character just read
      read a character
```

Converting this into C gives

```
#include <stdio.h>

/* copy input to output; 1st version */
main()
{
    int c;

    c = getchar();
    while (c != EOF) {
        putchar(c);
        c = getchar();
    }
}
```

The relational operator != means "not equal to."

What appears to be a character on the keyboard or screen is of course, like everything else, stored internally just as a bit pattern. The type `char` is specifically meant for storing such character data, but any integer type can be used. We used `int` for a subtle but important reason.

The problem is distinguishing the end of the input from valid data. The solution is that `getchar` returns a distinctive value when there is no more input, a value that cannot be confused with any real character. This value is called EOF, for "end of file." We must declare c to be a type big enough to hold any value that `getchar` returns. We can't use `char` since c must be big enough to hold EOF in addition to any possible `char`. Therefore we use `int`.

EOF is an integer defined in `<stdio.h>`, but the specific numeric value doesn't matter as long as it is not the same as any `char` value. By using the symbolic constant, we are assured that nothing in the program depends on the specific numeric value.

The program for copying would be written more concisely by experienced C programmers. In C, any assignment, such as

```
c = getchar()
```

is an expression and has a value, which is the value of the left hand side after the assignment. This means that an assignment can appear as part of a larger expression. If the assignment of a character to c is put inside the test part of a while loop, the copy program can be written this way:

```
#include <stdio.h>

/* copy input to output; 2nd version */
main( )
{
    int c;

    while ((c = getchar()) != EOF)
        putchar(c);
}
```

The while gets a character, assigns it to c, and then tests whether the character was the end-of-file signal. If it was not, the body of the while is executed, printing the character. The while then repeats. When the end of the input is finally reached, the while terminates and so does main.

This version centralizes the input—there is now only one reference to getchar—and shrinks the program. The resulting program is more compact, and, once the idiom is mastered, easier to read. You'll see this style often. (It's possible to get carried away and create impenetrable code, however, a tendency that we will try to curb.)

The parentheses around the assignment within the condition are necessary. The *precedence* of != is higher than that of =, which means that in the absence of parentheses the relational test != would be done before the assignment =. So the statement

```
c = getchar( ) != EOF
```

is equivalent to

```
c = (getchar( ) != EOF)
```

This has the undesired effect of setting c to 0 or 1, depending on whether or not the call of getchar encountered end of file. (More on this in Chapter 2.)

Exercise 1-6. Verify that the expression getchar( ) != EOF is 0 or 1. □

Exercise 1-7. Write a program to print the value of EOF. □

1.5.2 Character Counting

The next program counts characters; it is similar to the copy program.

```
#include <stdio.h>

/* count characters in input; 1st version */
main( )
{
    long nc;

    nc = 0;
    while (getchar( ) != EOF)
        ++nc;
    printf("%ld\n", nc);
}
```

The statement

```
++nc;
```

presents a new operator, ++, which means *increment by one*. You could instead write nc = nc+1 but ++nc is more concise and often more efficient. There is a corresponding operator -- to decrement by 1. The operators ++ and -- can be either prefix operators (++nc) or postfix (nc++); these two forms have different values in expressions, as will be shown in Chapter 2, but ++nc and nc++ both increment nc. For the moment we will stick to the prefix form.

The character counting program accumulates its count in a long variable instead of an int. long integers are at least 32 bits. Although on some machines, int and long are the same size, on others an int is 16 bits, with a maximum value of 32767, and it would take relatively little input to overflow an int counter. The conversion specification %ld tells printf that the corresponding argument is a long integer.

It may be possible to cope with even bigger numbers by using a double (double precision float). We will also use a for statement instead of a while, to illustrate another way to write the loop.

```
#include <stdio.h>

/* count characters in input; 2nd version */
main( )
{
    double nc;

    for (nc = 0; getchar( ) != EOF; ++nc)
        ;
    printf("%.0f\n", nc);
}
```

printf uses %f for both float and double; %.0f suppresses printing of the decimal point and the fraction part, which is zero.

The body of this for loop is empty, because all of the work is done in the test and increment parts. But the grammatical rules of C require that a for statement have a body. The isolated semicolon, called a *null statement*, is there to satisfy that requirement. We put it on a separate line to make it visible.

Before we leave the character counting program, observe that if the input contains no characters, the `while` or `for` test fails on the very first call to `getchar`, and the program produces zero, the right answer. This is important. One of the nice things about `while` and `for` is that they test at the top of the loop, before proceeding with the body. If there is nothing to do, nothing is done, even if that means never going through the loop body. Programs should act intelligently when given zero-length input. The `while` and `for` statements help ensure that programs do reasonable things with boundary conditions.

1.5.3 Line Counting

The next program counts input lines. As we mentioned above, the standard library ensures that an input text stream appears as a sequence of lines, each terminated by a newline. Hence, counting lines is just counting newlines:

```
#include <stdio.h>

/* count lines in input */
main( )
{
    int c, nl;

    nl = 0;
    while ((c = getchar()) != EOF)
        if (c == '\n')
            ++nl;
    printf("%d\n", nl);
}
```

The body of the `while` now consists of an `if`, which in turn controls the increment `++nl`. The `if` statement tests the parenthesized condition, and if the condition is true, executes the statement (or group of statements in braces) that follows. We have again indented to show what is controlled by what.

The double equals sign `==` is the C notation for "is equal to" (like Pascal's single `=` or Fortran's `.EQ.`). This symbol is used to distinguish the equality test from the single `=` that C uses for assignment. A word of caution: newcomers to C occasionally write `=` when they mean `==`. As we will see in Chapter 2, the result is usually a legal expression, so you will get no warning.

A character written between single quotes represents an integer value equal to the numerical value of the character in the machine's character set. This is called a *character constant,* although it is just another way to write a small integer. So, for example, `'A'` is a character constant; in the ASCII character set its value is 65, the internal representation of the character A. Of course `'A'` is to be preferred over 65: its meaning is obvious, and it is independent of a particular character set.

The escape sequences used in string constants are also legal in character

constants, so `'\n'` stands for the value of the newline character, which is 10 in
ASCII. You should note carefully that `'\n'` is a single character, and in
expressions is just an integer; on the other hand, `"\n"` is a string constant that
happens to contain only one character. The topic of strings versus characters is
discussed further in Chapter 2.

Exercise 1-8. Write a program to count blanks, tabs, and newlines. □

Exercise 1-9. Write a program to copy its input to its output, replacing each
string of one or more blanks by a single blank. □

Exercise 1-10. Write a program to copy its input to its output, replacing each
tab by \t, each backspace by \b, and each backslash by \\. This makes tabs
and backspaces visible in an unambiguous way. □

1.5.4 Word Counting

The fourth in our series of useful programs counts lines, words, and characters, with the loose definition that a word is any sequence of characters that
does not contain a blank, tab or newline. This is a bare-bones version of the
UNIX program wc.

```c
#include <stdio.h>

#define IN  1    /* inside a word */
#define OUT 0    /* outside a word */

/* count lines, words, and characters in input */
main()
{
    int c, nl, nw, nc, state;

    state = OUT;
    nl = nw = nc = 0;
    while ((c = getchar()) != EOF) {
        ++nc;
        if (c == '\n')
            ++nl;
        if (c == ' ' || c == '\n' || c == '\t')
            state = OUT;
        else if (state == OUT) {
            state = IN;
            ++nw;
        }
    }
    printf("%d %d %d\n", nl, nw, nc);
}
```

Every time the program encounters the first character of a word, it counts one more word. The variable `state` records whether the program is currently in a word or not; initially it is "not in a word," which is assigned the value `OUT`. We prefer the symbolic constants `IN` and `OUT` to the literal values 1 and 0 because they make the program more readable. In a program as tiny as this, it makes little difference, but in larger programs, the increase in clarity is well worth the modest extra effort to write it this way from the beginning. You'll also find that it's easier to make extensive changes in programs where magic numbers appear only as symbolic constants.

The line

```
nl = nw = nc = 0;
```

sets all three variables to zero. This is not a special case, but a consequence of the fact that an assignment is an expression with a value and assignments associate from right to left. It's as if we had written

```
nl = (nw = (nc = 0));
```

The operator `||` means OR, so the line

```
if (c == ' ' || c == '\n' || c == '\t')
```

says "if c is a blank *or* c is a newline *or* c is a tab". (Recall that the escape sequence `\t` is a visible representation of the tab character.) There is a corresponding operator `&&` for AND; its precedence is just higher than `||`. Expressions connected by `&&` or `||` are evaluated left to right, and it is guaranteed that evaluation will stop as soon as the truth or falsehood is known. If c is a blank, there is no need to test whether it is a newline or tab, so these tests are not made. This isn't particularly important here, but is significant in more complicated situations, as we will soon see.

The example also shows an `else`, which specifies an alternative action if the condition part of an `if` statement is false. The general form is

```
if (expression)
    statement₁
else
    statement₂
```

One and only one of the two statements associated with an `if-else` is performed. If the *expression* is true, *statement₁* is executed; if not, *statement₂* is executed. Each *statement* can be a single statement or several in braces. In the word count program, the one after the `else` is an `if` that controls two statements in braces.

Exercise 1-11. How would you test the word count program? What kinds of input are most likely to uncover bugs if there are any? □

Exercise 1-12. Write a program that prints its input one word per line. □

1.6 Arrays

Let us write a program to count the number of occurrences of each digit, of white space characters (blank, tab, newline), and of all other characters. This is artificial, but it permits us to illustrate several aspects of C in one program.

There are twelve categories of input, so it is convenient to use an array to hold the number of occurrences of each digit, rather than ten individual variables. Here is one version of the program:

```
#include <stdio.h>

/* count digits, white space, others */
main()
{
    int c, i, nwhite, nother;
    int ndigit[10];

    nwhite = nother = 0;
    for (i = 0; i < 10; ++i)
        ndigit[i] = 0;

    while ((c = getchar()) != EOF)
        if (c >= '0' && c <= '9')
            ++ndigit[c-'0'];
        else if (c == ' ' || c == '\n' || c == '\t')
            ++nwhite;
        else
            ++nother;

    printf("digits =");
    for (i = 0; i < 10; ++i)
        printf(" %d", ndigit[i]);
    printf(", white space = %d, other = %d\n",
        nwhite, nother);
}
```

The output of this program on itself is

```
digits = 9 3 0 0 0 0 0 0 0 1, white space = 123, other = 345
```

The declaration

```
int ndigit[10];
```

declares ndigit to be an array of 10 integers. Array subscripts always start at zero in C, so the elements are ndigit[0], ndigit[1], ..., ndigit[9]. This is reflected in the for loops that initialize and print the array.

A subscript can be any integer expression, which includes integer variables like i, and integer constants.

This particular program relies on the properties of the character representation of the digits. For example, the test

```
if (c >= '0' && c <= '9') ...
```

determines whether the character in c is a digit. If it is, the numeric value of that digit is

```
c - '0'
```

This works only if '0', '1', ..., '9' have consecutive increasing values. Fortunately, this is true for all character sets.

By definition, chars are just small integers, so char variables and constants are identical to ints in arithmetic expressions. This is natural and convenient; for example, c-'0' is an integer expression with a value between 0 and 9 corresponding to the character '0' to '9' stored in c, and is thus a valid subscript for the array ndigit.

The decision as to whether a character is a digit, white space, or something else is made with the sequence

```
if (c >= '0' && c <= '9')
    ++ndigit[c-'0'];
else if (c == ' ' || c == '\n' || c == '\t')
    ++nwhite;
else
    ++nother;
```

The pattern

```
if (condition₁)
    statement₁
else if (condition₂)
    statement₂
...
    ...
else
    statementₙ
```

occurs frequently in programs as a way to express a multi-way decision. The *conditions* are evaluated in order from the top until some *condition* is satisfied; at that point the corresponding *statement* part is executed, and the entire construction is finished. (Any *statement* can be several statements enclosed in braces.) If none of the conditions is satisfied, the *statement* after the final else is executed if it is present. If the final else and *statement* are omitted, as in the word count program, no action takes place. There can be any number of

```
else if (condition)
    statement
```

groups between the initial if and the final else.

As a matter of style, it is advisable to format this construction as we have shown; if each if were indented past the previous else, a long sequence of decisions would march off the right side of the page.

The `switch` statement, to be discussed in Chapter 3, provides another way to write a multi-way branch that is particularly suitable when the condition is whether some integer or character expression matches one of a set of constants. For contrast, we will present a `switch` version of this program in Section 3.4.

Exercise 1-13. Write a program to print a histogram of the lengths of words in its input. It is easy to draw the histogram with the bars horizontal; a vertical orientation is more challenging. □

Exercise 1-14. Write a program to print a histogram of the frequencies of different characters in its input. □

1.7 Functions

In C, a function is equivalent to a subroutine or function in Fortran, or a procedure or function in Pascal. A function provides a convenient way to encapsulate some computation, which can then be used without worrying about its implementation. With properly designed functions, it is possible to ignore *how* a job is done; knowing *what* is done is sufficient. C makes the use of functions easy, convenient and efficient; you will often see a short function defined and called only once, just because it clarifies some piece of code.

So far we have used only functions like `printf`, `getchar`, and `putchar` that have been provided for us; now it's time to write a few of our own. Since C has no exponentiation operator like the `**` of Fortran, let us illustrate the mechanics of function definition by writing a function `power(m,n)` to raise an integer m to a positive integer power n. That is, the value of `power(2,5)` is 32. This function is not a practical exponentiation routine, since it handles only positive powers of small integers, but it's good enough for illustration. (The standard library contains a function `pow(x,y)` that computes x^y.)

Here is the function `power` and a main program to exercise it, so you can see the whole structure at once.

```
#include <stdio.h>

int power(int m, int n);

/* test power function */
main()
{
    int i;

    for (i = 0; i < 10; ++i)
        printf("%d %d %d\n", i, power(2,i), power(-3,i));
    return 0;
}
```

```
/* power:   raise base to n-th power; n >= 0 */
int power(int base, int n)
{
    int i, p;

    p = 1;
    for (i = 1; i <= n; ++i)
        p = p * base;
    return p;
}
```

A function definition has this form:

> *return-type function-name* (*parameter declarations, if any*)
> {
> > *declarations*
> > *statements*
> }

Function definitions can appear in any order, and in one source file or several, although no function can be split between files. If the source program appears in several files, you may have to say more to compile and load it than if it all appears in one, but that is an operating system matter, not a language attribute. For the moment, we will assume that both functions are in the same file, so whatever you have learned about running C programs will still work.

The function `power` is called twice by `main`, in the line

```
printf("%d %d %d\n", i, power(2,i), power(-3,i));
```

Each call passes two arguments to `power`, which each time returns an integer to be formatted and printed. In an expression, `power(2,i)` is an integer just as 2 and `i` are. (Not all functions produce an integer value; we will take this up in Chapter 4.)

The first line of `power` itself,

```
int power(int base, int n)
```

declares the parameter types and names, and the type of the result that the function returns. The names used by `power` for its parameters are local to `power`, and are not visible to any other function: other routines can use the same names without conflict. This is also true of the variables `i` and `p`: the `i` in `power` is unrelated to the `i` in `main`.

We will generally use *parameter* for a variable named in the parenthesized list in a function definition, and *argument* for the value used in a call of the function. The terms *formal argument* and *actual argument* are sometimes used for the same distinction.

The value that `power` computes is returned to `main` by the `return` statement. Any expression may follow `return`:

```
return expression;
```

A function need not return a value; a `return` statement with no expression causes control, but no useful value, to be returned to the caller, as does "falling off the end" of a function by reaching the terminating right brace. And the calling function can ignore a value returned by a function.

You may have noticed that there is a `return` statement at the end of `main`. Since `main` is a function like any other, it may return a value to its caller, which is in effect the environment in which the program was executed. Typically, a return value of zero implies normal termination; non-zero values signal unusual or erroneous termination conditions. In the interests of simplicity, we have omitted `return` statements from our `main` functions up to this point, but we will include them hereafter, as a reminder that programs should return status to their environment.

The declaration

```
int power(int m, int n);
```

just before `main` says that `power` is a function that expects two `int` arguments and returns an `int`. This declaration, which is called a *function prototype*, has to agree with the definition and uses of `power`. It is an error if the definition of a function or any uses of it do not agree with its prototype.

Parameter names need not agree. Indeed, parameter names are optional in a function prototype, so for the prototype we could have written

```
int power(int, int);
```

Well-chosen names are good documentation, however, so we will often use them.

A note of history: The biggest change between ANSI C and earlier versions is how functions are declared and defined. In the original definition of C, the `power` function would have been written like this:

```
/* power:  raise base to n-th power; n >= 0 */
/*         (old-style version) */
power(base, n)
int base, n;
{
    int i, p;

    p = 1;
    for (i = 1; i <= n; ++i)
        p = p * base;
    return p;
}
```

The parameters are named between the parentheses, and their types are declared before the opening left brace; undeclared parameters are taken as `int`. (The body of the function is the same as before.)

The declaration of `power` at the beginning of the program would have looked like this:

```
int power();
```

No parameter list was permitted, so the compiler could not readily check that power was being called correctly. Indeed, since by default power would have been assumed to return an int, the entire declaration might well have been omitted.

The new syntax of function prototypes makes it much easier for a compiler to detect errors in the number of arguments or their types. The old style of declaration and definition still works in ANSI C, at least for a transition period, but we strongly recommend that you use the new form when you have a compiler that supports it.

Exercise 1-15. Rewrite the temperature conversion program of Section 1.2 to use a function for conversion. □

1.8 Arguments—Call by Value

One aspect of C functions may be unfamiliar to programmers who are used to some other languages, particularly Fortran. In C, all function arguments are passed "by value." This means that the called function is given the values of its arguments in temporary variables rather than the originals. This leads to some different properties than are seen with "call by reference" languages like Fortran or with var parameters in Pascal, in which the called routine has access to the original argument, not a local copy.

The main distinction is that in C the called function cannot directly alter a variable in the calling function; it can only alter its private, temporary copy.

Call by value is an asset, however, not a liability. It usually leads to more compact programs with fewer extraneous variables, because parameters can be treated as conveniently initialized local variables in the called routine. For example, here is a version of power that makes use of this property.

```
/* power:  raise base to n-th power; n>=0; version 2 */
int power(int base, int n)
{
    int p;

    for (p = 1; n > 0; --n)
        p = p * base;
    return p;
}
```

The parameter n is used as a temporary variable, and is counted down (a for loop that runs backwards) until it becomes zero; there is no longer a need for the variable i. Whatever is done to n inside power has no effect on the argument that power was originally called with.

When necessary, it is possible to arrange for a function to modify a variable in a calling routine. The caller must provide the *address* of the variable to be set (technically a *pointer* to the variable), and the called function must declare the parameter to be a pointer and access the variable indirectly through it. We will cover pointers in Chapter 5.

The story is different for arrays. When the name of an array is used as an argument, the value passed to the function is the location or address of the beginning of the array—there is no copying of array elements. By subscripting this value, the function can access and alter any element of the array. This is the topic of the next section.

1.9 Character Arrays

The most common type of array in C is the array of characters. To illustrate the use of character arrays and functions to manipulate them, let's write a program that reads a set of text lines and prints the longest. The outline is simple enough:

```
while (there's another line)
     if (it's longer than the previous longest)
          save it
          save its length
print longest line
```

This outline makes it clear that the program divides naturally into pieces. One piece gets a new line, another tests it, another saves it, and the rest controls the process.

Since things divide so nicely, it would be well to write them that way too. Accordingly, let us first write a separate function `getline` to fetch the next line of input. We will try to make the function useful in other contexts. At the minimum, `getline` has to return a signal about possible end of file; a more useful design would be to return the length of the line, or zero if end of file is encountered. Zero is an acceptable end-of-file return because it is never a valid line length. Every text line has at least one character; even a line containing only a newline has length 1.

When we find a line that is longer than the previous longest line, it must be saved somewhere. This suggests a second function, `copy`, to copy the new line to a safe place.

Finally, we need a main program to control `getline` and `copy`. Here is the result.

```
#include <stdio.h>
#define MAXLINE 1000      /* maximum input line size */

int getline(char line[], int maxline);
void copy(char to[], char from[]);

/* print longest input line */
main()
{
    int len;                /* current line length */
    int max;                /* maximum length seen so far */
    char line[MAXLINE];     /* current input line */
    char longest[MAXLINE];  /* longest line saved here */

    max = 0;
    while ((len = getline(line, MAXLINE)) > 0)
        if (len > max) {
            max = len;
            copy(longest, line);
        }
    if (max > 0)      /* there was a line */
        printf("%s", longest);
    return 0;
}

/* getline:  read a line into s, return length */
int getline(char s[], int lim)
{
    int c, i;

    for (i=0; i<lim-1 && (c=getchar())!=EOF && c!='\n'; ++i)
        s[i] = c;
    if (c == '\n') {
        s[i] = c;
        ++i;
    }
    s[i] = '\0';
    return i;
}

/* copy:  copy 'from' into 'to'; assume to is big enough */
void copy(char to[], char from[])
{
    int i;

    i = 0;
    while ((to[i] = from[i]) != '\0')
        ++i;
}
```

The functions `getline` and `copy` are declared at the beginning of the program, which we assume is contained in one file.

`main` and `getline` communicate through a pair of arguments and a returned value. In `getline`, the arguments are declared by the line

```
int getline(char s[], int lim)
```

which specifies that the first argument, `s`, is an array, and the second, `lim`, is an integer. The purpose of supplying the size of an array in a declaration is to set aside storage. The length of the array `s` is not necessary in `getline` since its size is set in `main`. `getline` uses `return` to send a value back to the caller, just as the function `power` did. This line also declares that `getline` returns an `int`; since `int` is the default return type, it could be omitted.

Some functions return a useful value; others, like `copy`, are used only for their effect and return no value. The return type of `copy` is `void`, which states explicitly that no value is returned.

`getline` puts the character `'\0'` (the *null character*, whose value is zero) at the end of the array it is creating, to mark the end of the string of characters. This convention is also used by the C language: when a string constant like

```
"hello\n"
```

appears in a C program, it is stored as an array of characters containing the characters of the string and terminated with a `'\0'` to mark the end.

h	e	l	l	o	\n	\0

The `%s` format specification in `printf` expects the corresponding argument to be a string represented in this form. `copy` also relies on the fact that its input argument is terminated by `'\0'`, and it copies this character into the output argument. (All of this implies that `'\0'` is not a part of normal text.)

It is worth mentioning in passing that even a program as small as this one presents some sticky design problems. For example, what should `main` do if it encounters a line which is bigger than its limit? `getline` works safely, in that it stops collecting when the array is full, even if no newline has been seen. By testing the length and the last character returned, `main` can determine whether the line was too long, and then cope as it wishes. In the interests of brevity, we have ignored the issue.

There is no way for a user of `getline` to know in advance how long an input line might be, so `getline` checks for overflow. On the other hand, the user of `copy` already knows (or can find out) how big the strings are, so we have chosen not to add error checking to it.

Exercise 1-16. Revise the main routine of the longest-line program so it will correctly print the length of arbitrarily long input lines, and as much as possible of the text. □

Exercise 1-17. Write a program to print all input lines that are longer than 80 characters. ☐

Exercise 1-18. Write a program to remove trailing blanks and tabs from each line of input, and to delete entirely blank lines. ☐

Exercise 1-19. Write a function `reverse(s)` that reverses the character string `s`. Use it to write a program that reverses its input a line at a time. ☐

1.10 External Variables and Scope

The variables in `main`, such as `line`, `longest`, etc., are private or local to `main`. Because they are declared within `main`, no other function can have direct access to them. The same is true of the variables in other functions; for example, the variable `i` in `getline` is unrelated to the `i` in `copy`. Each local variable in a function comes into existence only when the function is called, and disappears when the function is exited. This is why such variables are usually known as *automatic* variables, following terminology in other languages. We will use the term automatic henceforth to refer to these local variables. (Chapter 4 discusses the `static` storage class, in which local variables do retain their values between calls.)

Because automatic variables come and go with function invocation, they do not retain their values from one call to the next, and must be explicitly set upon each entry. If they are not set, they will contain garbage.

As an alternative to automatic variables, it is possible to define variables that are *external* to all functions, that is, variables that can be accessed by name by any function. (This mechanism is rather like Fortran COMMON or Pascal variables declared in the outermost block.) Because external variables are globally accessible, they can be used instead of argument lists to communicate data between functions. Furthermore, because external variables remain in existence permanently, rather than appearing and disappearing as functions are called and exited, they retain their values even after the functions that set them have returned.

An external variable must be *defined*, exactly once, outside of any function; this sets aside storage for it. The variable must also be *declared* in each function that wants to access it; this states the type of the variable. The declaration may be an explicit `extern` statement or may be implicit from context. To make the discussion concrete, let us rewrite the longest-line program with `line`, `longest`, and `max` as external variables. This requires changing the calls, declarations, and bodies of all three functions.

```c
#include <stdio.h>

#define MAXLINE 1000    /* maximum input line size */

int max;                /* maximum length seen so far */
char line[MAXLINE];     /* current input line */
char longest[MAXLINE];  /* longest line saved here */

int getline(void);
void copy(void);



/* print longest input line; specialized version */
main()
{
    int len;
    extern int max;
    extern char longest[];

    max = 0;
    while ((len = getline()) > 0)
        if (len > max) {
            max = len;
            copy();
        }
    if (max > 0)    /* there was a line */
        printf("%s", longest);
    return 0;
}



/* getline:  specialized version */
int getline(void)
{
    int c, i;
    extern char line[];

    for (i = 0; i < MAXLINE-1
        && (c=getchar()) != EOF && c != '\n'; ++i)
            line[i] = c;
    if (c == '\n') {
        line[i] = c;
        ++i;
    }
    line[i] = '\0';
    return i;
}
```

```
/* copy:  specialized version */
void copy(void)
{
    int i;
    extern char line[], longest[];

    i = 0;
    while ((longest[i] = line[i]) != '\0')
        ++i;
}
```

The external variables in `main`, `getline`, and `copy` are defined by the first lines of the example above, which state their type and cause storage to be allocated for them. Syntactically, external definitions are just like definitions of local variables, but since they occur outside of functions, the variables are external. Before a function can use an external variable, the name of the variable must be made known to the function. One way to do this is to write an `extern` declaration in the function; the declaration is the same as before except for the added keyword `extern`.

In certain circumstances, the `extern` declaration can be omitted. If the definition of an external variable occurs in the source file before its use in a particular function, then there is no need for an `extern` declaration in the function. The `extern` declarations in `main`, `getline` and `copy` are thus redundant. In fact, common practice is to place definitions of all external variables at the beginning of the source file, and then omit all `extern` declarations.

If the program is in several source files, and a variable is defined in *file1* and used in *file2* and *file3*, then `extern` declarations are needed in *file2* and *file3* to connect the occurrences of the variable. The usual practice is to collect `extern` declarations of variables and functions in a separate file, historically called a *header*, that is included by `#include` at the front of each source file. The suffix `.h` is conventional for header names. The functions of the standard library, for example, are declared in headers like `<stdio.h>`. This topic is discussed at length in Chapter 4, and the library itself in Chapter 7 and Appendix B.

Since the specialized versions of `getline` and `copy` have no arguments, logic would suggest that their prototypes at the beginning of the file should be `getline()` and `copy()`. But for compatibility with older C programs the standard takes an empty list as an old-style declaration, and turns off all argument list checking; the word `void` must be used for an explicitly empty list. We will discuss this further in Chapter 4.

You should note that we are using the words *definition* and *declaration* carefully when we refer to external variables in this section. "Definition" refers to the place where the variable is created or assigned storage; "declaration" refers to places where the nature of the variable is stated but no storage is allocated.

By the way, there is a tendency to make everything in sight an `extern` variable because it appears to simplify communications—argument lists are short and variables are always there when you want them. But external variables are always there even when you don't want them. Relying too heavily on external variables is fraught with peril since it leads to programs whose data connections are not at all obvious—variables can be changed in unexpected and even inadvertent ways, and the program is hard to modify. The second version of the longest-line program is inferior to the first, partly for these reasons, and partly because it destroys the generality of two useful functions by wiring into them the names of the variables they manipulate.

At this point we have covered what might be called the conventional core of C. With this handful of building blocks, it's possible to write useful programs of considerable size, and it would probably be a good idea if you paused long enough to do so. These exercises suggest programs of somewhat greater complexity than the ones earlier in this chapter.

Exercise 1-20. Write a program `detab` that replaces tabs in the input with the proper number of blanks to space to the next tab stop. Assume a fixed set of tab stops, say every *n* columns. Should *n* be a variable or a symbolic parameter? □

Exercise 1-21. Write a program `entab` that replaces strings of blanks by the minimum number of tabs and blanks to achieve the same spacing. Use the same tab stops as for `detab`. When either a tab or a single blank would suffice to reach a tab stop, which should be given preference? □

Exercise 1-22. Write a program to "fold" long input lines into two or more shorter lines after the last non-blank character that occurs before the *n*-th column of input. Make sure your program does something intelligent with very long lines, and if there are no blanks or tabs before the specified column. □

Exercise 1-23. Write a program to remove all comments from a C program. Don't forget to handle quoted strings and character constants properly. C comments do not nest. □

Exercise 1-24. Write a program to check a C program for rudimentary syntax errors like unbalanced parentheses, brackets and braces. Don't forget about quotes, both single and double, escape sequences, and comments. (This program is hard if you do it in full generality.) □

CHAPTER 2: **Types, Operators, and Expressions**

Variables and constants are the basic data objects manipulated in a program. Declarations list the variables to be used, and state what type they have and perhaps what their initial values are. Operators specify what is to be done to them. Expressions combine variables and constants to produce new values. The type of an object determines the set of values it can have and what operations can be performed on it. These building blocks are the topics of this chapter.

The ANSI standard has made many small changes and additions to basic types and expressions. There are now `signed` and `unsigned` forms of all integer types, and notations for unsigned constants and hexadecimal character constants. Floating-point operations may be done in single precision; there is also a `long double` type for extended precision. String constants may be concatenated at compile time. Enumerations have become part of the language, formalizing a feature of long standing. Objects may be declared `const`, which prevents them from being changed. The rules for automatic coercions among arithmetic types have been augmented to handle the richer set of types.

2.1 Variable Names

Although we didn't say so in Chapter 1, there are some restrictions on the names of variables and symbolic constants. Names are made up of letters and digits; the first character must be a letter. The underscore "_" counts as a letter; it is sometimes useful for improving the readability of long variable names. Don't begin variable names with underscore, however, since library routines often use such names. Upper case and lower case letters are distinct, so x and X are two different names. Traditional C practice is to use lower case for variable names, and all upper case for symbolic constants.

At least the first 31 characters of an internal name are significant. For function names and external variables, the number may be less than 31, because external names may be used by assemblers and loaders over which the language has no control. For external names, the standard guarantees uniqueness only for 6 characters and a single case. Keywords like `if`, `else`, `int`, `float`, etc., are reserved: you can't use them as variable names. They must be in lower case.

It's wise to choose variable names that are related to the purpose of the variable, and that are unlikely to get mixed up typographically. We tend to use short names for local variables, especially loop indices, and longer names for external variables.

2.2 Data Types and Sizes

There are only a few basic data types in C:

char	a single byte, capable of holding one character in the local character set.
int	an integer, typically reflecting the natural size of integers on the host machine.
float	single-precision floating point.
double	double-precision floating point.

In addition, there are a number of qualifiers that can be applied to these basic types. short and long apply to integers:

```
short int sh;
long int counter;
```

The word int can be omitted in such declarations, and typically is.

The intent is that short and long should provide different lengths of integers where practical; int will normally be the natural size for a particular machine. short is often 16 bits, long 32 bits, and int either 16 or 32 bits. Each compiler is free to choose appropriate sizes for its own hardware, subject only to the restriction that shorts and ints are at least 16 bits, longs are at least 32 bits, and short is no longer than int, which is no longer than long.

The qualifier signed or unsigned may be applied to char or any integer. unsigned numbers are always positive or zero, and obey the laws of arithmetic modulo 2^n, where n is the number of bits in the type. So, for instance, if chars are 8 bits, unsigned char variables have values between 0 and 255, while signed chars have values between −128 and 127 (in a two's complement machine). Whether plain chars are signed or unsigned is machine-dependent, but printable characters are always positive.

The type long double specifies extended-precision floating point. As with integers, the sizes of floating-point objects are implementation-defined; float, double and long double could represent one, two or three distinct sizes.

The standard headers <limits.h> and <float.h> contain symbolic constants for all of these sizes, along with other properties of the machine and compiler. These are discussed in Appendix B.

Exercise 2-1. Write a program to determine the ranges of char, short, int, and `long` variables, both `signed` and `unsigned`, by printing appropriate values from standard headers and by direct computation. Harder if you compute them: determine the ranges of the various floating-point types. □

2.3 Constants

An integer constant like 1234 is an `int`. A `long` constant is written with a terminal 1 (ell) or L, as in 123456789L; an integer too big to fit into an `int` will also be taken as a `long`. Unsigned constants are written with a terminal u or U, and the suffix ul or UL indicates `unsigned long`.

Floating-point constants contain a decimal point (123.4) or an exponent (1e-2) or both; their type is `double`, unless suffixed. The suffixes f or F indicate a `float` constant; l or L indicate a `long double`.

The value of an integer can be specified in octal or hexadecimal instead of decimal. A leading 0 (zero) on an integer constant means octal; a leading 0x or 0X means hexadecimal. For example, decimal 31 can be written as 037 in octal and 0x1f or 0X1F in hex. Octal and hexadecimal constants may also be followed by L to make them `long` and U to make them `unsigned`: 0XFUL is an `unsigned long` constant with value 15 decimal.

A *character constant* is an integer, written as one character within single quotes, such as `'x'`. The value of a character constant is the numeric value of the character in the machine's character set. For example, in the ASCII character set the character constant `'0'` has the value 48, which is unrelated to the numeric value 0. If we write `'0'` instead of a numeric value like 48 that depends on character set, the program is independent of the particular value and easier to read. Character constants participate in numeric operations just as any other integers, although they are most often used in comparisons with other characters.

Certain characters can be represented in character and string constants by escape sequences like \n (newline); these sequences look like two characters, but represent only one. In addition, an arbitrary byte-sized bit pattern can be specified by

      `'\`*ooo*`'`

where *ooo* is one to three octal digits (0...7) or by

      `'\x`*hh*`'`

where *hh* is one or more hexadecimal digits (0...9, a...f, A...F). So we might write

```
#define VTAB '\013'    /* ASCII vertical tab */
#define BELL '\007'    /* ASCII bell character */
```

or, in hexadecimal,

```
#define VTAB '\xb'    /* ASCII vertical tab */
#define BELL '\x7'    /* ASCII bell character */
```

The complete set of escape sequences is

\a	alert (bell) character	\\	backslash
\b	backspace	\?	question mark
\f	formfeed	\'	single quote
\n	newline	\"	double quote
\r	carriage return	\\ooo	octal number
\t	horizontal tab	\xhh	hexadecimal number
\v	vertical tab		

The character constant `'\0'` represents the character with value zero, the null character. `'\0'` is often written instead of 0 to emphasize the character nature of some expression, but the numeric value is just 0.

A *constant expression* is an expression that involves only constants. Such expressions may be evaluated during compilation rather than run-time, and accordingly may be used in any place that a constant can occur, as in

```
#define MAXLINE 1000
char line[MAXLINE+1];
```

or

```
#define LEAP 1   /* in leap years */
int days[31+28+LEAP+31+30+31+30+31+31+30+31+30+31];
```

A *string constant*, or *string literal*, is a sequence of zero or more characters surrounded by double quotes, as in

```
"I am a string"
```

or

```
""   /* the empty string */
```

The quotes are not part of the string, but serve only to delimit it. The same escape sequences used in character constants apply in strings; `\"` represents the double-quote character. String constants can be concatenated at compile time:

```
"hello," " world"
```

is equivalent to

```
"hello, world"
```

This is useful for splitting long strings across several source lines.

Technically, a string constant is an array of characters. The internal representation of a string has a null character `'\0'` at the end, so the physical storage required is one more than the number of characters written between the quotes. This representation means that there is no limit to how long a string can be, but programs must scan a string completely to determine its length. The standard library function `strlen(s)` returns the length of its character string argument s, excluding the terminal `'\0'`. Here is our version:

```
/* strlen:  return length of s */
int strlen(char s[])
{
    int i;

    i = 0;
    while (s[i] != '\0')
        ++i;
    return i;
}
```

strlen and other string functions are declared in the standard header
`<string.h>`.

Be careful to distinguish between a character constant and a string that contains a single character: `'x'` is not the same as `"x"`. The former is an integer,
used to produce the numeric value of the letter *x* in the machine's character set.
The latter is an array of characters that contains one character (the letter *x*)
and a `'\0'`.

There is one other kind of constant, the *enumeration constant*. An
enumeration is a list of constant integer values, as in

```
enum boolean { NO, YES };
```

The first name in an enum has value 0, the next 1, and so on, unless explicit
values are specified. If not all values are specified, unspecified values continue
the progression from the last specified value, as in the second of these examples:

```
enum escapes { BELL = '\a', BACKSPACE = '\b', TAB = '\t',
               NEWLINE = '\n', VTAB = '\v', RETURN = '\r' };

enum months { JAN = 1, FEB, MAR, APR, MAY, JUN,
              JUL, AUG, SEP, OCT, NOV, DEC };
                      /* FEB is 2, MAR is 3, etc. */
```

Names in different enumerations must be distinct. Values need not be distinct
in the same enumeration.

Enumerations provide a convenient way to associate constant values with
names, an alternative to #define with the advantage that the values can be
generated for you. Although variables of enum types may be declared, compilers need not check that what you store in such a variable is a valid value for
the enumeration. Nevertheless, enumeration variables offer the chance of
checking and so are often better than #defines. In addition, a debugger may
be able to print values of enumeration variables in their symbolic form.

2.4 Declarations

All variables must be declared before use, although certain declarations can be made implicitly by context. A declaration specifies a type, and contains a list of one or more variables of that type, as in

```
int   lower, upper, step;
char  c, line[1000];
```

Variables can be distributed among declarations in any fashion; the lists above could equally well be written as

```
int   lower;
int   upper;
int   step;
char  c;
char  line[1000];
```

This latter form takes more space, but is convenient for adding a comment to each declaration or for subsequent modifications.

A variable may also be initialized in its declaration. If the name is followed by an equals sign and an expression, the expression serves as an initializer, as in

```
char   esc = '\\';
int    i = 0;
int    limit = MAXLINE+1;
float  eps = 1.0e-5;
```

If the variable in question is not automatic, the initialization is done once only, conceptually before the program starts executing, and the initializer must be a constant expression. An explicitly initialized automatic variable is initialized each time the function or block it is in is entered; the initializer may be any expression. External and static variables are initialized to zero by default. Automatic variables for which there is no explicit initializer have undefined (i.e., garbage) values.

The qualifier const can be applied to the declaration of any variable to specify that its value will not be changed. For an array, the const qualifier says that the elements will not be altered.

```
const double e = 2.71828182845905;
const char msg[] = "warning: ";
```

The const declaration can also be used with array arguments, to indicate that the function does not change that array:

```
int strlen(const char[]);
```

The result is implementation-defined if an attempt is made to change a const.

2.5 Arithmetic Operators

The binary arithmetic operators are +, −, *, /, and the modulus operator %. Integer division truncates any fractional part. The expression

```
x % y
```

produces the remainder when x is divided by y, and thus is zero when y divides x exactly. For example, a year is a leap year if it is divisible by 4 but not by 100, except that years divisible by 400 *are* leap years. Therefore

```
if ((year % 4 == 0 && year % 100 != 0) || year % 400 == 0)
    printf("%d is a leap year\n", year);
else
    printf("%d is not a leap year\n", year);
```

The % operator cannot be applied to float or double. The direction of truncation for / and the sign of the result for % are machine-dependent for negative operands, as is the action taken on overflow or underflow.

The binary + and − operators have the same precedence, which is lower than the precedence of *, /, and %, which is in turn lower than unary + and −. Arithmetic operators associate left to right.

Table 2-1 at the end of this chapter summarizes precedence and associativity for all operators.

2.6 Relational and Logical Operators

The relational operators are

```
>    >=    <    <=
```

They all have the same precedence. Just below them in precedence are the equality operators:

```
==    !=
```

Relational operators have lower precedence than arithmetic operators, so an expression like i < lim-1 is taken as i < (lim-1), as would be expected.

More interesting are the logical operators && and ||. Expressions connected by && or || are evaluated left to right, and evaluation stops as soon as the truth or falsehood of the result is known. Most C programs rely on these properties. For example, here is a loop from the input function getline that we wrote in Chapter 1:

```
for (i=0; i<lim-1 && (c=getchar()) != '\n' && c != EOF; ++i)
    s[i] = c;
```

Before reading a new character it is necessary to check that there is room to store it in the array s, so the test i < lim-1 *must* be made first. Moreover, if this test fails, we must not go on and read another character.

Similarly, it would be unfortunate if c were tested against EOF before getchar is called; therefore the call and assignment must occur before the character in c is tested.

The precedence of && is higher than that of ¦¦, and both are lower than relational and equality operators, so expressions like

```
i<lim-1 && (c = getchar()) != '\n' && c != EOF
```

need no extra parentheses. But since the precedence of != is higher than assignment, parentheses are needed in

```
(c = getchar()) != '\n'
```

to achieve the desired result of assignment to c and then comparison with '\n'.

By definition, the numeric value of a relational or logical expression is 1 if the relation is true, and 0 if the relation is false.

The unary negation operator ! converts a non-zero operand into 0, and a zero operand into 1. A common use of ! is in constructions like

```
if (!valid)
```

rather than

```
if (valid == 0)
```

It's hard to generalize about which form is better. Constructions like !valid read nicely ("if not valid"), but more complicated ones can be hard to understand.

Exercise 2-2. Write a loop equivalent to the for loop above without using && or ¦¦. □

2.7 Type Conversions

When an operator has operands of different types, they are converted to a common type according to a small number of rules. In general, the only automatic conversions are those that convert a "narrower" operand into a "wider" one without losing information, such as converting an integer to floating point in an expression like f + i. Expressions that don't make sense, like using a float as a subscript, are disallowed. Expressions that might lose information, like assigning a longer integer type to a shorter, or a floating-point type to an integer, may draw a warning, but they are not illegal.

A char is just a small integer, so chars may be freely used in arithmetic expressions. This permits considerable flexibility in certain kinds of character transformations. One is exemplified by this naive implementation of the function atoi, which converts a string of digits into its numeric equivalent.

```
/* atoi:  convert s to integer */
int atoi(char s[])
{
    int i, n;

    n = 0;
    for (i = 0; s[i] >= '0' && s[i] <= '9'; ++i)
        n = 10 * n + (s[i] - '0');
    return n;
}
```

As we discussed in Chapter 1, the expression

```
s[i] - '0'
```

gives the numeric value of the character stored in `s[i]`, because the values of
`'0'`, `'1'`, etc., form a contiguous increasing sequence.

Another example of `char` to `int` conversion is the function `lower`, which
maps a single character to lower case *for the ASCII character set*. If the character is not an upper case letter, `lower` returns it unchanged.

```
/* lower:  convert c to lower case; ASCII only */
int lower(int c)
{
    if (c >= 'A' && c <= 'Z')
        return c + 'a' - 'A';
    else
        return c;
}
```

This works for ASCII because corresponding upper case and lower case letters
are a fixed distance apart as numeric values and each alphabet is contiguous—
there is nothing but letters between A and Z. This latter observation is not true
of the EBCDIC character set, however, so this code would convert more than
just letters in EBCDIC.

The standard header `<ctype.h>`, described in Appendix B, defines a family
of functions that provide tests and conversions that are independent of character
set. For example, the function `tolower(c)` returns the lower case value of `c`
if `c` is upper case, so `tolower` is a portable replacement for the function
`lower` shown above. Similarly, the test

```
c >= '0' && c <= '9'
```

can be replaced by

```
isdigit(c)
```

We will use the `<ctype.h>` functions from now on.

There is one subtle point about the conversion of characters to integers. The
language does not specify whether variables of type `char` are signed or
unsigned quantities. When a `char` is converted to an `int`, can it ever produce
a negative integer? The answer varies from machine to machine, reflecting

differences in architecture. On some machines a `char` whose leftmost bit is 1 will be converted to a negative integer ("sign extension"). On others, a `char` is promoted to an `int` by adding zeros at the left end, and thus is always positive.

The definition of C guarantees that any character in the machine's standard printing character set will never be negative, so these characters will always be positive quantities in expressions. But arbitrary bit patterns stored in character variables may appear to be negative on some machines, yet positive on others. For portability, specify `signed` or `unsigned` if non-character data is to be stored in `char` variables.

Relational expressions like `i > j` and logical expressions connected by `&&` and `||` are defined to have value 1 if true, and 0 if false. Thus the assignment

        d = c >= '0' && c <= '9'

sets d to 1 if c is a digit, and 0 if not. However, functions like `isdigit` may return any non-zero value for true. In the test part of `if`, `while`, `for`, etc., "true" just means "non-zero," so this makes no difference.

Implicit arithmetic conversions work much as expected. In general, if an operator like `+` or `*` that takes two operands (a binary operator) has operands of different types, the "lower" type is *promoted* to the "higher" type before the operation proceeds. The result is of the higher type. Section 6 of Appendix A states the conversion rules precisely. If there are no `unsigned` operands, however, the following informal set of rules will suffice:

> If either operand is `long double`, convert the other to `long double`.
>
> Otherwise, if either operand is `double`, convert the other to `double`.
>
> Otherwise, if either operand is `float`, convert the other to `float`.
>
> Otherwise, convert `char` and `short` to `int`.
>
> Then, if either operand is `long`, convert the other to `long`.

Notice that `float`s in an expression are not automatically converted to `double`; this is a change from the original definition. In general, mathematical functions like those in `<math.h>` will use double precision. The main reason for using `float` is to save storage in large arrays, or, less often, to save time on machines where double-precision arithmetic is particularly expensive.

Conversion rules are more complicated when `unsigned` operands are involved. The problem is that comparisons between signed and unsigned values are machine-dependent, because they depend on the sizes of the various integer types. For example, suppose that `int` is 16 bits and `long` is 32 bits. Then `-1L < 1U`, because `1U`, which is an `int`, is promoted to a `signed long`. But `-1L > 1UL`, because `-1L` is promoted to `unsigned long` and thus appears to be a large positive number.

Conversions take place across assignments; the value of the right side is converted to the type of the left, which is the type of the result.

A character is converted to an integer, either by sign extension or not, as described above.

Longer integers are converted to shorter ones or to `chars` by dropping the excess high-order bits. Thus in

```
int  i;
char c;

i = c;
c = i;
```

the value of `c` is unchanged. This is true whether or not sign extension is involved. Reversing the order of assignments might lose information, however.

If `x` is `float` and `i` is `int`, then `x = i` and `i = x` both cause conversions; `float` to `int` causes truncation of any fractional part. When `double` is converted to `float`, whether the value is rounded or truncated is implementation-dependent.

Since an argument of a function call is an expression, type conversions also take place when arguments are passed to functions. In the absence of a function prototype, `char` and `short` become `int`, and `float` becomes `double`. This is why we have declared function arguments to be `int` and `double` even when the function is called with `char` and `float`.

Finally, explicit type conversions can be forced ("coerced") in any expression, with a unary operator called a *cast*. In the construction

   (*type-name*) *expression*

the *expression* is converted to the named type by the conversion rules above. The precise meaning of a cast is as if the *expression* were assigned to a variable of the specified type, which is then used in place of the whole construction. For example, the library routine `sqrt` expects a `double` argument, and will produce nonsense if inadvertently handed something else. (`sqrt` is declared in `<math.h>`.) So if n is an integer, we can use

```
sqrt((double) n)
```

to convert the value of n to `double` before passing it to `sqrt`. Note that the cast produces the *value* of n in the proper type; n itself is not altered. The cast operator has the same high precedence as other unary operators, as summarized in the table at the end of this chapter.

If arguments are declared by a function prototype, as they normally should be, the declaration causes automatic coercion of any arguments when the function is called. Thus, given a function prototype for `sqrt`:

```
double sqrt(double);
```

the call

```
root2 = sqrt(2);
```

coerces the integer 2 into the `double` value 2.0 without any need for a cast.

The standard library includes a portable implementation of a pseudo-random number generator and a function for initializing the seed; the former illustrates a cast:

```
unsigned long int next = 1;

/* rand:  return pseudo-random integer on 0..32767 */
int rand(void)
{
    next = next * 1103515245 + 12345;
    return (unsigned int)(next/65536) % 32768;
}

/* srand:  set seed for rand() */
void srand(unsigned int seed)
{
    next = seed;
}
```

Exercise 2-3. Write the function htoi(s), which converts a string of hexa-decimal digits (including an optional 0x or 0X) into its equivalent integer value. The allowable digits are 0 through 9, a through f, and A through F. □

2.8 Increment and Decrement Operators

C provides two unusual operators for incrementing and decrementing variables. The increment operator ++ adds 1 to its operand, while the decrement operator -- subtracts 1. We have frequently used ++ to increment variables, as in

```
if (c == '\n')
    ++nl;
```

The unusual aspect is that ++ and -- may be used either as prefix operators (before the variable, as in ++n), or postfix (after the variable: n++). In both cases, the effect is to increment n. But the expression ++n increments n *before* its value is used, while n++ increments n *after* its value has been used. This means that in a context where the value is being used, not just the effect, ++n and n++ are different. If n is 5, then

```
x = n++;
```

sets x to 5, but

```
x = ++n;
```

sets x to 6. In both cases, n becomes 6. The increment and decrement operators can only be applied to variables; an expression like (i+j)++ is illegal.

In a context where no value is wanted, just the incrementing effect, as in

```
if (c == '\n')
    nl++;
```

prefix and postfix are the same. But there are situations where one or the other is specifically called for. For instance, consider the function `squeeze(s,c)`, which removes all occurrences of the character c from the string s.

```
/* squeeze:  delete all c from s */
void squeeze(char s[], int c)
{
    int i, j;

    for (i = j = 0; s[i] != '\0'; i++)
        if (s[i] != c)
            s[j++] = s[i];
    s[j] = '\0';
}
```

Each time a non-c occurs, it is copied into the current j position and only then is j incremented to be ready for the next character. This is exactly equivalent to

```
if (s[i] != c) {
    s[j] = s[i];
    j++;
}
```

Another example of a similar construction comes from the `getline` function that we wrote in Chapter 1, where we can replace

```
if (c == '\n') {
    s[i] = c;
    ++i;
}
```

by the more compact

```
if (c == '\n')
    s[i++] = c;
```

As a third example, consider the standard function `strcat(s,t)`, which concatenates the string t to the end of the string s. `strcat` assumes that there is enough space in s to hold the combination. As we have written it, `strcat` returns no value; the standard library version returns a pointer to the resulting string.

```
/* strcat:  concatenate t to end of s; s must be big enough */
void strcat(char s[], char t[])
{
    int i, j;

    i = j = 0;
    while (s[i] != '\0')     /* find end of s */
        i++;
    while ((s[i++] = t[j++]) != '\0')   /* copy t */
        ;
}
```

As each character is copied from t to s, the postfix ++ is applied to both i and j to make sure that they are in position for the next pass through the loop.

Exercise 2-4. Write an alternate version of squeeze(s1,s2) that deletes each character in s1 that matches any character in the *string* s2. □

Exercise 2-5. Write the function any(s1,s2), which returns the first location in the string s1 where any character from the string s2 occurs, or −1 if s1 contains no characters from s2. (The standard library function strpbrk does the same job but returns a pointer to the location.) □

2.9 Bitwise Operators

C provides six operators for bit manipulation; these may only be applied to integral operands, that is, char, short, int, and long, whether signed or unsigned.

    & bitwise AND
    | bitwise inclusive OR
    ^ bitwise exclusive OR
    << left shift
    >> right shift
    ~ one's complement (unary)

The bitwise AND operator & is often used to mask off some set of bits; for example,

```
n = n & 0177;
```

sets to zero all but the low-order 7 bits of n.
The bitwise OR operator | is used to turn bits on:

```
x = x | SET_ON;
```

sets to one in x the bits that are set to one in SET_ON.
The bitwise exclusive OR operator ^ sets a one in each bit position where its operands have different bits, and zero where they are the same.

One must distinguish the bitwise operators & and ¦ from the logical operators && and ¦¦, which imply left-to-right evaluation of a truth value. For example, if x is 1 and y is 2, then x & y is zero while x && y is one.

The shift operators << and >> perform left and right shifts of their left operand by the number of bit positions given by the right operand, which must be positive. Thus x << 2 shifts the value of x left by two positions, filling vacated bits with zero; this is equivalent to multiplication by 4. Right shifting an unsigned quantity always fills vacated bits with zero. Right shifting a signed quantity will fill with sign bits ("arithmetic shift") on some machines and with 0-bits ("logical shift") on others.

The unary operator ~ yields the one's complement of an integer; that is, it converts each 1-bit into a 0-bit and vice versa. For example,

```
x = x & ~077
```

sets the last six bits of x to zero. Note that x & ~077 is independent of word length, and is thus preferable to, for example, x & 0177700, which assumes that x is a 16-bit quantity. The portable form involves no extra cost, since ~077 is a constant expression that can be evaluated at compile time.

As an illustration of some of the bit operators, consider the function getbits(x,p,n) that returns the (right adjusted) n-bit field of x that begins at position p. We assume that bit position 0 is at the right end and that n and p are sensible positive values. For example, getbits(x,4,3) returns the three bits in bit positions 4, 3 and 2, right adjusted.

```
/* getbits:  get n bits from position p */
unsigned getbits(unsigned x, int p, int n)
{
    return (x >> (p+1-n)) & ~(~0 << n);
}
```

The expression x >> (p+1-n) moves the desired field to the right end of the word. ~0 is all 1-bits; shifting it left n bit positions with ~0<<n places zeros in the rightmost n bits; complementing that with ~ makes a mask with ones in the rightmost n bits.

Exercise 2-6. Write a function setbits(x,p,n,y) that returns x with the n bits that begin at position p set to the rightmost n bits of y, leaving the other bits unchanged. □

Exercise 2-7. Write a function invert(x,p,n) that returns x with the n bits that begin at position p inverted (i.e., 1 changed into 0 and vice versa), leaving the others unchanged. □

Exercise 2-8. Write a function rightrot(x,n) that returns the value of the integer x rotated to the right by n bit positions. □

2.10 Assignment Operators and Expressions

Expressions such as

```
i = i + 2
```

in which the variable on the left hand side is repeated immediately on the right, can be written in the compressed form

```
i += 2
```

The operator += is called an *assignment operator.*

Most binary operators (operators like + that have a left and right operand) have a corresponding assignment operator *op =*, where *op* is one of

```
+    -    *    /    %    <<    >>    &    ^    |
```

If $expr_1$ and $expr_2$ are expressions, then

$$expr_1 \; op = \; expr_2$$

is equivalent to

$$expr_1 = (expr_1) \; op \; (expr_2)$$

except that $expr_1$ is computed only once. Notice the parentheses around $expr_2$:

```
x *= y + 1
```

means

```
x = x * (y + 1)
```

rather than

```
x = x * y + 1
```

As an example, the function `bitcount` counts the number of 1-bits in its integer argument.

```
/* bitcount:   count 1 bits in x */
int bitcount(unsigned x)
{
    int b;

    for (b = 0; x != 0; x >>= 1)
        if (x & 01)
            b++;
    return b;
}
```

Declaring the argument x to be `unsigned` ensures that when it is right-shifted, vacated bits will be filled with zeros, not sign bits, regardless of the machine the program is run on.

Quite apart from conciseness, assignment operators have the advantage that they correspond better to the way people think. We say "add 2 to i" or "increment i by 2," not "take i, add 2, then put the result back in i." Thus the expression i += 2 is preferable to i = i+2. In addition, for a complicated expression like

```
yyval[yypv[p3+p4] + yypv[p1+p2]] += 2
```

the assignment operator makes the code easier to understand, since the reader doesn't have to check painstakingly that two long expressions are indeed the same, or to wonder why they're not. And an assignment operator may even help a compiler to produce efficient code.

We have already seen that the assignment statement has a value and can occur in expressions; the most common example is

```
while ((c = getchar()) != EOF)
    ...
```

The other assignment operators (+=, -=, etc.) can also occur in expressions, although this is less frequent.

In all such expressions, the type of an assignment expression is the type of its left operand, and the value is the value after the assignment.

Exercise 2-9. In a two's complement number system, x &= (x-1) deletes the rightmost 1-bit in x. Explain why. Use this observation to write a faster version of bitcount. □

2.11 Conditional Expressions

The statements

```
if (a > b)
    z = a;
else
    z = b;
```

compute in z the maximum of a and b. The *conditional expression*, written with the ternary operator "?:", provides an alternate way to write this and similar constructions. In the expression

$$expr_1 \; ? \; expr_2 \; : \; expr_3$$

the expression $expr_1$ is evaluated first. If it is non-zero (true), then the expression $expr_2$ is evaluated, and that is the value of the conditional expression. Otherwise $expr_3$ is evaluated, and that is the value. Only one of $expr_2$ and $expr_3$ is evaluated. Thus to set z to the maximum of a and b,

```
z = (a > b) ? a : b;     /* z = max(a, b) */
```

It should be noted that the conditional expression is indeed an expression, and it can be used wherever any other expression can be. If $expr_2$ and $expr_3$

are of different types, the type of the result is determined by the conversion rules discussed earlier in this chapter. For example, if f is a float and n is an int, then the expression

```
(n > 0) ? f : n
```

is of type float regardless of whether n is positive.

Parentheses are not necessary around the first expression of a conditional expression, since the precedence of ?: is very low, just above assignment. They are advisable anyway, however, since they make the condition part of the expression easier to see.

The conditional expression often leads to succinct code. For example, this loop prints n elements of an array, 10 per line, with each column separated by one blank, and with each line (including the last) terminated by a newline.

```
for (i = 0; i < n; i++)
    printf("%6d%c", a[i], (i%10==9 || i==n-1) ? '\n' : ' ');
```

A newline is printed after every tenth element, and after the n-th. All other elements are followed by one blank. This might look tricky, but it's more compact than the equivalent if-else. Another good example is

```
printf("You have %d item%s.\n", n, n==1 ? "" : "s");
```

Exercise 2-10. Rewrite the function lower, which converts upper case letters to lower case, with a conditional expression instead of if-else. □

2.12 Precedence and Order of Evaluation

Table 2-1 summarizes the rules for precedence and associativity of all operators, including those that we have not yet discussed. Operators on the same line have the same precedence; rows are in order of decreasing precedence, so, for example, *, /, and % all have the same precedence, which is higher than that of binary + and -. The "operator" ( ) refers to function call. The operators -> and . are used to access members of structures; they will be covered in Chapter 6, along with sizeof (size of an object). Chapter 5 discusses * (indirection through a pointer) and & (address of an object), and Chapter 3 discusses the comma operator.

Note that the precedence of the bitwise operators &, ^, and | falls below == and !=. This implies that bit-testing expressions like

```
if ((x & MASK) == 0) ...
```

must be fully parenthesized to give proper results.

C, like most languages, does not specify the order in which the operands of an operator are evaluated. (The exceptions are &&, ||, ?:, and ','.) For example, in a statement like

TABLE 2-1. PRECEDENCE AND ASSOCIATIVITY OF OPERATORS

OPERATORS	ASSOCIATIVITY
( ) [ ] -> .	left to right
! ~ ++ -- + - * & (*type*) sizeof	right to left
* / %	left to right
+ -	left to right
<< >>	left to right
< <= > >=	left to right
== !=	left to right
&	left to right
^	left to right
¦	left to right
&&	left to right
¦¦	left to right
?:	right to left
= += -= *= /= %= &= ^= ¦= <<= >>=	right to left
,	left to right

Unary +, -, and * have higher precedence than the binary forms.

```
x = f() + g();
```

f may be evaluated before g or vice versa; thus if either f or g alters a variable on which the other depends, x can depend on the order of evaluation. Intermediate results can be stored in temporary variables to ensure a particular sequence.

Similarly, the order in which function arguments are evaluated is not specified, so the statement

```
printf("%d %d\n", ++n, power(2, n));    /* WRONG */
```

can produce different results with different compilers, depending on whether n is incremented before power is called. The solution, of course, is to write

```
++n;
printf("%d %d\n", n, power(2, n));
```

Function calls, nested assignment statements, and increment and decrement operators cause "side effects"—some variable is changed as a by-product of the evaluation of an expression. In any expression involving side effects, there can be subtle dependencies on the order in which variables taking part in the expression are updated. One unhappy situation is typified by the statement

```
a[i] = i++;
```

The question is whether the subscript is the old value of i or the new.

Compilers can interpret this in different ways, and generate different answers depending on their interpretation. The standard intentionally leaves most such matters unspecified. When side effects (assignment to variables) take place within an expression is left to the discretion of the compiler, since the best order depends strongly on machine architecture. (The standard does specify that all side effects on arguments take effect before a function is called, but that would not help in the call to `printf` above.)

The moral is that writing code that depends on order of evaluation is a bad programming practice in any language. Naturally, it is necessary to know what things to avoid, but if you don't know *how* they are done on various machines, you won't be tempted to take advantage of a particular implementation.

CHAPTER 3: **Control Flow**

The control-flow statements of a language specify the order in which computations are performed. We have already met the most common control-flow constructions in earlier examples; here we will complete the set, and be more precise about the ones discussed before.

3.1 Statements and Blocks

An expression such as `x = 0` or `i++` or `printf(...)` becomes a *statement* when it is followed by a semicolon, as in

```
x = 0;
i++;
printf(...);
```

In C, the semicolon is a statement terminator, rather than a separator as it is in languages like Pascal.

Braces { and } are used to group declarations and statements together into a *compound statement*, or *block*, so that they are syntactically equivalent to a single statement. The braces that surround the statements of a function are one obvious example; braces around multiple statements after an `if`, `else`, `while`, or `for` are another. (Variables can be declared inside *any* block; we will talk about this in Chapter 4.) There is no semicolon after the right brace that ends a block.

3.2 If-Else

The `if-else` statement is used to express decisions. Formally, the syntax is

```
if (expression)
        statement₁
else
        statement₂
```

where the `else` part is optional. The *expression* is evaluated; if it is true (that is, if *expression* has a non-zero value), *statement*$_1$ is executed. If it is false (*expression* is zero) and if there is an `else` part, *statement*$_2$ is executed instead.

Since an `if` simply tests the numeric value of an expression, certain coding shortcuts are possible. The most obvious is writing

```
if (expression)
```

instead of

```
if (expression != 0)
```

Sometimes this is natural and clear; at other times it can be cryptic.

Because the `else` part of an `if-else` is optional, there is an ambiguity when an `else` is omitted from a nested `if` sequence. This is resolved by associating the `else` with the closest previous `else`-less `if`. For example, in

```
if (n > 0)
    if (a > b)
        z = a;
    else
        z = b;
```

the `else` goes with the inner `if`, as we have shown by indentation. If that isn't what you want, braces must be used to force the proper association:

```
if (n > 0) {
    if (a > b)
        z = a;
}
else
    z = b;
```

The ambiguity is especially pernicious in situations like this:

```
if (n >= 0)
    for (i = 0; i < n; i++)
        if (s[i] > 0) {
            printf("...");
            return i;
        }
else            /* WRONG */
    printf("error -- n is negative\n");
```

The indentation shows unequivocally what you want, but the compiler doesn't get the message, and associates the `else` with the inner `if`. This kind of bug can be hard to find; it's a good idea to use braces when there are nested `if`s.

By the way, notice that there is a semicolon after `z = a` in

```
if (a > b)
    z = a;
else
    z = b;
```

This is because grammatically, a *statement* follows the `if`, and an expression statement like "`z = a;`" is always terminated by a semicolon.

3.3 Else-If

The construction

```
if (expression)
      statement
else if (expression)
      statement
else if (expression)
      statement
else if (expression)
      statement
else
      statement
```

occurs so often that it is worth a brief separate discussion. This sequence of `if` statements is the most general way of writing a multi-way decision. The *expressions* are evaluated in order; if any *expression* is true, the *statement* associated with it is executed, and this terminates the whole chain. As always, the code for each *statement* is either a single statement, or a group in braces.

The last `else` part handles the "none of the above" or default case where none of the other conditions is satisfied. Sometimes there is no explicit action for the default; in that case the trailing

```
else
      statement
```

can be omitted, or it may be used for error checking to catch an "impossible" condition.

To illustrate a three-way decision, here is a binary search function that decides if a particular value x occurs in the sorted array v. The elements of v must be in increasing order. The function returns the position (a number between 0 and n-1) if x occurs in v, and -1 if not.

Binary search first compares the input value x to the middle element of the array v. If x is less than the middle value, searching focuses on the lower half of the table, otherwise on the upper half. In either case, the next step is to compare x to the middle element of the selected half. This process of dividing the range in two continues until the value is found or the range is empty.

```
/* binsearch:  find x in v[0] <= v[1] <= ... <= v[n-1] */
int binsearch(int x, int v[], int n)
{
    int low, high, mid;

    low = 0;
    high = n - 1;
    while (low <= high) {
        mid = (low+high) / 2;
        if (x < v[mid])
            high = mid - 1;
        else if (x > v[mid])
            low = mid + 1;
        else    /* found match */
            return mid;
    }
    return -1;   /* no match */
}
```

The fundamental decision is whether x is less than, greater than, or equal to the middle element v[mid] at each step; this is a natural for else-if.

Exercise 3-1. Our binary search makes two tests inside the loop, when one would suffice (at the price of more tests outside). Write a version with only one test inside the loop and measure the difference in run-time. □

3.4 Switch

The switch statement is a multi-way decision that tests whether an expression matches one of a number of *constant* integer values, and branches accordingly.

```
switch (expression ) {
    case const-expr:    statements
    case const-expr:    statements
    default:  statements
}
```

Each case is labeled by one or more integer-valued constants or constant expressions. If a case matches the expression value, execution starts at that case. All case expressions must be different. The case labeled default is executed if none of the other cases are satisfied. A default is optional; if it isn't there and if none of the cases match, no action at all takes place. Cases and the default clause can occur in any order.

In Chapter 1 we wrote a program to count the occurrences of each digit, white space, and all other characters, using a sequence of if ... else if ... else. Here is the same program with a switch:

```c
#include <stdio.h>

main()   /* count digits, white space, others */
{
    int c, i, nwhite, nother, ndigit[10];

    nwhite = nother = 0;
    for (i = 0; i < 10; i++)
        ndigit[i] = 0;
    while ((c = getchar()) != EOF) {
        switch (c) {
        case '0': case '1': case '2': case '3': case '4':
        case '5': case '6': case '7': case '8': case '9':
            ndigit[c-'0']++;
            break;
        case ' ':
        case '\n':
        case '\t':
            nwhite++;
            break;
        default:
            nother++;
            break;
        }
    }
    printf("digits =");
    for (i = 0; i < 10; i++)
        printf(" %d", ndigit[i]);
    printf(", white space = %d, other = %d\n",
        nwhite, nother);
    return 0;
}
```

The `break` statement causes an immediate exit from the `switch`. Because cases serve just as labels, after the code for one case is done, execution *falls through* to the next unless you take explicit action to escape. `break` and `return` are the most common ways to leave a `switch`. A `break` statement can also be used to force an immediate exit from `while`, `for`, and `do` loops, as will be discussed later in this chapter.

Falling through cases is a mixed blessing. On the positive side, it allows several cases to be attached to a single action, as with the digits in this example. But it also implies that normally each case must end with a `break` to prevent falling through to the next. Falling through from one case to another is not robust, being prone to disintegration when the program is modified. With the exception of multiple labels for a single computation, fall-throughs should be used sparingly, and commented.

As a matter of good form, put a `break` after the last case (the `default` here) even though it's logically unnecessary. Some day when another case gets added at the end, this bit of defensive programming will save you.

Exercise 3-2. Write a function escape(s,t) that converts characters like newline and tab into visible escape sequences like \n and \t as it copies the string t to s. Use a switch. Write a function for the other direction as well, converting escape sequences into the real characters. □

3.5 Loops—While and For

We have already encountered the while and for loops. In

```
while (expression)
    statement
```

the *expression* is evaluated. If it is non-zero, *statement* is executed and *expression* is re-evaluated. This cycle continues until *expression* becomes zero, at which point execution resumes after *statement*.

The for statement

```
for (expr₁; expr₂; expr₃)
    statement
```

is equivalent to

```
expr₁;
while (expr₂) {
    statement
    expr₃;
}
```

except for the behavior of continue, which is described in Section 3.7.

Grammatically, the three components of a for loop are expressions. Most commonly, $expr_1$ and $expr_3$ are assignments or function calls and $expr_2$ is a relational expression. Any of the three parts can be omitted, although the semicolons must remain. If $expr_1$ or $expr_3$ is omitted, it is simply dropped from the expansion. If the test, $expr_2$, is not present, it is taken as permanently true, so

```
for (;;) {
    ...
}
```

is an "infinite" loop, presumably to be broken by other means, such as a break or return.

Whether to use while or for is largely a matter of personal preference. For example, in

```
while ((c = getchar()) == ' ' || c == '\n' || c == '\t')
    ;   /* skip white space characters */
```

there is no initialization or re-initialization, so the while is most natural.

The for is preferable when there is a simple initialization and increment, since it keeps the loop control statements close together and visible at the top of the loop. This is most obvious in

```
for (i = 0; i < n; i++)
    ...
```

which is the C idiom for processing the first n elements of an array, the analog of the Fortran DO loop or the Pascal `for`. The analogy is not perfect, however, since the index and limit of a C `for` loop can be altered from within the loop, and the index variable i retains its value when the loop terminates for any reason. Because the components of the `for` are arbitrary expressions, `for` loops are not restricted to arithmetic progressions. Nonetheless, it is bad style to force unrelated computations into the initialization and increment of a `for`, which are better reserved for loop control operations.

As a larger example, here is another version of `atoi` for converting a string to its numeric equivalent. This one is slightly more general than the one in Chapter 2; it copes with optional leading white space and an optional + or − sign. (Chapter 4 shows `atof`, which does the same conversion for floating-point numbers.)

The structure of the program reflects the form of the input:

> *skip white space, if any*
> *get sign, if any*
> *get integer part and convert it*

Each step does its part, and leaves things in a clean state for the next. The whole process terminates on the first character that could not be part of a number.

```
#include <ctype.h>

/* atoi:  convert s to integer; version 2 */
int atoi(char s[])
{
    int i, n, sign;

    for (i = 0; isspace(s[i]); i++)   /* skip white space */
        ;
    sign = (s[i] == '-') ? -1 : 1;
    if (s[i] == '+' || s[i] == '-')   /* skip sign */
        i++;
    for (n = 0; isdigit(s[i]); i++)
        n = 10 * n + (s[i] - '0');
    return sign * n;
}
```

The standard library provides a more elaborate function `strtol` for conversion of strings to long integers; see Section 5 of Appendix B.

The advantages of keeping loop control centralized are even more obvious when there are several nested loops. The following function is a Shell sort for sorting an array of integers. The basic idea of this sorting algorithm, which was invented in 1959 by D. L. Shell, is that in early stages, far-apart elements are compared, rather than adjacent ones as in simpler interchange sorts. This tends to eliminate large amounts of disorder quickly, so later stages have less work to do. The interval between compared elements is gradually decreased to one, at which point the sort effectively becomes an adjacent interchange method.

```c
/* shellsort:  sort v[0]...v[n-1] into increasing order */
void shellsort(int v[], int n)
{
    int gap, i, j, temp;

    for (gap = n/2; gap > 0; gap /= 2)
        for (i = gap; i < n; i++)
            for (j=i-gap; j>=0 && v[j]>v[j+gap]; j-=gap) {
                temp = v[j];
                v[j] = v[j+gap];
                v[j+gap] = temp;
            }
}
```

There are three nested loops. The outermost controls the gap between compared elements, shrinking it from n/2 by a factor of two each pass until it becomes zero. The middle loop steps along the elements. The innermost loop compares each pair of elements that is separated by gap and reverses any that are out of order. Since gap is eventually reduced to one, all elements are eventually ordered correctly. Notice how the generality of the for makes the outer loop fit the same form as the others, even though it is not an arithmetic progression.

One final C operator is the comma ",", which most often finds use in the for statement. A pair of expressions separated by a comma is evaluated left to right, and the type and value of the result are the type and value of the right operand. Thus in a for statement, it is possible to place multiple expressions in the various parts, for example to process two indices in parallel. This is illustrated in the function reverse(s), which reverses the string s in place.

```c
#include <string.h>

/* reverse:  reverse string s in place */
void reverse(char s[])
{
    int c, i, j;

    for (i = 0, j = strlen(s)-1; i < j; i++, j--) {
        c = s[i];
        s[i] = s[j];
        s[j] = c;
    }
}
```

The commas that separate function arguments, variables in declarations, etc., are *not* comma operators, and do not guarantee left to right evaluation.

Comma operators should be used sparingly. The most suitable uses are for constructs strongly related to each other, as in the `for` loop in `reverse`, and in macros where a multistep computation has to be a single expression. A comma expression might also be appropriate for the exchange of elements in `reverse`, where the exchange can be thought of as a single operation:

```
for (i = 0, j = strlen(s)-1; i < j; i++, j--)
    c = s[i], s[i] = s[j], s[j] = c;
```

Exercise 3-3. Write a function `expand(s1,s2)` that expands shorthand notations like `a-z` in the string `s1` into the equivalent complete list `abc...xyz` in `s2`. Allow for letters of either case and digits, and be prepared to handle cases like `a-b-c` and `a-z0-9` and `-a-z`. Arrange that a leading or trailing `-` is taken literally. ☐

3.6 Loops—Do-while

As we discussed in Chapter 1, the `while` and `for` loops test the termination condition at the top. By contrast, the third loop in C, the `do-while`, tests at the bottom *after* making each pass through the loop body; the body is always executed at least once.

The syntax of the `do` is

```
do
     statement
while (expression);
```

The *statement* is executed, then *expression* is evaluated. If it is true, *statement* is evaluated again, and so on. When the expression becomes false, the loop terminates. Except for the sense of the test, `do-while` is equivalent to the Pascal `repeat-until` statement.

Experience shows that `do-while` is much less used than `while` and `for`. Nonetheless, from time to time it is valuable, as in the following function `itoa`, which converts a number to a character string (the inverse of `atoi`). The job is slightly more complicated than might be thought at first, because the easy methods of generating the digits generate them in the wrong order. We have chosen to generate the string backwards, then reverse it.

```
/* itoa:   convert n to characters in s */
void itoa(int n, char s[])
{
    int i, sign;

    if ((sign = n) < 0)   /* record sign */
        n = -n;           /* make n positive */
    i = 0;
    do {        /* generate digits in reverse order */
        s[i++] = n % 10 + '0';   /* get next digit */
    } while ((n /= 10) > 0);       /* delete it */
    if (sign < 0)
        s[i++] = '-';
    s[i] = '\0';
    reverse(s);
}
```

The do-while is necessary, or at least convenient, since at least one character must be installed in the array s, even if n is zero. We also used braces around the single statement that makes up the body of the do-while, even though they are unnecessary, so the hasty reader will not mistake the while part for the *beginning* of a while loop.

Exercise 3-4. In a two's complement number representation, our version of itoa does not handle the largest negative number, that is, the value of n equal to $-(2^{wordsize-1})$. Explain why not. Modify it to print that value correctly, regardless of the machine on which it runs. ☐

Exercise 3-5. Write the function itob(n,s,b) that converts the integer n into a base b character representation in the string s. In particular, itob(n,s,16) formats n as a hexadecimal integer in s. ☐

Exercise 3-6. Write a version of itoa that accepts three arguments instead of two. The third argument is a minimum field width; the converted number must be padded with blanks on the left if necessary to make it wide enough. ☐

3.7 Break and Continue

It is sometimes convenient to be able to exit from a loop other than by testing at the top or bottom. The break statement provides an early exit from for, while, and do, just as from switch. A break causes the innermost enclosing loop or switch to be exited immediately.

The following function, trim, removes trailing blanks, tabs, and newlines from the end of a string, using a break to exit from a loop when the rightmost non-blank, non-tab, non-newline is found.

```
/* trim:  remove trailing blanks, tabs, newlines */
int trim(char s[])
{
    int n;

    for (n = strlen(s)-1; n >= 0; n--)
        if (s[n] != ' ' && s[n] != '\t' && s[n] != '\n')
            break;
    s[n+1] = '\0';
    return n;
}
```

`strlen` returns the length of the string. The `for` loop starts at the end and scans backwards looking for the first character that is not a blank or tab or newline. The loop is broken when one is found, or when n becomes negative (that is, when the entire string has been scanned). You should verify that this is correct behavior even when the string is empty or contains only white space characters.

The `continue` statement is related to `break`, but less often used; it causes the next iteration of the enclosing `for`, `while`, or do loop to begin. In the `while` and do, this means that the test part is executed immediately; in the `for`, control passes to the increment step. The `continue` statement applies only to loops, not to `switch`. A `continue` inside a `switch` inside a loop causes the next loop iteration.

As an example, this fragment processes only the non-negative elements in the array a; negative values are skipped.

```
for (i = 0; i < n; i++) {
    if (a[i] < 0)    /* skip negative elements */
        continue;
    ...   /* do positive elements */
}
```

The `continue` statement is often used when the part of the loop that follows is complicated, so that reversing a test and indenting another level would nest the program too deeply.

3.8 Goto and Labels

C provides the infinitely-abusable `goto` statement, and labels to branch to. Formally, the `goto` is never necessary, and in practice it is almost always easy to write code without it. We have not used `goto` in this book.

Nevertheless, there are a few situations where `goto`s may find a place. The most common is to abandon processing in some deeply nested structure, such as breaking out of two or more loops at once. The `break` statement cannot be used directly since it only exits from the innermost loop. Thus:

```
for ( ... )
    for ( ... ) {
        ...
        if (disaster)
            goto error;
    }
    ...

error:
    clean up the mess
```

This organization is handy if the error-handling code is non-trivial, and if errors can occur in several places.

A label has the same form as a variable name, and is followed by a colon. It can be attached to any statement in the same function as the goto. The scope of a label is the entire function.

As another example, consider the problem of determining whether two arrays a and b have an element in common. One possibility is

```
for (i = 0; i < n; i++)
    for (j = 0; j < m; j++)
        if (a[i] == b[j])
            goto found;
/* didn't find any common element */
...
found:
/* got one:  a[i] == b[j] */
...
```

Code involving a goto can always be written without one, though perhaps at the price of some repeated tests or an extra variable. For example, the array search becomes

```
found = 0;
for (i = 0; i < n && !found; i++)
    for (j = 0; j < m && !found; j++)
        if (a[i] == b[j])
            found = 1;
if (found)
    /* got one:  a[i-1] == b[j-1] */
    ...
else
    /* didn't find any common element */
    ...
```

With a few exceptions like those cited here, code that relies on goto statements is generally harder to understand and to maintain than code without gotos. Although we are not dogmatic about the matter, it does seem that goto statements should be used rarely, if at all.

CHAPTER 4: **Functions and Program Structure**

Functions break large computing tasks into smaller ones, and enable people to build on what others have done instead of starting over from scratch. Appropriate functions hide details of operation from parts of the program that don't need to know about them, thus clarifying the whole, and easing the pain of making changes.

C has been designed to make functions efficient and easy to use; C programs generally consist of many small functions rather than a few big ones. A program may reside in one or more source files. Source files may be compiled separately and loaded together, along with previously compiled functions from libraries. We will not go into that process here, however, since the details vary from system to system.

Function declaration and definition is the area where the ANSI standard has made the most visible changes to C. As we saw first in Chapter 1, it is now possible to declare the types of arguments when a function is declared. The syntax of function definition also changes, so that declarations and definitions match. This makes it possible for a compiler to detect many more errors than it could before. Furthermore, when arguments are properly declared, appropriate type coercions are performed automatically.

The standard clarifies the rules on the scope of names; in particular, it requires that there be only one definition of each external object. Initialization is more general: automatic arrays and structures may now be initialized.

The C preprocessor has also been enhanced. New preprocessor facilities include a more complete set of conditional compilation directives, a way to create quoted strings from macro arguments, and better control over the macro expansion process.

4.1 Basics of Functions

To begin, let us design and write a program to print each line of its input that contains a particular "pattern" or string of characters. (This is a special case of the UNIX program grep.) For example, searching for the pattern of

67

letters "ould" in the set of lines

```
Ah Love! could you and I with Fate conspire
To grasp this sorry Scheme of Things entire,
Would not we shatter it to bits -- and then
Re-mould it nearer to the Heart's Desire!
```

will produce the output

```
Ah Love! could you and I with Fate conspire
Would not we shatter it to bits -- and then
Re-mould it nearer to the Heart's Desire!
```

The job falls neatly into three pieces:

```
while (there's another line)
    if (the line contains the pattern)
        print it
```

Although it's certainly possible to put the code for all of this in `main`, a better way is to use the structure to advantage by making each part a separate function. Three small pieces are easier to deal with than one big one, because irrelevant details can be buried in the functions, and the chance of unwanted interactions is minimized. And the pieces may even be useful in other programs.

"While there's another line" is `getline`, a function that we wrote in Chapter 1, and "print it" is `printf`, which someone has already provided for us. This means we need only write a routine to decide whether the line contains an occurrence of the pattern.

We can solve that problem by writing a function `strindex(s,t)` that returns the position or index in the string `s` where the string `t` begins, or -1 if `s` doesn't contain `t`. Because C arrays begin at position zero, indexes will be zero or positive, and so a negative value like -1 is convenient for signaling failure. When we later need more sophisticated pattern matching, we only have to replace `strindex`; the rest of the code can remain the same. (The standard library provides a function `strstr` that is similar to `strindex`, except that it returns a pointer instead of an index.)

Given this much design, filling in the details of the program is straightforward. Here is the whole thing, so you can see how the pieces fit together. For now, the pattern to be searched for is a literal string, which is not the most general of mechanisms. We will return shortly to a discussion of how to initialize character arrays, and in Chapter 5 will show how to make the pattern a parameter that is set when the program is run. There is also a slightly different version of `getline`; you might find it instructive to compare it to the one in Chapter 1.

```
#include <stdio.h>
#define MAXLINE 1000     /* maximum input line length */

int getline(char line[], int max);
int strindex(char source[], char searchfor[]);

char pattern[] = "ould";    /* pattern to search for */

/* find all lines matching pattern */
main()
{
    char line[MAXLINE];
    int found = 0;

    while (getline(line, MAXLINE) > 0)
        if (strindex(line, pattern) >= 0) {
            printf("%s", line);
            found++;
        }
    return found;
}

/* getline:  get line into s, return length */
int getline(char s[], int lim)
{
    int c, i;

    i = 0;
    while (--lim > 0 && (c=getchar()) != EOF && c != '\n')
        s[i++] = c;
    if (c == '\n')
        s[i++] = c;
    s[i] = '\0';
    return i;
}

/* strindex:  return index of t in s, -1 if none */
int strindex(char s[], char t[])
{
    int i, j, k;

    for (i = 0; s[i] != '\0'; i++) {
        for (j=i, k=0; t[k]!='\0' && s[j]==t[k]; j++, k++)
            ;
        if (k > 0 && t[k] == '\0')
            return i;
    }
    return -1;
}
```

Each function definition has the form

> *return-type function-name(argument declarations)*
> {
>   *declarations and statements*
> }

Various parts may be absent; a minimal function is

```
dummy() {}
```

which does nothing and returns nothing. A do-nothing function like this is sometimes useful as a place holder during program development. If the return type is omitted, `int` is assumed.

A program is just a set of definitions of variables and functions. Communication between the functions is by arguments and values returned by the functions, and through external variables. The functions can occur in any order in the source file, and the source program can be split into multiple files, so long as no function is split.

The `return` statement is the mechanism for returning a value from the called function to its caller. Any expression can follow `return`:

```
return expression;
```

The *expression* will be converted to the return type of the function if necessary. Parentheses are often used around the *expression*, but they are optional.

The calling function is free to ignore the returned value. Furthermore, there need be no expression after `return`; in that case, no value is returned to the caller. Control also returns to the caller with no value when execution "falls off the end" of the function by reaching the closing right brace. It is not illegal, but probably a sign of trouble, if a function returns a value from one place and no value from another. In any case, if a function fails to return a value, its "value" is certain to be garbage.

The pattern-searching program returns a status from `main`, the number of matches found. This value is available for use by the environment that called the program.

The mechanics of how to compile and load a C program that resides on multiple source files vary from one system to the next. On the UNIX system, for example, the `cc` command mentioned in Chapter 1 does the job. Suppose that the three functions are stored in three files called `main.c`, `getline.c`, and `strindex.c`. Then the command

```
cc main.c getline.c strindex.c
```

compiles the three files, placing the resulting object code in files `main.o`, `getline.o`, and `strindex.o`, then loads them all into an executable file called `a.out`. If there is an error, say in `main.c`, that file can be recompiled by itself and the result loaded with the previous object files, with the command

```
cc main.c getline.o strindex.o
```

The `cc` command uses the ".c" versus ".o" naming convention to distinguish source files from object files.

Exercise 4-1. Write the function `strrindex(s,t)`, which returns the position of the *rightmost* occurrence of t in s, or – 1 if there is none. □

4.2 Functions Returning Non-integers

So far our examples of functions have returned either no value (void) or an int. What if a function must return some other type? Many numerical functions like `sqrt`, `sin`, and `cos` return `double`; other specialized functions return other types. To illustrate how to deal with this, let us write and use the function `atof(s)`, which converts the string s to its double-precision floating-point equivalent. `atof` is an extension of `atoi`, which we showed versions of in Chapters 2 and 3. It handles an optional sign and decimal point, and the presence or absence of either integer part or fractional part. Our version is *not* a high-quality input conversion routine; that would take more space than we care to use. The standard library includes an `atof`; the header `<stdlib.h>` declares it.

First, `atof` itself must declare the type of value it returns, since it is not int. The type name precedes the function name:

```
#include <ctype.h>

/* atof:  convert string s to double */
double atof(char s[])
{
    double val, power;
    int i, sign;

    for (i = 0; isspace(s[i]); i++)  /* skip white space */
        ;
    sign = (s[i] == '-') ? -1 : 1;
    if (s[i] == '+' || s[i] == '-')
        i++;
    for (val = 0.0; isdigit(s[i]); i++)
        val = 10.0 * val + (s[i] - '0');
    if (s[i] == '.')
        i++;
    for (power = 1.0; isdigit(s[i]); i++) {
        val = 10.0 * val + (s[i] - '0');
        power *= 10.0;
    }
    return sign * val / power;
}
```

Second, and just as important, the calling routine must know that `atof` returns a non-int value. One way to ensure this is to declare `atof` explicitly in the calling routine. The declaration is shown in this primitive calculator (barely adequate for check-book balancing), which reads one number per line, optionally preceded by a sign, and adds them up, printing the running sum after each input:

```
#include <stdio.h>

#define MAXLINE 100

/* rudimentary calculator */
main()
{
    double sum, atof(char []);
    char line[MAXLINE];
    int getline(char line[], int max);

    sum = 0;
    while (getline(line, MAXLINE) > 0)
        printf("\t%g\n", sum += atof(line));
    return 0;
}
```

The declaration

```
    double sum, atof(char []);
```

says that sum is a double variable, and that atof is a function that takes one char[] argument and returns a double.

The function atof must be declared and defined consistently. If atof itself and the call to it in main have inconsistent types in the same source file, the error will be detected by the compiler. But if (as is more likely) atof were compiled separately, the mismatch would not be detected, atof would return a double that main would treat as an int, and meaningless answers would result.

In the light of what we have said about how declarations must match definitions, this might seem surprising. The reason a mismatch can happen is that if there is no function prototype, a function is implicitly declared by its first appearance in an expression, such as

```
    sum += atof(line)
```

If a name that has not been previously declared occurs in an expression and is followed by a left parenthesis, it is declared by context to be a function name, the function is assumed to return an int, and nothing is assumed about its arguments. Furthermore, if a function declaration does not include arguments, as in

```
    double atof();
```

that too is taken to mean that nothing is to be assumed about the arguments of atof; all parameter checking is turned off. This special meaning of the empty argument list is intended to permit older C programs to compile with new compilers. But it's a bad idea to use it with new programs. If the function takes arguments, declare them; if it takes no arguments, use `void`.

Given `atof`, properly declared, we could write `atoi` (convert a string to `int`) in terms of it:

```
/* atoi:  convert string s to integer using atof */
int atoi(char s[])
{
    double atof(char s[]);

    return (int) atof(s);
}
```

Notice the structure of the declarations and the `return` statement. The value of the expression in

```
return expression;
```

is converted to the type of the function before the return is taken. Therefore, the value of `atof`, a `double`, is converted automatically to `int` when it appears in this `return`, since the function `atoi` returns an `int`. This operation does potentially discard information, however, so some compilers warn of it. The cast states explicitly that the operation is intended, and suppresses any warning.

Exercise 4-2. Extend `atof` to handle scientific notation of the form

```
123.45e-6
```

where a floating-point number may be followed by e or E and an optionally signed exponent. □

4.3 External Variables

A C program consists of a set of external objects, which are either variables or functions. The adjective "external" is used in contrast to "internal," which describes the arguments and variables defined inside functions. External variables are defined outside of any function, and are thus potentially available to many functions. Functions themselves are always external, because C does not allow functions to be defined inside other functions. By default, external variables and functions have the property that all references to them by the same name, even from functions compiled separately, are references to the same thing. (The standard calls this property *external linkage*.) In this sense, external variables are analogous to Fortran COMMON blocks or variables in the outermost block in Pascal. We will see later how to define external variables and functions that are visible only within a single source file.

Because external variables are globally accessible, they provide an alternative to function arguments and return values for communicating data between functions. Any function may access an external variable by referring to it by name, if the name has been declared somehow.

If a large number of variables must be shared among functions, external variables are more convenient and efficient than long argument lists. As pointed out in Chapter 1, however, this reasoning should be applied with some caution, for it can have a bad effect on program structure, and lead to programs with too many data connections between functions.

External variables are also useful because of their greater scope and lifetime. Automatic variables are internal to a function; they come into existence when the function is entered, and disappear when it is left. External variables, on the other hand, are permanent, so they retain values from one function invocation to the next. Thus if two functions must share some data, yet neither calls the other, it is often most convenient if the shared data is kept in external variables rather than passed in and out via arguments.

Let us examine this issue further with a larger example. The problem is to write a calculator program that provides the operators +, −, *, and /. Because it is easier to implement, the calculator will use reverse Polish notation instead of infix. (Reverse Polish is used by some pocket calculators, and in languages like Forth and Postscript.)

In reverse Polish notation, each operator follows its operands; an infix expression like

```
( 1 - 2 ) * ( 4 + 5 )
```

is entered as

```
1 2 - 4 5 + *
```

Parentheses are not needed; the notation is unambiguous as long as we know how many operands each operator expects.

The implementation is simple. Each operand is pushed onto a stack; when an operator arrives, the proper number of operands (two for binary operators) is popped, the operator is applied to them, and the result is pushed back onto the stack. In the example above, for instance, 1 and 2 are pushed, then replaced by their difference, −1. Next, 4 and 5 are pushed and then replaced by their sum, 9. The product of −1 and 9, which is −9, replaces them on the stack. The value on the top of the stack is popped and printed when the end of the input line is encountered.

The structure of the program is thus a loop that performs the proper operation on each operator and operand as it appears:

```
while (next operator or operand is not end-of-file indicator)
    if (number)
        push it
    else if (operator)
        pop operands
        do operation
        push result
    else if (newline)
        pop and print top of stack
    else
        error
```

The operations of pushing and popping a stack are trivial, but by the time
error detection and recovery are added, they are long enough that it is better to
put each in a separate function than to repeat the code throughout the whole
program. And there should be a separate function for fetching the next input
operator or operand.

The main design decision that has not yet been discussed is where the stack
is, that is, which routines access it directly. One possibility is to keep it in
main, and pass the stack and the current stack position to the routines that
push and pop it. But main doesn't need to know about the variables that control the stack; it only does push and pop operations. So we have decided to
store the stack and its associated information in external variables accessible to
the push and pop functions but not to main.

Translating this outline into code is easy enough. If for now we think of the
program as existing in one source file, it will look like this:

```
#includes
#defines

function declarations for main

main() { ... }

external variables for push and pop

void push(double f) { ... }
double pop(void) { ... }

int getop(char s[]) { ... }

routines called by getop
```

Later we will discuss how this might be split into two or more source files.

The function main is a loop containing a big switch on the type of operator or operand; this is a more typical use of switch than the one shown in Section 3.4.

```c
#include <stdio.h>
#include <stdlib.h>    /* for atof() */

#define MAXOP   100    /* max size of operand or operator */
#define NUMBER  '0'    /* signal that a number was found */

int getop(char []);
void push(double);
double pop(void);

/* reverse Polish calculator */
main()
{
    int type;
    double op2;
    char s[MAXOP];

    while ((type = getop(s)) != EOF) {
        switch (type) {
        case NUMBER:
            push(atof(s));
            break;
        case '+':
            push(pop() + pop());
            break;
        case '*':
            push(pop() * pop());
            break;
        case '-':
            op2 = pop();
            push(pop() - op2);
            break;
        case '/':
            op2 = pop();
            if (op2 != 0.0)
                push(pop() / op2);
            else
                printf("error: zero divisor\n");
            break;
        case '\n':
            printf("\t%.8g\n", pop());
            break;
        default:
            printf("error: unknown command %s\n", s);
            break;
        }
    }
    return 0;
}
```

Because + and * are commutative operators, the order in which the popped operands are combined is irrelevant, but for − and / the left and right operands must be distinguished. In

```
push(pop() - pop());     /* WRONG */
```

the order in which the two calls of pop are evaluated is not defined. To guarantee the right order, it is necessary to pop the first value into a temporary variable as we did in main.

```
#define MAXVAL   100    /* maximum depth of val stack */

int sp = 0;             /* next free stack position */
double val[MAXVAL];     /* value stack */

/* push:  push f onto value stack */
void push(double f)
{
    if (sp < MAXVAL)
        val[sp++] = f;
    else
        printf("error: stack full, can't push %g\n", f);
}



/* pop:  pop and return top value from stack */
double pop(void)
{
    if (sp > 0)
        return val[--sp];
    else {
        printf("error: stack empty\n");
        return 0.0;
    }
}
```

A variable is external if it is defined outside of any function. Thus the stack and stack index that must be shared by push and pop are defined outside of these functions. But main itself does not refer to the stack or stack position—the representation can be hidden.

Let us now turn to the implementation of getop, the function that fetches the next operator or operand. The task is easy. Skip blanks and tabs. If the next character is not a digit or a decimal point, return it. Otherwise, collect a string of digits (which might include a decimal point), and return NUMBER, the signal that a number has been collected.

```c
#include <ctype.h>

int getch(void);
void ungetch(int);

/* getop:  get next operator or numeric operand */
int getop(char s[])
{
    int i, c;

    while ((s[0] = c = getch()) == ' ' || c == '\t')
        ;
    s[1] = '\0';
    if (!isdigit(c) && c != '.')
        return c;       /* not a number */
    i = 0;
    if (isdigit(c))     /* collect integer part */
        while (isdigit(s[++i] = c = getch()))
            ;
    if (c == '.')       /* collect fraction part */
        while (isdigit(s[++i] = c = getch()))
            ;
    s[i] = '\0';
    if (c != EOF)
        ungetch(c);
    return NUMBER;
}
```

What are getch and ungetch? It is often the case that a program cannot determine that it has read enough input until it has read too much. One instance is collecting the characters that make up a number: until the first non-digit is seen, the number is not complete. But then the program has read one character too far, a character that it is not prepared for.

The problem would be solved if it were possible to "un-read" the unwanted character. Then, every time the program reads one character too many, it could push it back on the input, so the rest of the code could behave as if it had never been read. Fortunately, it's easy to simulate un-getting a character, by writing a pair of cooperating functions. getch delivers the next input character to be considered; ungetch remembers the characters put back on the input, so that subsequent calls to getch will return them before reading new input.

How they work together is simple. ungetch puts the pushed-back characters into a shared buffer—a character array. getch reads from the buffer if there is anything there, and calls getchar if the buffer is empty. There must also be an index variable that records the position of the current character in the buffer.

Since the buffer and the index are shared by getch and ungetch and must retain their values between calls, they must be external to both routines. Thus we can write getch, ungetch, and their shared variables as:

```
#define BUFSIZE 100

char buf[BUFSIZE];   /* buffer for ungetch */
int  bufp = 0;       /* next free position in buf */

int getch(void) /* get a (possibly pushed back) character */
{
    return (bufp > 0) ? buf[--bufp] : getchar();
}

void ungetch(int c) /* push character back on input */
{
    if (bufp >= BUFSIZE)
        printf("ungetch: too many characters\n");
    else
        buf[bufp++] = c;
}
```

The standard library includes a function `ungetc` that provides one character of pushback; we will discuss it in Chapter 7. We have used an array for the pushback, rather than a single character, to illustrate a more general approach.

Exercise 4-3. Given the basic framework, it's straightforward to extend the calculator. Add the modulus (%) operator and provisions for negative numbers. ☐

Exercise 4-4. Add commands to print the top element of the stack without popping, to duplicate it, and to swap the top two elements. Add a command to clear the stack. ☐

Exercise 4-5. Add access to library functions like `sin`, `exp`, and `pow`. See `<math.h>` in Appendix B, Section 4. ☐

Exercise 4-6. Add commands for handling variables. (It's easy to provide twenty-six variables with single-letter names.) Add a variable for the most recently printed value. ☐

Exercise 4-7. Write a routine `ungets(s)` that will push back an entire string onto the input. Should `ungets` know about `buf` and `bufp`, or should it just use `ungetch`? ☐

Exercise 4-8. Suppose that there will never be more than one character of pushback. Modify `getch` and `ungetch` accordingly. ☐

Exercise 4-9. Our `getch` and `ungetch` do not handle a pushed-back EOF correctly. Decide what their properties ought to be if an EOF is pushed back, then implement your design. ☐

Exercise 4-10. An alternate organization uses `getline` to read an entire input line; this makes `getch` and `ungetch` unnecessary. Revise the calculator to use this approach. ☐

4.4 Scope Rules

The functions and external variables that make up a C program need not all
be compiled at the same time; the source text of the program may be kept in
several files, and previously compiled routines may be loaded from libraries.
Among the questions of interest are

- How are declarations written so that variables are properly declared during
  compilation?
- How are declarations arranged so that all the pieces will be properly con-
  nected when the program is loaded?
- How are declarations organized so there is only one copy?
- How are external variables initialized?

Let us discuss these topics by reorganizing the calculator program into several
files. As a practical matter, the calculator is too small to be worth splitting, but
it is a fine illustration of the issues that arise in larger programs.

The *scope* of a name is the part of the program within which the name can
be used. For an automatic variable declared at the beginning of a function, the
scope is the function in which the name is declared. Local variables of the same
name in different functions are unrelated. The same is true of the parameters
of the function, which are in effect local variables.

The scope of an external variable or a function lasts from the point at which
it is declared to the end of the file being compiled. For example, if `main`, `sp`,
`val`, `push`, and `pop` are defined in one file, in the order shown above, that is,

```
main() { ... }

int sp = 0;
double val[MAXVAL];

void push(double f) { ... }

double pop(void) { ... }
```

then the variables `sp` and `val` may be used in `push` and `pop` simply by naming them; no further declarations are needed. But these names are not visible in
`main`, nor are `push` and `pop` themselves.

On the other hand, if an external variable is to be referred to before it is
defined, or if it is defined in a different source file from the one where it is
being used, then an `extern` declaration is mandatory.

It is important to distinguish between the *declaration* of an external variable
and its *definition*. A declaration announces the properties of a variable (pri-
marily its type); a definition also causes storage to be set aside. If the lines

```
int sp;
double val[MAXVAL];
```

appear outside of any function, they *define* the external variables `sp` and `val`, cause storage to be set aside, and also serve as the declaration for the rest of that source file. On the other hand, the lines

```
    extern int sp;
    extern double val[];
```

declare for the rest of the source file that `sp` is an `int` and that `val` is a `double` array (whose size is determined elsewhere), but they do not create the variables or reserve storage for them.

There must be only one *definition* of an external variable among all the files that make up the source program; other files may contain `extern` declarations to access it. (There may also be `extern` declarations in the file containing the definition.) Array sizes must be specified with the definition, but are optional with an `extern` declaration.

Initialization of an external variable goes only with the definition.

Although it is not a likely organization for this program, the functions `push` and `pop` could be defined in one file, and the variables `val` and `sp` defined and initialized in another. Then these definitions and declarations would be necessary to tie them together:

In file1:

```
    extern int sp;
    extern double val[];

    void push(double f) { ... }

    double pop(void) { ... }
```

In file2:

```
    int sp = 0;
    double val[MAXVAL];
```

Because the `extern` declarations in *file1* lie ahead of and outside the function definitions, they apply to all functions; one set of declarations suffices for all of *file1*. This same organization would also be needed if the definitions of `sp` and `val` followed their use in one file.

4.5 Header Files

Let us now consider dividing the calculator program into several source files, as it might be if each of the components were substantially bigger. The `main` function would go in one file, which we will call `main.c`; `push`, `pop`, and their variables go into a second file, `stack.c`; `getop` goes into a third, `getop.c`. Finally, `getch` and `ungetch` go into a fourth file, `getch.c`; we separate them from the others because they would come from a separately-compiled library in a realistic program.

There is one more thing to worry about—the definitions and declarations shared among the files. As much as possible, we want to centralize this, so that there is only one copy to get right and keep right as the program evolves. Accordingly, we will place this common material in a *header file*, calc.h, which will be included as necessary. (The #include line is described in Section 4.11.) The resulting program then looks like this:

calc.h:

```
#define NUMBER '0'
void push(double);
double pop(void);
int getop(char []);
int getch(void);
void ungetch(int);
```

main.c:

```
#include <stdio.h>
#include <stdlib.h>
#include "calc.h"
#define MAXOP 100
main() {
    ...
}
```

getop.c:

```
#include <stdio.h>
#include <ctype.h>
#include "calc.h"
getop() {
    ...
}
```

getch.c:

```
#include <stdio.h>
#define BUFSIZE 100
char buf[BUFSIZE];
int bufp = 0;
int getch(void) {
    ...
}
void ungetch(int) {
    ...
}
```

stack.c:

```
#include <stdio.h>
#include "calc.h"
#define MAXVAL 100
int sp = 0;
double val[MAXVAL];
void push(double) {
    ...
}
double pop(void) {
    ...
}
```

There is a tradeoff between the desire that each file have access only to the information it needs for its job and the practical reality that it is harder to maintain more header files. Up to some moderate program size, it is probably best to have one header file that contains everything that is to be shared between any two parts of the program; that is the decision we made here. For a much larger program, more organization and more headers would be needed.

4.6 Static Variables

The variables `sp` and `val` in `stack.c`, and `buf` and `bufp` in `getch.c`, are for the private use of the functions in their respective source files, and are not meant to be accessed by anything else. The `static` declaration, applied to an external variable or function, limits the scope of that object to the rest of the source file being compiled. External `static` thus provides a way to hide names like `buf` and `bufp` in the `getch-ungetch` combination, which must be external so they can be shared, yet which should not be visible to users of `getch` and `ungetch`.

Static storage is specified by prefixing the normal declaration with the word `static`. If the two routines and the two variables are compiled in one file, as in

```
static char buf[BUFSIZE];    /* buffer for ungetch */
static int  bufp = 0;        /* next free position in buf */

int getch(void) { ... }

void ungetch(int c) { ... }
```

then no other routine will be able to access `buf` and `bufp`, and those names will not conflict with the same names in other files of the same program. In the same way, the variables that `push` and `pop` use for stack manipulation can be hidden, by declaring `sp` and `val` to be `static`.

The external `static` declaration is most often used for variables, but it can be applied to functions as well. Normally, function names are global, visible to any part of the entire program. If a function is declared `static`, however, its name is invisible outside of the file in which it is declared.

The `static` declaration can also be applied to internal variables. Internal `static` variables are local to a particular function just as automatic variables are, but unlike automatics, they remain in existence rather than coming and going each time the function is activated. This means that internal `static` variables provide private, permanent storage within a single function.

Exercise 4-11. Modify `getop` so that it doesn't need to use `ungetch`. Hint: use an internal `static` variable. □

4.7 Register Variables

A `register` declaration advises the compiler that the variable in question will be heavily used. The idea is that `register` variables are to be placed in machine registers, which may result in smaller and faster programs. But compilers are free to ignore the advice.

The `register` declaration looks like

```
register int  x;
register char c;
```

and so on. The `register` declaration can only be applied to automatic variables and to the formal parameters of a function. In this latter case, it looks like

```
f(register unsigned m, register long n)
{
    register int i;
    ...
}
```

In practice, there are restrictions on register variables, reflecting the realities of underlying hardware. Only a few variables in each function may be kept in registers, and only certain types are allowed. Excess register declarations are harmless, however, since the word `register` is ignored for excess or disallowed declarations. And it is not possible to take the address of a register variable (a topic to be covered in Chapter 5), regardless of whether the variable is actually placed in a register. The specific restrictions on number and types of register variables vary from machine to machine.

4.8 Block Structure

C is not a block-structured language in the sense of Pascal or similar languages, because functions may not be defined within other functions. On the other hand, variables can be defined in a block-structured fashion within a function. Declarations of variables (including initializations) may follow the left brace that introduces *any* compound statement, not just the one that begins a function. Variables declared in this way hide any identically named variables in outer blocks, and remain in existence until the matching right brace. For example, in

```
if (n > 0) {
    int i;  /* declare a new i */

    for (i = 0; i < n; i++)
        ...
}
```

the scope of the variable i is the "true" branch of the if; this i is unrelated to any i outside the block. An automatic variable declared and initialized in a block is initialized each time the block is entered. A `static` variable is initialized only the first time the block is entered.

Automatic variables, including formal parameters, also hide external variables and functions of the same name. Given the declarations

```
        int x;
        int y;

        f(double x)
        {
            double y;
            ...
        }
```

then within the function f, occurrences of x refer to the parameter, which is a double; outside of f, they refer to the external int. The same is true of the variable y.

As a matter of style, it's best to avoid variable names that conceal names in an outer scope; the potential for confusion and error is too great.

4.9 Initialization

Initialization has been mentioned in passing many times so far, but always peripherally to some other topic. This section summarizes some of the rules, now that we have discussed the various storage classes.

In the absence of explicit initialization, external and static variables are guaranteed to be initialized to zero; automatic and register variables have undefined (i.e., garbage) initial values.

Scalar variables may be initialized when they are defined, by following the name with an equals sign and an expression:

```
        int   x = 1;
        char squote = '\'';
        long day = 1000L * 60L * 60L * 24L;   /* milliseconds/day */
```

For external and static variables, the initializer must be a constant expression; the initialization is done once, conceptually before the program begins execution. For automatic and register variables, it is done each time the function or block is entered.

For automatic and register variables, the initializer is not restricted to being a constant: it may be any expression involving previously defined values, even function calls. For example, the initializations of the binary search program in Section 3.3 could be written as

```
        int binsearch(int x, int v[], int n)
        {
            int low = 0;
            int high = n - 1;
            int mid;
            ...
        }
```

instead of

```
int low, high, mid;

low = 0;
high = n - 1;
```

In effect, initializations of automatic variables are just shorthand for assignment statements. Which form to prefer is largely a matter of taste. We have generally used explicit assignments, because initializers in declarations are harder to see and further away from the point of use.

An array may be initialized by following its declaration with a list of initializers enclosed in braces and separated by commas. For example, to initialize an array days with the number of days in each month:

```
int days[] = { 31, 28, 31, 30, 31, 30, 31, 31, 30, 31, 30, 31 };
```

When the size of the array is omitted, the compiler will compute the length by counting the initializers, of which there are 12 in this case.

If there are fewer initializers for an array than the number specified, the missing elements will be zero for external, static, and automatic variables. It is an error to have too many initializers. There is no way to specify repetition of an initializer, nor to initialize an element in the middle of an array without supplying all the preceding values as well.

Character arrays are a special case of initialization; a string may be used instead of the braces and commas notation:

```
char pattern[] = "ould";
```

is a shorthand for the longer but equivalent

```
char pattern[] = { 'o', 'u', 'l', 'd', '\0' };
```

In this case, the array size is five (four characters plus the terminating '\0').

4.10   Recursion

C functions may be used recursively; that is, a function may call itself either directly or indirectly. Consider printing a number as a character string. As we mentioned before, the digits are generated in the wrong order: low-order digits are available before high-order digits, but they have to be printed the other way around.

There are two solutions to this problem. One is to store the digits in an array as they are generated, then print them in the reverse order, as we did with itoa in Section 3.6. The alternative is a recursive solution, in which printd first calls itself to cope with any leading digits, then prints the trailing digit. Again, this version can fail on the largest negative number.

```
#include <stdio.h>

/* printd:  print n in decimal */
void printd(int n)
{
    if (n < 0) {
        putchar('-');
        n = -n;
    }
    if (n / 10)
        printd(n / 10);
    putchar(n % 10 + '0');
}
```

When a function calls itself recursively, each invocation gets a fresh set of all the automatic variables, independent of the previous set. Thus in `printd(123)` the first `printd` receives the argument n = 123. It passes 12 to a second `printd`, which in turn passes 1 to a third. The third-level `printd` prints 1, then returns to the second level. That `printd` prints 2, then returns to the first level. That one prints 3 and terminates.

Another good example of recursion is quicksort, a sorting algorithm developed by C. A. R. Hoare in 1962. Given an array, one element is chosen and the others are partitioned into two subsets—those less than the partition element and those greater than or equal to it. The same process is then applied recursively to the two subsets. When a subset has fewer than two elements, it doesn't need any sorting; this stops the recursion.

Our version of quicksort is not the fastest possible, but it's one of the simplest. We use the middle element of each subarray for partitioning.

```
/* qsort:  sort v[left]...v[right] into increasing order */
void qsort(int v[], int left, int right)
{
    int i, last;
    void swap(int v[], int i, int j);

    if (left >= right)     /* do nothing if array contains */
        return;            /* fewer than two elements */
    swap(v, left, (left + right)/2); /* move partition elem */
    last = left;                     /* to v[0] */
    for (i = left+1; i <= right; i++)    /* partition */
        if (v[i] < v[left])
            swap(v, ++last, i);
    swap(v, left, last);             /* restore partition elem */
    qsort(v, left, last-1);
    qsort(v, last+1, right);
}
```

We moved the swapping operation into a separate function `swap` because it occurs three times in `qsort`.

```
/* swap:  interchange v[i] and v[j] */
void swap(int v[], int i, int j)
{
    int temp;

    temp = v[i];
    v[i] = v[j];
    v[j] = temp;
}
```

The standard library includes a version of qsort that can sort objects of any type.

Recursion may provide no saving in storage, since somewhere a stack of the values being processed must be maintained. Nor will it be faster. But recursive code is more compact, and often much easier to write and understand than the non-recursive equivalent. Recursion is especially convenient for recursively defined data structures like trees; we will see a nice example in Section 6.5.

Exercise 4-12. Adapt the ideas of printd to write a recursive version of itoa; that is, convert an integer into a string by calling a recursive routine. □

Exercise 4-13. Write a recursive version of the function reverse(s), which reverses the string s in place. □

4.11 The C Preprocessor

C provides certain language facilities by means of a preprocessor, which is conceptually a separate first step in compilation. The two most frequently used features are #include, to include the contents of a file during compilation, and #define, to replace a token by an arbitrary sequence of characters. Other features described in this section include conditional compilation and macros with arguments.

4.11.1 File Inclusion

File inclusion makes it easy to handle collections of #defines and declarations (among other things). Any source line of the form

        #include "*filename*"

or

        #include <*filename*>

is replaced by the contents of the file *filename*. If the *filename* is quoted, searching for the file typically begins where the source program was found; if it is not found there, or if the name is enclosed in < and >, searching follows an implementation-defined rule to find the file. An included file may itself contain

`#include` lines.

There are often several `#include` lines at the beginning of a source file, to include common `#define` statements and `extern` declarations, or to access the function prototype declarations for library functions from headers like `<stdio.h>`. (Strictly speaking, these need not be files; the details of how headers are accessed are implementation-dependent.)

`#include` is the preferred way to tie the declarations together for a large program. It guarantees that all the source files will be supplied with the same definitions and variable declarations, and thus eliminates a particularly nasty kind of bug. Naturally, when an included file is changed, all files that depend on it must be recompiled.

4.11.2 Macro Substitution

A definition has the form

> `#define`   *name*   *replacement text*

It calls for a macro substitution of the simplest kind—subsequent occurrences of the token *name* will be replaced by the *replacement text*. The name in a `#define` has the same form as a variable name; the replacement text is arbitrary. Normally the replacement text is the rest of the line, but a long definition may be continued onto several lines by placing a `\` at the end of each line to be continued. The scope of a name defined with `#define` is from its point of definition to the end of the source file being compiled. A definition may use previous definitions. Substitutions are made only for tokens, and do not take place within quoted strings. For example, if YES is a defined name, there would be no substitution in `printf("YES")` or in YESMAN.

Any name may be defined with any replacement text. For example,

> `#define  forever  for (;;)   /* infinite loop */`

defines a new word, `forever`, for an infinite loop.

It is also possible to define macros with arguments, so the replacement text can be different for different calls of the macro. As an example, define a macro called `max`:

> `#define  max(A, B)  ((A) > (B) ? (A) : (B))`

Although it looks like a function call, a use of `max` expands into in-line code. Each occurrence of a formal parameter (here A or B) will be replaced by the corresponding actual argument. Thus the line

> `x = max(p+q, r+s);`

will be replaced by the line

> `x = ((p+q) > (r+s) ? (p+q) : (r+s));`

So long as the arguments are treated consistently, this macro will serve for any data type; there is no need for different kinds of `max` for different data types, as there would be with functions.

If you examine the expansion of `max`, you will notice some pitfalls. The expressions are evaluated twice; this is bad if they involve side effects like increment operators or input and output. For instance,

```
max(i++, j++)   /* WRONG */
```

will increment the larger value twice. Some care also has to be taken with parentheses to make sure the order of evaluation is preserved; consider what happens when the macro

```
#define  square(x)  x * x    /* WRONG */
```

is invoked as `square(z+1)`.

Nonetheless, macros are valuable. One practical example comes from `<stdio.h>`, in which `getchar` and `putchar` are often defined as macros to avoid the run-time overhead of a function call per character processed. The functions in `<ctype.h>` are also usually implemented as macros.

Names may be undefined with `#undef`, usually to ensure that a routine is really a function, not a macro:

```
#undef getchar

int getchar(void) { ... }
```

Formal parameters are not replaced within quoted strings. If, however, a parameter name is preceded by a # in the replacement text, the combination will be expanded into a quoted string with the parameter replaced by the actual argument. This can be combined with string concatenation to make, for example, a debugging print macro:

```
#define  dprint(expr)  printf(#expr " = %g\n", expr)
```

When this is invoked, as in

```
dprint(x/y);
```

the macro is expanded into

```
printf("x/y" " = %g\n", x/y);
```

and the strings are concatenated, so the effect is

```
printf("x/y = %g\n", x/y);
```

Within the actual argument, each " is replaced by \" and each \ by \\, so the result is a legal string constant.

The preprocessor operator ## provides a way to concatenate actual arguments during macro expansion. If a parameter in the replacement text is adjacent to a ##, the parameter is replaced by the actual argument, the ## and surrounding white space are removed, and the result is re-scanned. For example, the macro `paste` concatenates its two arguments:

```
#define  paste(front, back)  front ## back
```

so `paste(name, 1)` creates the token `name 1`.

The rules for nested uses of `##` are arcane; further details may be found in Appendix A.

Exercise 4-14. Define a macro `swap(t,x,y)` that interchanges two arguments of type `t`. (Block structure will help.) □

4.11.3 Conditional Inclusion

It is possible to control preprocessing itself with conditional statements that are evaluated during preprocessing. This provides a way to include code selectively, depending on the value of conditions evaluated during compilation.

The `#if` line evaluates a constant integer expression (which may not include `sizeof`, casts, or `enum` constants). If the expression is non-zero, subsequent lines until an `#endif` or `#elif` or `#else` are included. (The preprocessor statement `#elif` is like `else if`.) The expression `defined(`*name*`)` in a `#if` is 1 if the *name* has been defined, and 0 otherwise.

For example, to make sure that the contents of a file `hdr.h` are included only once, the contents of the file are surrounded with a conditional like this:

```
#if !defined(HDR)
#define HDR

/* contents of hdr.h go here */

#endif
```

The first inclusion of `hdr.h` defines the name `HDR`; subsequent inclusions will find the name defined and skip down to the `#endif`. A similar style can be used to avoid including files multiple times. If this style is used consistently, then each header can itself include any other headers on which it depends, without the user of the header having to deal with the interdependence.

This sequence tests the name `SYSTEM` to decide which version of a header to include:

```
#if SYSTEM == SYSV
    #define HDR "sysv.h"
#elif SYSTEM == BSD
    #define HDR "bsd.h"
#elif SYSTEM == MSDOS
    #define HDR "msdos.h"
#else
    #define HDR "default.h"
#endif
#include HDR
```

The `#ifdef` and `#ifndef` lines are specialized forms that test whether a name is defined. The first example of `#if` above could have been written

```
#ifndef HDR
#define HDR

/* contents of hdr.h go here */

#endif
```

CHAPTER 5: **Pointers and Arrays**

A pointer is a variable that contains the address of a variable. Pointers are much used in C, partly because they are sometimes the only way to express a computation, and partly because they usually lead to more compact and efficient code than can be obtained in other ways. Pointers and arrays are closely related; this chapter also explores this relationship and shows how to exploit it.

Pointers have been lumped with the goto statement as a marvelous way to create impossible-to-understand programs. This is certainly true when they are used carelessly, and it is easy to create pointers that point somewhere unexpected. With discipline, however, pointers can also be used to achieve clarity and simplicity. This is the aspect that we will try to illustrate.

The main change in ANSI C is to make explicit the rules about how pointers can be manipulated, in effect mandating what good programmers already practice and good compilers already enforce. In addition, the type void * (pointer to void) replaces char * as the proper type for a generic pointer.

5.1 Pointers and Addresses

Let us begin with a simplified picture of how memory is organized. A typical machine has an array of consecutively numbered or addressed memory cells that may be manipulated individually or in contiguous groups. One common situation is that any byte can be a char, a pair of one-byte cells can be treated as a short integer, and four adjacent bytes form a long. A pointer is a group of cells (often two or four) that can hold an address. So if c is a char and p is a pointer that points to it, we could represent the situation this way:

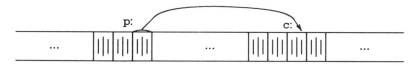

The unary operator & gives the address of an object, so the statement

93

```
p = &c;
```

assigns the address of c to the variable p, and p is said to "point to" c. The &
operator only applies to objects in memory: variables and array elements. It
cannot be applied to expressions, constants, or register variables.

The unary operator * is the *indirection* or *dereferencing* operator; when
applied to a pointer, it accesses the object the pointer points to. Suppose that x
and y are integers and ip is a pointer to int. This artificial sequence shows
how to declare a pointer and how to use & and *:

```
int x = 1, y = 2, z[10];
int *ip;            /* ip is a pointer to int */

ip = &x;            /* ip now points to x */
y = *ip;            /* y is now 1 */
*ip = 0;            /* x is now 0 */
ip = &z[0];         /* ip now points to z[0] */
```

The declarations of x, y, and z are what we've seen all along. The declaration
of the pointer ip,

```
int *ip;
```

is intended as a mnemonic; it says that the expression *ip is an int. The syntax of the declaration for a variable mimics the syntax of expressions in which
the variable might appear. This reasoning applies to function declarations as
well. For example,

```
double *dp, atof(char *);
```

says that in an expression *dp and atof(s) have values of type double, and
that the argument of atof is a pointer to char.

You should also note the implication that a pointer is constrained to point to
a particular kind of object: every pointer points to a specific data type. (There
is one exception: a "pointer to void" is used to hold any type of pointer but
cannot be dereferenced itself. We'll come back to it in Section 5.11.)

If ip points to the integer x, then *ip can occur in any context where x
could, so

```
*ip = *ip + 10;
```

increments *ip by 10.

The unary operators * and & bind more tightly than arithmetic operators, so
the assignment

```
y = *ip + 1
```

takes whatever ip points at, adds 1, and assigns the result to y, while

```
*ip += 1
```

increments what ip points to, as do

```
    ++*ip
```

and

```
    (*ip)++
```

The parentheses are necessary in this last example; without them, the expression would increment `ip` instead of what it points to, because unary operators like `*` and `++` associate right to left.

Finally, since pointers are variables, they can be used without dereferencing. For example, if `iq` is another pointer to `int`,

```
    iq = ip
```

copies the contents of `ip` into `iq`, thus making `iq` point to whatever `ip` pointed to.

5.2 Pointers and Function Arguments

Since C passes arguments to functions by value, there is no direct way for the called function to alter a variable in the calling function. For instance, a sorting routine might exchange two out-of-order elements with a function called `swap`. It is not enough to write

```
    swap(a, b);
```

where the `swap` function is defined as

```
    void swap(int x, int y)  /* WRONG */
    {
        int temp;

        temp = x;
        x = y;
        y = temp;
    }
```

Because of call by value, `swap` can't affect the arguments a and b in the routine that called it. The function above only swaps *copies* of a and b.

The way to obtain the desired effect is for the calling program to pass *pointers* to the values to be changed:

```
    swap(&a, &b);
```

Since the operator `&` produces the address of a variable, `&a` is a pointer to a. In `swap` itself, the parameters are declared to be pointers, and the operands are accessed indirectly through them.

```
void swap(int *px, int *py)  /* interchange *px and *py */
{
    int temp;

    temp = *px;
    *px = *py;
    *py = temp;
}
```

Pictorially:

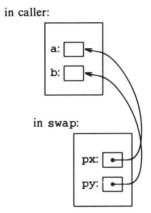

in caller:

a:

b:

in swap:

px:

py:

Pointer arguments enable a function to access and change objects in the function that called it. As an example, consider a function `getint` that performs free-format input conversion by breaking a stream of characters into integer values, one integer per call. `getint` has to return the value it found and also signal end of file when there is no more input. These values have to be passed back by separate paths, for no matter what value is used for EOF, that could also be the value of an input integer.

One solution is to have `getint` return the end of file status as its function value, while using a pointer argument to store the converted integer back in the calling function. This is the scheme used by `scanf` as well; see Section 7.4.

The following loop fills an array with integers by calls to `getint`:

```
int n, array[SIZE], getint(int *);

for (n = 0; n < SIZE && getint(&array[n]) != EOF; n++)
    ;
```

Each call sets `array[n]` to the next integer found in the input and increments n. Notice that it is essential to pass the address of `array[n]` to `getint`. Otherwise there is no way for `getint` to communicate the converted integer back to the caller.

Our version of `getint` returns EOF for end of file, zero if the next input is not a number, and a positive value if the input contains a valid number.

```
#include <ctype.h>

int getch(void);
void ungetch(int);

/* getint:  get next integer from input into *pn */
int getint(int *pn)
{
    int c, sign;

    while (isspace(c = getch()))    /* skip white space */
        ;
    if (!isdigit(c) && c != EOF && c != '+' && c != '-') {
        ungetch(c);     /* it's not a number */
        return 0;
    }
    sign = (c == '-') ? -1 : 1;
    if (c == '+' || c == '-')
        c = getch();
    for (*pn = 0; isdigit(c); c = getch())
        *pn = 10 * *pn + (c - '0');
    *pn *= sign;
    if (c != EOF)
        ungetch(c);
    return c;
}
```

Throughout `getint`, `*pn` is used as an ordinary `int` variable. We have also used `getch` and `ungetch` (described in Section 4.3) so the one extra character that must be read can be pushed back onto the input.

Exercise 5-1. As written, `getint` treats a + or – not followed by a digit as a valid representation of zero. Fix it to push such a character back on the input. □

Exercise 5-2. Write `getfloat`, the floating-point analog of `getint`. What type does `getfloat` return as its function value? □

5.3 Pointers and Arrays

In C, there is a strong relationship between pointers and arrays, strong enough that pointers and arrays should be discussed simultaneously. Any operation that can be achieved by array subscripting can also be done with pointers. The pointer version will in general be faster but, at least to the uninitiated, somewhat harder to understand.

The declaration

```
int a[10];
```

defines an array a of size 10, that is, a block of 10 consecutive objects named a[0], a[1], ..., a[9].

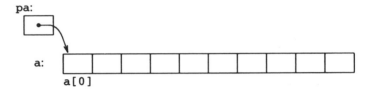

The notation a[i] refers to the i-th element of the array. If pa is a pointer to an integer, declared as

```
int *pa;
```

then the assignment

```
pa = &a[0];
```

sets pa to point to element zero of a; that is, pa contains the address of a[0].

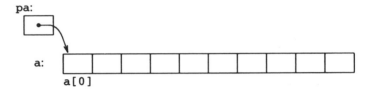

Now the assignment

```
x = *pa;
```

will copy the contents of a[0] into x.

If pa points to a particular element of an array, then by definition pa+1 points to the next element, pa+i points i elements after pa, and pa-i points i elements before. Thus, if pa points to a[0],

```
*(pa+1)
```

refers to the contents of a[1], pa+i is the address of a[i], and *(pa+i) is the contents of a[i].

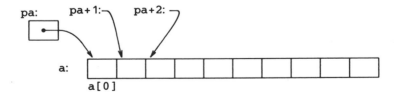

These remarks are true regardless of the type or size of the variables in the array a. The meaning of "adding 1 to a pointer," and by extension, all pointer arithmetic, is that pa+1 points to the next object, and pa+i points to the i-th object beyond pa.

The correspondence between indexing and pointer arithmetic is very close. By definition, the value of a variable or expression of type array is the address of element zero of the array. Thus after the assignment

```
pa = &a[0];
```

pa and a have identical values. Since the name of an array is a synonym for the location of the initial element, the assignment pa=&a[0] can also be written as

```
pa = a;
```

Rather more surprising, at least at first sight, is the fact that a reference to a[i] can also be written as *(a+i). In evaluating a[i], C converts it to *(a+i) immediately; the two forms are equivalent. Applying the operator & to both parts of this equivalence, it follows that &a[i] and a+i are also identical: a+i is the address of the i-th element beyond a. As the other side of this coin, if pa is a pointer, expressions may use it with a subscript; pa[i] is identical to *(pa+i). In short, an array-and-index expression is equivalent to one written as a pointer and offset.

There is one difference between an array name and a pointer that must be kept in mind. A pointer is a variable, so pa=a and pa++ are legal. But an array name is not a variable; constructions like a=pa and a++ are illegal.

When an array name is passed to a function, what is passed is the location of the initial element. Within the called function, this argument is a local variable, and so an array name parameter is a pointer, that is, a variable containing an address. We can use this fact to write another version of strlen, which computes the length of a string.

```
/* strlen:  return length of string s */
int strlen(char *s)
{
    int n;

    for (n = 0; *s != '\0'; s++)
        n++;
    return n;
}
```

Since s is a pointer, incrementing it is perfectly legal; s++ has no effect on the character string in the function that called strlen, but merely increments strlen's private copy of the pointer. That means that calls like

```
strlen("hello, world");   /* string constant */
strlen(array);            /* char array[100]; */
strlen(ptr);              /* char *ptr; */
```

all work.

As formal parameters in a function definition,

```
        char s[ ];
```
and
```
        char *s;
```
are equivalent; we prefer the latter because it says more explicitly that the parameter is a pointer. When an array name is passed to a function, the function can at its convenience believe that it has been handed either an array or a pointer, and manipulate it accordingly. It can even use both notations if it seems appropriate and clear.

It is possible to pass part of an array to a function, by passing a pointer to the beginning of the subarray. For example, if a is an array,
```
        f(&a[2])
```
and
```
        f(a+2)
```
both pass to the function f the address of the subarray that starts at a[2]. Within f, the parameter declaration can read
```
        f(int arr[]) { ... }
```
or
```
        f(int *arr) { ... }
```
So as far as f is concerned, the fact that the parameter refers to part of a larger array is of no consequence.

If one is sure that the elements exist, it is also possible to index backwards in an array; p[-1], p[-2], and so on are syntactically legal, and refer to the elements that immediately precede p[0]. Of course, it is illegal to refer to objects that are not within the array bounds.

5.4   Address Arithmetic

If p is a pointer to some element of an array, then p++ increments p to point to the next element, and p+=i increments it to point i elements beyond where it currently does. These and similar constructions are the simplest forms of pointer or address arithmetic.

C is consistent and regular in its approach to address arithmetic; its integration of pointers, arrays, and address arithmetic is one of the strengths of the language. Let us illustrate by writing a rudimentary storage allocator. There are two routines. The first, alloc(n), returns a pointer p to n consecutive character positions, which can be used by the caller of alloc for storing characters. The second, afree(p), releases the storage thus acquired so it can be re-used later. The routines are "rudimentary" because the calls to afree must be made in the opposite order to the calls made on alloc. That is, the storage

managed by `alloc` and `afree` is a stack, or last-in, first-out list. The standard library provides analogous functions called `malloc` and `free` that have no
such restrictions; in Section 8.7 we will show how they can be implemented.

The easiest implementation is to have `alloc` hand out pieces of a large
character array that we will call `allocbuf`. This array is private to `alloc`
and `afree`. Since they deal in pointers, not array indices, no other routine
need know the name of the array, which can be declared `static` in the source
file containing `alloc` and `afree`, and thus be invisible outside it. In practical
implementations, the array may well not even have a name; it might instead be
obtained by calling `malloc` or by asking the operating system for a pointer to
some unnamed block of storage.

The other information needed is how much of `allocbuf` has been used.
We use a pointer, called `allocp`, that points to the next free element. When
`alloc` is asked for n characters, it checks to see if there is enough room left in
`allocbuf`. If so, `alloc` returns the current value of `allocp` (i.e., the beginning of the free block), then increments it by n to point to the next free area. If
there is no room, `alloc` returns zero. `afree(p)` merely sets `allocp` to p if
p is inside `allocbuf`.

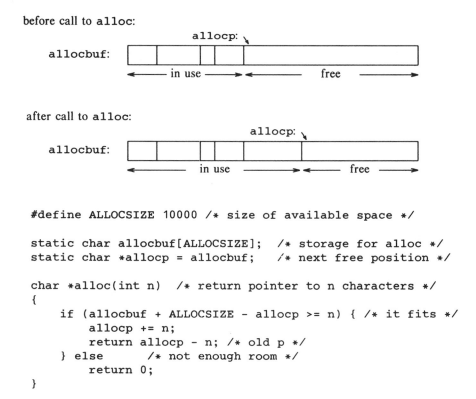

```
#define ALLOCSIZE 10000 /* size of available space */

static char allocbuf[ALLOCSIZE];  /* storage for alloc */
static char *allocp = allocbuf;   /* next free position */

char *alloc(int n)  /* return pointer to n characters */
{
    if (allocbuf + ALLOCSIZE - allocp >= n) { /* it fits */
        allocp += n;
        return allocp - n; /* old p */
    } else       /* not enough room */
        return 0;
}
```

```
void afree(char *p)   /* free storage pointed to by p */
{
    if (p >= allocbuf && p < allocbuf + ALLOCSIZE)
        allocp = p;
}
```

In general a pointer can be initialized just as any other variable can, though normally the only meaningful values are zero or an expression involving the addresses of previously defined data of appropriate type. The declaration

```
static char *allocp = allocbuf;
```

defines `allocp` to be a character pointer and initializes it to point to the beginning of `allocbuf`, which is the next free position when the program starts. This could have also been written

```
static char *allocp = &allocbuf[0];
```

since the array name *is* the address of the zeroth element.

The test

```
if (allocbuf + ALLOCSIZE - allocp >= n) {  /* it fits */
```

checks if there's enough room to satisfy a request for n characters. If there is, the new value of `allocp` would be at most one beyond the end of `allocbuf`. If the request can be satisfied, `alloc` returns a pointer to the beginning of a block of characters (notice the declaration of the function itself). If not, `alloc` must return some signal that no space is left. C guarantees that zero is never a valid address for data, so a return value of zero can be used to signal an abnormal event, in this case, no space.

Pointers and integers are not interchangeable. Zero is the sole exception: the constant zero may be assigned to a pointer, and a pointer may be compared with the constant zero. The symbolic constant `NULL` is often used in place of zero, as a mnemonic to indicate more clearly that this is a special value for a pointer. `NULL` is defined in `<stdio.h>`. We will use `NULL` henceforth.

Tests like

```
if (allocbuf + ALLOCSIZE - allocp >= n) {  /* it fits */
```

and

```
if (p >= allocbuf && p < allocbuf + ALLOCSIZE)
```

show several important facets of pointer arithmetic. First, pointers may be compared under certain circumstances. If p and q point to members of the same array, then relations like ==, !=, <, >=, etc., work properly. For example,

```
p < q
```

is true if p points to an earlier member of the array than q does. Any pointer can be meaningfully compared for equality or inequality with zero. But the behavior is undefined for arithmetic or comparisons with pointers that do not point to members of the same array. (There is one exception: the address of the first element past the end of an array can be used in pointer arithmetic.)

Second, we have already observed that a pointer and an integer may be added or subtracted. The construction

```
p + n
```

means the address of the n-th object beyond the one p currently points to. This is true regardless of the kind of object p points to; n is scaled according to the size of the objects p points to, which is determined by the declaration of p. If an int is four bytes, for example, the int will be scaled by four.

Pointer subtraction is also valid: if p and q point to elements of the same array, and p<q, then q-p+1 is the number of elements from p to q inclusive. This fact can be used to write yet another version of strlen:

```
/* strlen:  return length of string s */
int strlen(char *s)
{
    char *p = s;

    while (*p != '\0')
        p++;
    return p - s;
}
```

In its declaration, p is initialized to s, that is, to point to the first character of the string. In the while loop, each character in turn is examined until the '\0' at the end is seen. Because p points to characters, p++ advances p to the next character each time, and p-s gives the number of characters advanced over, that is, the string length. (The number of characters in the string could be too large to store in an int. The header <stddef.h> defines a type ptrdiff_t that is large enough to hold the signed difference of two pointer values. If we were being very cautious, however, we would use size_t for the return type of strlen, to match the standard library version. size_t is the unsigned integer type returned by the sizeof operator.)

Pointer arithmetic is consistent: if we had been dealing with floats, which occupy more storage than chars, and if p were a pointer to float, p++ would advance to the next float. Thus we could write another version of alloc that maintains floats instead of chars, merely by changing char to float throughout alloc and afree. All the pointer manipulations automatically take into account the size of the object pointed to.

The valid pointer operations are assignment of pointers of the same type, adding or subtracting a pointer and an integer, subtracting or comparing two pointers to members of the same array, and assigning or comparing to zero. All other pointer arithmetic is illegal. It is not legal to add two pointers, or to multiply or divide or shift or mask them, or to add float or double to them, or even, except for void *, to assign a pointer of one type to a pointer of another type without a cast.

5.5 Character Pointers and Functions

A *string constant*, written as

```
"I am a string"
```

is an array of characters. In the internal representation, the array is terminated with the null character ′\0′ so that programs can find the end. The length in storage is thus one more than the number of characters between the double quotes.

Perhaps the most common occurrence of string constants is as arguments to functions, as in

```
printf("hello, world\n");
```

When a character string like this appears in a program, access to it is through a character pointer; printf receives a pointer to the beginning of the character array. That is, a string constant is accessed by a pointer to its first element.

String constants need not be function arguments. If pmessage is declared as

```
char *pmessage;
```

then the statement

```
pmessage = "now is the time";
```

assigns to pmessage a pointer to the character array. This is *not* a string copy; only pointers are involved. C does not provide any operators for processing an entire string of characters as a unit.

There is an important difference between these definitions:

```
char amessage[] = "now is the time";   /* an array */
char *pmessage = "now is the time";    /* a pointer */
```

amessage is an array, just big enough to hold the sequence of characters and ′\0′ that initializes it. Individual characters within the array may be changed but amessage will always refer to the same storage. On the other hand, pmessage is a pointer, initialized to point to a string constant; the pointer may subsequently be modified to point elsewhere, but the result is undefined if you try to modify the string contents.

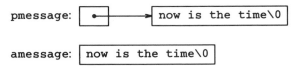

We will illustrate more aspects of pointers and arrays by studying versions of two useful functions adapted from the standard library. The first function is strcpy(s,t), which copies the string t to the string s. It would be nice just to say s=t but this copies the pointer, not the characters. To copy the characters, we need a loop. The array version is first:

```
/* strcpy:  copy t to s; array subscript version */
void strcpy(char *s, char *t)
{
    int i;

    i = 0;
    while ((s[i] = t[i]) != '\0')
        i++;
}
```

For contrast, here is a version of `strcpy` with pointers:

```
/* strcpy:  copy t to s; pointer version 1 */
void strcpy(char *s, char *t)
{
    while ((*s = *t) != '\0') {
        s++;
        t++;
    }
}
```

Because arguments are passed by value, `strcpy` can use the parameters `s` and `t` in any way it pleases. Here they are conveniently initialized pointers, which are marched along the arrays a character at a time, until the `'\0'` that terminates `t` has been copied to `s`.

In practice, `strcpy` would not be written as we showed it above. Experienced C programmers would prefer

```
/* strcpy:  copy t to s; pointer version 2 */
void strcpy(char *s, char *t)
{
    while ((*s++ = *t++) != '\0')
        ;
}
```

This moves the increment of `s` and `t` into the test part of the loop. The value of `*t++` is the character that `t` pointed to before `t` was incremented; the postfix `++` doesn't change `t` until after this character has been fetched. In the same way, the character is stored into the old `s` position before `s` is incremented. This character is also the value that is compared against `'\0'` to control the loop. The net effect is that characters are copied from `t` to `s`, up to and including the terminating `'\0'`.

As the final abbreviation, observe that a comparison against `'\0'` is redundant, since the question is merely whether the expression is zero. So the function would likely be written as

```
/* strcpy:  copy t to s; pointer version 3 */
void strcpy(char *s, char *t)
{
    while (*s++ = *t++)
        ;
}
```

Although this may seem cryptic at first sight, the notational convenience is considerable, and the idiom should be mastered, because you will see it frequently in C programs.

The `strcpy` in the standard library (`<string.h>`) returns the target string as its function value.

The second routine that we will examine is `strcmp(s,t)`, which compares the character strings s and t, and returns negative, zero or positive if s is lexicographically less than, equal to, or greater than t. The value is obtained by subtracting the characters at the first position where s and t disagree.

```
/* strcmp:  return <0 if s<t, 0 if s==t, >0 if s>t */
int strcmp(char *s, char *t)
{
    int i;

    for (i = 0; s[i] == t[i]; i++)
        if (s[i] == '\0')
            return 0;
    return s[i] - t[i];
}
```

The pointer version of `strcmp`:

```
/* strcmp:  return <0 if s<t, 0 if s==t, >0 if s>t */
int strcmp(char *s, char *t)
{
    for ( ; *s == *t; s++, t++)
        if (*s == '\0')
            return 0;
    return *s - *t;
}
```

Since ++ and -- are either prefix or postfix operators, other combinations of * and ++ and -- occur, although less frequently. For example,

```
*--p
```

decrements p before fetching the character that p points to. In fact, the pair of expressions

```
*p++ = val;    /* push val onto stack */
val = *--p;    /* pop top of stack into val */
```

are the standard idioms for pushing and popping a stack; see Section 4.3.

The header `<string.h>` contains declarations for the functions mentioned in this section, plus a variety of other string-handling functions from the standard library.

Exercise 5-3. Write a pointer version of the function `strcat` that we showed in Chapter 2: `strcat(s,t)` copies the string t to the end of s. □

Exercise 5-4. Write the function `strend(s,t)`, which returns 1 if the string t occurs at the end of the string s, and zero otherwise. □

Exercise 5-5. Write versions of the library functions `strncpy`, `strncat`, and `strncmp`, which operate on at most the first n characters of their argument strings. For example, `strncpy(s,t,n)` copies at most n characters of t to s. Full descriptions are in Appendix B. □

Exercise 5-6. Rewrite appropriate programs from earlier chapters and exercises with pointers instead of array indexing. Good possibilities include `getline` (Chapters 1 and 4), `atoi`, `itoa`, and their variants (Chapters 2, 3, and 4), `reverse` (Chapter 3), and `strindex` and `getop` (Chapter 4). □

5.6 Pointer Arrays; Pointers to Pointers

Since pointers are variables themselves, they can be stored in arrays just as other variables can. Let us illustrate by writing a program that will sort a set of text lines into alphabetic order, a stripped-down version of the UNIX program sort.

In Chapter 3 we presented a Shell sort function that would sort an array of integers, and in Chapter 4 we improved on it with a quicksort. The same algorithms will work, except that now we have to deal with lines of text, which are of different lengths, and which, unlike integers, can't be compared or moved in a single operation. We need a data representation that will cope efficiently and conveniently with variable-length text lines.

This is where the array of pointers enters. If the lines to be sorted are stored end-to-end in one long character array, then each line can be accessed by a pointer to its first character. The pointers themselves can be stored in an array. Two lines can be compared by passing their pointers to `strcmp`. When two out-of-order lines have to be exchanged, the pointers in the pointer array are exchanged, not the text lines themselves.

This eliminates the twin problems of complicated storage management and high overhead that would go with moving the lines themselves.

The sorting process has three steps:

read all the lines of input
sort them
print them in order

As usual, it's best to divide the program into functions that match this natural division, with the main routine controlling the other functions. Let us defer the sorting step for a moment, and concentrate on the data structure and the input and output.

The input routine has to collect and save the characters of each line, and build an array of pointers to the lines. It will also have to count the number of input lines, since that information is needed for sorting and printing. Since the input function can only cope with a finite number of input lines, it can return some illegal line count like –1 if too much input is presented.

The output routine only has to print the lines in the order in which they appear in the array of pointers.

```
#include <stdio.h>
#include <string.h>

#define MAXLINES 5000          /* max #lines to be sorted */

char *lineptr[MAXLINES];       /* pointers to text lines */

int readlines(char *lineptr[], int nlines);
void writelines(char *lineptr[], int nlines);

void qsort(char *lineptr[], int left, int right);

/* sort input lines */
main()
{
    int nlines;     /* number of input lines read */

    if ((nlines = readlines(lineptr, MAXLINES)) >= 0) {
        qsort(lineptr, 0, nlines-1);
        writelines(lineptr, nlines);
        return 0;
    } else {
        printf("error: input too big to sort\n");
        return 1;
    }
}
```

```
#define MAXLEN 1000    /* max length of any input line */
int getline(char *, int);
char *alloc(int);

/* readlines:  read input lines */
int readlines(char *lineptr[], int maxlines)
{
    int len, nlines;
    char *p, line[MAXLEN];

    nlines = 0;
    while ((len = getline(line, MAXLEN)) > 0)
        if (nlines >= maxlines || (p = alloc(len)) == NULL)
            return -1;
        else {
            line[len-1] = '\0'; /* delete newline */
            strcpy(p, line);
            lineptr[nlines++] = p;
        }
    return nlines;
}

/* writelines:  write output lines */
void writelines(char *lineptr[], int nlines)
{
    int i;

    for (i = 0; i < nlines; i++)
        printf("%s\n", lineptr[i]);
}
```

The function `getline` is from Section 1.9.

The main new thing is the declaration for `lineptr`:

```
char *lineptr[MAXLINES]
```

says that `lineptr` is an array of `MAXLINES` elements, each element of which is a pointer to a `char`. That is, `lineptr[i]` is a character pointer, and `*lineptr[i]` is the character it points to, the first character of the i-th saved text line.

Since `lineptr` is itself the name of an array, it can be treated as a pointer in the same manner as in our earlier examples, and `writelines` can be written instead as

```
/* writelines:  write output lines */
void writelines(char *lineptr[], int nlines)
{
    while (nlines-- > 0)
        printf("%s\n", *lineptr++);
}
```

Initially *lineptr points to the first line; each increment advances it to the next line pointer while nlines is counted down.

With input and output under control, we can proceed to sorting. The quicksort from Chapter 4 needs minor changes: the declarations have to be modified, and the comparison operation must be done by calling strcmp. The algorithm remains the same, which gives us some confidence that it will still work.

```
/* qsort:  sort v[left]...v[right] into increasing order */
void qsort(char *v[], int left, int right)
{
    int i, last;
    void swap(char *v[], int i, int j);

    if (left >= right)    /* do nothing if array contains */
        return;           /* fewer than two elements */
    swap(v, left, (left + right)/2);
    last = left;
    for (i = left+1; i <= right; i++)
        if (strcmp(v[i], v[left]) < 0)
            swap(v, ++last, i);
    swap(v, left, last);
    qsort(v, left, last-1);
    qsort(v, last+1, right);
}
```

Similarly, the swap routine needs only trivial changes:

```
/* swap:  interchange v[i] and v[j] */
void swap(char *v[], int i, int j)
{
    char *temp;

    temp = v[i];
    v[i] = v[j];
    v[j] = temp;
}
```

Since any individual element of v (alias lineptr) is a character pointer, temp must be also, so one can be copied to the other.

Exercise 5-7. Rewrite readlines to store lines in an array supplied by main, rather than calling alloc to maintain storage. How much faster is the program? ☐

5.7 Multi-dimensional Arrays

C provides rectangular multi-dimensional arrays, although in practice they are much less used than arrays of pointers. In this section, we will show some of their properties.

Consider the problem of date conversion, from day of the month to day of the year and vice versa. For example, March 1 is the 60th day of a non-leap year, and the 61st day of a leap year. Let us define two functions to do the conversions: `day_of_year` converts the month and day into the day of the year, and `month_day` converts the day of the year into the month and day. Since this latter function computes two values, the month and day arguments will be pointers:

```
month_day(1988, 60, &m, &d)
```

sets `m` to 2 and `d` to 29 (February 29th).

These functions both need the same information, a table of the number of days in each month ("thirty days hath September ..."). Since the number of days per month differs for leap years and non-leap years, it's easier to separate them into two rows of a two-dimensional array than to keep track of what happens to February during computation. The array and the functions for performing the transformations are as follows:

```
static char daytab[2][13] = {
    {0, 31, 28, 31, 30, 31, 30, 31, 31, 30, 31, 30, 31},
    {0, 31, 29, 31, 30, 31, 30, 31, 31, 30, 31, 30, 31}
};

/* day_of_year:  set day of year from month & day */
int day_of_year(int year, int month, int day)
{
    int i, leap;

    leap = year%4 == 0 && year%100 != 0 || year%400 == 0;
    for (i = 1; i < month; i++)
        day += daytab[leap][i];
    return day;
}

    /* month_day:  set month, day from day of year */
    void month_day(int year, int yearday, int *pmonth, int *pday)
    {
        int i, leap;

        leap = year%4 == 0 && year%100 != 0 || year%400 == 0;
        for (i = 1; yearday > daytab[leap][i]; i++)
            yearday -= daytab[leap][i];
        *pmonth = i;
        *pday = yearday;
    }
```

Recall that the arithmetic value of a logical expression, such as the one for `leap`, is either zero (false) or one (true), so it can be used as a subscript of the array `daytab`.

The array `daytab` has to be external to both `day_of_year` and

month_day, so they can both use it. We made it char to illustrate a legiti-
mate use of char for storing small non-character integers.

   daytab is the first two-dimensional array we have dealt with. In C, a two-
dimensional array is really a one-dimensional array, each of whose elements is
an array. Hence subscripts are written as

```
daytab[i][j]     /* [row][col] */
```

rather than

```
daytab[i,j]      /* WRONG */
```

Other than this notational distinction, a two-dimensional array can be treated in
much the same way as in other languages. Elements are stored by rows, so the
rightmost subscript, or column, varies fastest as elements are accessed in storage
order.

   An array is initialized by a list of initializers in braces; each row of a two-
dimensional array is initialized by a corresponding sub-list. We started the
array daytab with a column of zero so that month numbers can run from the
natural 1 to 12 instead of 0 to 11. Since space is not at a premium here, this is
clearer than adjusting the indices.

   If a two-dimensional array is to be passed to a function, the parameter
declaration in the function must include the number of columns; the number of
rows is irrelevant, since what is passed is, as before, a pointer to an array of
rows, where each row is an array of 13 ints. In this particular case, it is a
pointer to objects that are arrays of 13 ints. Thus if the array daytab is to
be passed to a function f, the declaration of f would be

```
f(int daytab[2][13]) { ... }
```

It could also be

```
f(int daytab[][13]) { ... }
```

since the number of rows is irrelevant, or it could be

```
f(int (*daytab)[13]) { ... }
```

which says that the parameter is a pointer to an array of 13 integers. The
parentheses are necessary since brackets [] have higher precedence than *.
Without parentheses, the declaration

```
int *daytab[13]
```

is an array of 13 pointers to integers. More generally, only the first dimension
(subscript) of an array is free; all the others have to be specified.

   Section 5.12 has a further discussion of complicated declarations.

Exercise 5-8. There is no error checking in day_of_year or month_day.
Remedy this defect. □

5.8   Initialization of Pointer Arrays

Consider the problem of writing a function `month_name(n)`, which returns a pointer to a character string containing the name of the n-th month. This is an ideal application for an internal `static` array. `month_name` contains a private array of character strings, and returns a pointer to the proper one when called. This section shows how that array of names is initialized.

The syntax is similar to previous initializations:

```
/* month_name:  return name of n-th month */
char *month_name(int n)
{
    static char *name[] = {
        "Illegal month",
        "January", "February", "March",
        "April", "May", "June",
        "July", "August", "September",
        "October", "November", "December"
    };

    return (n < 1 || n > 12) ? name[0] : name[n];
}
```

The declaration of `name`, which is an array of character pointers, is the same as `lineptr` in the sorting example. The initializer is a list of character strings; each is assigned to the corresponding position in the array. The characters of the i-th string are placed somewhere, and a pointer to them is stored in `name[i]`. Since the size of the array `name` is not specified, the compiler counts the initializers and fills in the correct number.

5.9   Pointers vs. Multi-dimensional Arrays

Newcomers to C are sometimes confused about the difference between a two-dimensional array and an array of pointers, such as `name` in the example above. Given the definitions

```
int a[10][20];
int *b[10];
```

then `a[3][4]` and `b[3][4]` are both syntactically legal references to a single `int`. But `a` is a true two-dimensional array: 200 `int`-sized locations have been set aside, and the conventional rectangular subscript calculation $20 \times row + col$ is used to find the element `a[row][col]`. For `b`, however, the definition only allocates 10 pointers and does not initialize them; initialization must be done explicitly, either statically or with code. Assuming that each element of `b` does point to a twenty-element array, then there will be 200 `ints` set aside, plus ten cells for the pointers. The important advantage of the pointer array is that the rows of the array may be of different lengths. That is, each element of `b` need not point to a twenty-element vector; some may point to two elements, some to fifty, and some to none at all.

Although we have phrased this discussion in terms of integers, by far the most frequent use of arrays of pointers is to store character strings of diverse lengths, as in the function `month_name`. Compare the declaration and picture for an array of pointers:

```
char *name[] = { "Illegal month", "Jan, "Feb", "Mar" };
```

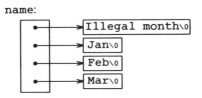

name:

with those for a two-dimensional array:

```
char aname[][15] = { "Illegal month", "Jan", "Feb", "Mar" };
```

aname:

Illegal month\0 Jan\0		Feb\0	Mar\0
0	15	30	45

Exercise 5-9. Rewrite the routines `day_of_year` and `month_day` with pointers instead of indexing. □

5.10 Command-line Arguments

In environments that support C, there is a way to pass command-line arguments or parameters to a program when it begins executing. When `main` is called, it is called with two arguments. The first (conventionally called `argc`, for argument count) is the number of command-line arguments the program was invoked with; the second (`argv`, for argument vector) is a pointer to an array of character strings that contain the arguments, one per string. We customarily use multiple levels of pointers to manipulate these character strings.

The simplest illustration is the program `echo`, which echoes its command-line arguments on a single line, separated by blanks. That is, the command

```
echo hello, world
```

prints the output

```
hello, world
```

By convention, `argv[0]` is the name by which the program was invoked, so `argc` is at least 1. If `argc` is 1, there are no command-line arguments after the program name. In the example above, `argc` is 3, and `argv[0]`, `argv[1]`, and `argv[2]` are "echo", "hello,", and "world" respectively. The first optional argument is `argv[1]` and the last is `argv[argc-1]`; additionally, the standard requires that `argv[argc]` be a null pointer.

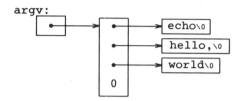

The first version of echo treats `argv` as an array of character pointers:

```c
#include <stdio.h>

/* echo command-line arguments; 1st version */
main(int argc, char *argv[])
{
    int i;

    for (i = 1; i < argc; i++)
        printf("%s%s", argv[i], (i < argc-1) ? " " : "");
    printf("\n");
    return 0;
}
```

Since `argv` is a pointer to an array of pointers, we can manipulate the pointer rather than index the array. This next variation is based on incrementing `argv`, which is a pointer to pointer to char, while `argc` is counted down:

```c
#include <stdio.h>

/* echo command-line arguments; 2nd version */
main(int argc, char *argv[])
{
    while (--argc > 0)
        printf("%s%s", *++argv, (argc > 1) ? " " : "");
    printf("\n");
    return 0;
}
```

Since `argv` is a pointer to the beginning of the array of argument strings, incrementing it by 1 (`++argv`) makes it point at the original `argv[1]` instead of `argv[0]`. Each successive increment moves it along to the next argument; `*argv` is then the pointer to that argument. At the same time, `argc` is decremented; when it becomes zero, there are no arguments left to print.

Alternatively, we could write the `printf` statement as

```
        printf((argc > 1) ? "%s " : "%s", *++argv);
```

This shows that the format argument of `printf` can be an expression too.

As a second example, let us make some enhancements to the pattern-finding program from Section 4.1. If you recall, we wired the search pattern deep into the program, an obviously unsatisfactory arrangement. Following the lead of the UNIX program `grep`, let us change the program so the pattern to be matched is specified by the first argument on the command line.

```
#include <stdio.h>
#include <string.h>
#define MAXLINE 1000

int getline(char *line, int max);

/* find:  print lines that match pattern from 1st arg */
main(int argc, char *argv[])
{
    char line[MAXLINE];
    int found = 0;

    if (argc != 2)
        printf("Usage: find pattern\n");
    else
        while (getline(line, MAXLINE) > 0)
            if (strstr(line, argv[1]) != NULL) {
                printf("%s", line);
                found++;
            }
    return found;
}
```

The standard library function `strstr(s,t)` returns a pointer to the first occurrence of the string `t` in the string `s`, or `NULL` if there is none. It is declared in `<string.h>`.

The model can now be elaborated to illustrate further pointer constructions. Suppose we want to allow two optional arguments. One says "print all lines *except* those that match the pattern;" the second says "precede each printed line by its line number."

A common convention for C programs on UNIX systems is that an argument that begins with a minus sign introduces an optional flag or parameter. If we choose `-x` (for "except") to signal the inversion, and `-n` ("number") to request line numbering, then the command

```
find -x -n pattern
```

will print each line that doesn't match the pattern, preceded by its line number.

Optional arguments should be permitted in any order, and the rest of the program should be independent of the number of arguments that were present. Furthermore, it is convenient for users if option arguments can be combined, as in

        find -nx *pattern*

Here is the program:

```
#include <stdio.h>
#include <string.h>
#define MAXLINE 1000

int getline(char *line, int max);

/* find:  print lines that match pattern from 1st arg */
main(int argc, char *argv[])
{
    char line[MAXLINE];
    long lineno = 0;
    int c, except = 0, number = 0, found = 0;

    while (--argc > 0 && (*++argv)[0] == '-')
        while (c = *++argv[0])
            switch (c) {
            case 'x':
                except = 1;
                break;
            case 'n':
                number = 1;
                break;
            default:
                printf("find: illegal option %c\n", c);
                argc = 0;
                found = -1;
                break;
            }
    if (argc != 1)
        printf("Usage: find -x -n pattern\n");
    else
        while (getline(line, MAXLINE) > 0) {
            lineno++;
            if ((strstr(line, *argv) != NULL) != except) {
                if (number)
                    printf("%ld:", lineno);
                printf("%s", line);
                found++;
            }
        }
    return found;
}
```

`argc` is decremented and `argv` is incremented before each optional argument. At the end of the loop, if there are no errors, `argc` tells how many arguments remain unprocessed and `argv` points to the first of these. Thus `argc`

should be 1 and `*argv` should point at the pattern. Notice that `*++argv` is a pointer to an argument string, so `(*++argv)[0]` is its first character. (An alternate valid form would be `**++argv`.) Because `[ ]` binds tighter than `*` and `++`, the parentheses are necessary; without them the expression would be taken as `*++(argv[0])`. In fact, that is what we used in the inner loop, where the task is to walk along a specific argument string. In the inner loop, the expression `*++argv[0]` increments the pointer `argv[0]`!

It is rare that one uses pointer expressions more complicated than these; in such cases, breaking them into two or three steps will be more intuitive.

Exercise 5-10. Write the program `expr`, which evaluates a reverse Polish expression from the command line, where each operator or operand is a separate argument. For example,

        expr   2   3   4   +   *

evaluates $2 \times (3+4)$. □

Exercise 5-11. Modify the programs `entab` and `detab` (written as exercises in Chapter 1) to accept a list of tab stops as arguments. Use the default tab settings if there are no arguments. □

Exercise 5-12. Extend `entab` and `detab` to accept the shorthand

        entab -*m* +*n*

to mean tab stops every *n* columns, starting at column *m*. Choose convenient (for the user) default behavior. □

Exercise 5-13. Write the program `tail`, which prints the last *n* lines of its input. By default, *n* is 10, let us say, but it can be changed by an optional argument, so that

        tail -*n*

prints the last *n* lines. The program should behave rationally no matter how unreasonable the input or the value of *n*. Write the program so it makes the best use of available storage; lines should be stored as in the sorting program of Section 5.6, not in a two-dimensional array of fixed size. □

5.11 Pointers to Functions

In C, a function itself is not a variable, but it is possible to define pointers to functions, which can be assigned, placed in arrays, passed to functions, returned by functions, and so on. We will illustrate this by modifying the sorting procedure written earlier in this chapter so that if the optional argument -n is given, it will sort the input lines numerically instead of lexicographically.

A sort often consists of three parts—a comparison that determines the ordering of any pair of objects, an exchange that reverses their order, and a sorting algorithm that makes comparisons and exchanges until the objects are in order. The sorting algorithm is independent of the comparison and exchange operations, so by passing different comparison and exchange functions to it, we can arrange to sort by different criteria. This is the approach taken in our new sort.

Lexicographic comparison of two lines is done by strcmp, as before; we will also need a routine numcmp that compares two lines on the basis of numeric value and returns the same kind of condition indication as strcmp does. These functions are declared ahead of main and a pointer to the appropriate one is passed to qsort. We have skimped on error processing for arguments, so as to concentrate on the main issues.

```c
#include <stdio.h>
#include <string.h>

#define MAXLINES 5000      /* max #lines to be sorted */
char *lineptr[MAXLINES];   /* pointers to text lines */

int readlines(char *lineptr[], int nlines);
void writelines(char *lineptr[], int nlines);

void qsort(void *lineptr[], int left, int right,
           int (*comp)(void *, void *));
int numcmp(char *, char *);

/* sort input lines */
main(int argc, char *argv[])
{
    int nlines;          /* number of input lines read */
    int numeric = 0;     /* 1 if numeric sort */

    if (argc > 1 && strcmp(argv[1], "-n") == 0)
        numeric = 1;
    if ((nlines = readlines(lineptr, MAXLINES)) >= 0) {
        qsort((void **) lineptr, 0, nlines-1,
          (int (*)(void*,void*))(numeric ? numcmp : strcmp));
        writelines(lineptr, nlines);
        return 0;
    } else {
        printf("input too big to sort\n");
        return 1;
    }
}
```

In the call to qsort, strcmp and numcmp are addresses of functions. Since they are known to be functions, the & operator is not necessary, in the same way that it is not needed before an array name.

We have written qsort so it can process any data type, not just character strings. As indicated by the function prototype, qsort expects an array of pointers, two integers, and a function with two pointer arguments. The generic pointer type void * is used for the pointer arguments. Any pointer can be cast to void * and back again without loss of information, so we can call qsort by casting arguments to void *. The elaborate cast of the function argument casts the arguments of the comparison function. These will generally have no effect on actual representation, but assure the compiler that all is well.

```
/* qsort:  sort v[left]...v[right] into increasing order */
void qsort(void *v[], int left, int right,
           int (*comp)(void *, void *))
{
    int i, last;
    void swap(void *v[], int, int);

    if (left >= right)    /* do nothing if array contains */
        return;           /* fewer than two elements */
    swap(v, left, (left + right)/2);
    last = left;
    for (i = left+1; i <= right; i++)
        if ((*comp)(v[i], v[left]) < 0)
            swap(v, ++last, i);
    swap(v, left, last);
    qsort(v, left, last-1, comp);
    qsort(v, last+1, right, comp);
}
```

The declarations should be studied with some care. The fourth parameter of qsort is

```
int (*comp)(void *, void *)
```

which says that comp is a pointer to a function that has two void * arguments and returns an int.

The use of comp in the line

```
if ((*comp)(v[i], v[left]) < 0)
```

is consistent with the declaration: comp is a pointer to a function, *comp is the function, and

```
(*comp)(v[i], v[left])
```

is the call to it. The parentheses are needed so the components are correctly associated; without them,

```
int *comp(void *, void *)    /* WRONG */
```

says that comp is a function returning a pointer to an int, which is very different.

We have already shown strcmp, which compares two strings. Here is numcmp, which compares two strings on a leading numeric value, computed by calling `atof`:

```
#include <stdlib.h>

/* numcmp:  compare s1 and s2 numerically */
int numcmp(char *s1, char *s2)
{
    double v1, v2;

    v1 = atof(s1);
    v2 = atof(s2);
    if (v1 < v2)
        return -1;
    else if (v1 > v2)
        return 1;
    else
        return 0;
}
```

The `swap` function, which exchanges two pointers, is identical to what we presented earlier in the chapter, except that the declarations are changed to `void *`.

```
void swap(void *v[], int i, int j)
{
    void *temp;

    temp = v[i];
    v[i] = v[j];
    v[j] = temp;
}
```

A variety of other options can be added to the sorting program; some make challenging exercises.

Exercise 5-14. Modify the sort program to handle a `-r` flag, which indicates sorting in reverse (decreasing) order. Be sure that `-r` works with `-n`. □

Exercise 5-15. Add the option `-f` to fold upper and lower case together, so that case distinctions are not made during sorting; for example, a and A compare equal. □

Exercise 5-16. Add the `-d` ("directory order") option, which makes comparisons only on letters, numbers and blanks. Make sure it works in conjunction with `-f`. □

Exercise 5-17. Add a field-handling capability, so sorting may be done on fields within lines, each field sorted according to an independent set of options. (The index for this book was sorted with `-df` for the index category and `-n` for the page numbers.) □

5.12 Complicated Declarations

C is sometimes castigated for the syntax of its declarations, particularly ones that involve pointers to functions. The syntax is an attempt to make the declaration and the use agree; it works well for simple cases, but it can be confusing for the harder ones, because declarations cannot be read left to right, and because parentheses are over-used. The difference between

```
    int *f();        /* f: function returning pointer to int */
```
and
```
    int (*pf)();     /* pf: pointer to function returning int */
```

illustrates the problem: * is a prefix operator and it has lower precedence than ( ), so parentheses are necessary to force the proper association.

Although truly complicated declarations rarely arise in practice, it is important to know how to understand them, and, if necessary, how to create them. One good way to synthesize declarations is in small steps with `typedef`, which is discussed in Section 6.7. As an alternative, in this section we will present a pair of programs that convert from valid C to a word description and back again. The word description reads left to right.

The first, `dcl`, is the more complex. It converts a C declaration into a word description, as in these examples:

```
char **argv
    argv:  pointer to pointer to char
int (*daytab)[13]
    daytab:  pointer to array[13] of int
int *daytab[13]
    daytab:  array[13] of pointer to int
void *comp()
    comp:  function returning pointer to void
void (*comp)()
    comp:  pointer to function returning void
char (*(*x())[])()
    x: function returning pointer to array[] of
    pointer to function returning char
char (*(*x[3])())[5]
    x: array[3] of pointer to function returning
    pointer to array[5] of char
```

`dcl` is based on the grammar that specifies a declarator, which is spelled out precisely in Appendix A, Section 8.5; this is a simplified form:

> *dcl:*   *optional ∗'s direct-dcl*
> *direct-dcl:* *name*
>   *(dcl)*
>   *direct-dcl( )*
>   *direct-dcl[optional size]*

In words, a *dcl* is a *direct-dcl*, perhaps preceded by ∗'s. A *direct-dcl* is a

name, or a parenthesized *dcl*, or a *direct-dcl* followed by parentheses, or a
direct-dcl followed by brackets with an optional size.

This grammar can be used to parse declarations. For instance, consider this
declarator:

```
(*pfa[])()
```

pfa will be identified as a *name* and thus as a *direct-dcl*. Then pfa[] is also
a *direct-dcl*. Then *pfa[] is a recognized as a *dcl*, so (*pfa[]) is a *direct-dcl*. Then (*pfa[])() is a *direct-dcl* and thus a *dcl*. We can also illustrate
the parse with a parse tree like this (where *direct-dcl* has been abbreviated to
dir-dcl):

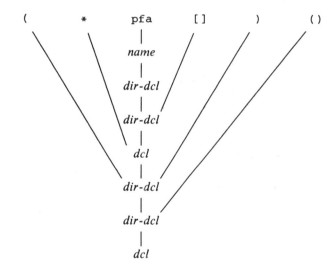

The heart of the dcl program is a pair of functions, dcl and dirdcl, that
parse a declaration according to this grammar. Because the grammar is recursively defined, the functions call each other recursively as they recognize pieces
of a declaration; the program is called a recursive-descent parser.

```c
/* dcl:  parse a declarator */
void dcl(void)
{
    int ns;

    for (ns = 0; gettoken() == '*'; )   /* count *'s */
        ns++;
    dirdcl();
    while (ns-- > 0)
        strcat(out, " pointer to");
}
```

```
/* dirdcl:  parse a direct declarator */
void dirdcl(void)
{
    int type;

    if (tokentype == '(') {            /* ( dcl ) */
        dcl();
        if (tokentype != ')')
            printf("error: missing )\n");
    } else if (tokentype == NAME)     /* variable name */
        strcpy(name, token);
    else
        printf("error: expected name or (dcl)\n");
    while ((type=gettoken()) == PARENS || type == BRACKETS)
        if (type == PARENS)
            strcat(out, " function returning");
        else {
            strcat(out, " array");
            strcat(out, token);
            strcat(out, " of");
        }
}
```

Since the programs are intended to be illustrative, not bullet-proof, there are significant restrictions on dcl. It can only handle a simple data type like char or int. It does not handle argument types in functions, or qualifiers like const. Spurious blanks confuse it. It doesn't do much error recovery, so invalid declarations will also confuse it. These improvements are left as exercises.

Here are the global variables and the main routine:

```
#include <stdio.h>
#include <string.h>
#include <ctype.h>

#define  MAXTOKEN  100

enum { NAME, PARENS, BRACKETS };

void dcl(void);
void dirdcl(void);

int  gettoken(void);
int  tokentype;              /* type of last token */
char token[MAXTOKEN];        /* last token string */
char name[MAXTOKEN];         /* identifier name */
char datatype[MAXTOKEN];     /* data type = char, int, etc. */
char out[1000];              /* output string */
```

```
main()  /* convert declaration to words */
{
    while (gettoken() != EOF) {    /* 1st token on line */
        strcpy(datatype, token);   /* is the datatype */
        out[0] = '\0';
        dcl();        /* parse rest of line */
        if (tokentype != '\n')
            printf("syntax error\n");
        printf("%s: %s %s\n", name, out, datatype);
    }
    return 0;
}
```

The function `gettoken` skips blanks and tabs, then finds the next token in the input; a "token" is a name, a pair of parentheses, a pair of brackets perhaps including a number, or any other single character.

```
int gettoken(void)  /* return next token */
{
    int c, getch(void);
    void ungetch(int);
    char *p = token;

    while ((c = getch()) == ' ' || c == '\t')
        ;
    if (c == '(') {
        if ((c = getch()) == ')') {
            strcpy(token, "()");
            return tokentype = PARENS;
        } else {
            ungetch(c);
            return tokentype = '(';
        }
    } else if (c == '[') {
        for (*p++ = c; (*p++ = getch()) != ']'; )
            ;
        *p = '\0';
        return tokentype = BRACKETS;
    } else if (isalpha(c)) {
        for (*p++ = c; isalnum(c = getch()); )
            *p++ = c;
        *p = '\0';
        ungetch(c);
        return tokentype = NAME;
    } else
        return tokentype = c;
}
```

`getch` and `ungetch` were discussed in Chapter 4.

Going in the other direction is easier, especially if we do not worry about generating redundant parentheses. The program `undcl` converts a word description like "**x** is a function returning a pointer to an array of pointers to functions returning **char**," which we will express as

```
x () * [] * () char
```

to

```
char (*(*x())[])()
```

The abbreviated input syntax lets us reuse the `gettoken` function. `undcl` also uses the same external variables as `dcl` does.

```
/* undcl:  convert word description to declaration */
main()
{
    int type;
    char temp[MAXTOKEN];

    while (gettoken() != EOF) {
        strcpy(out, token);
        while ((type = gettoken()) != '\n')
            if (type == PARENS || type == BRACKETS)
                strcat(out, token);
            else if (type == '*') {
                sprintf(temp, "(*%s)", out);
                strcpy(out, temp);
            } else if (type == NAME) {
                sprintf(temp, "%s %s", token, out);
                strcpy(out, temp);
            } else
                printf("invalid input at %s\n", token);
        printf("%s\n", out);
    }
    return 0;
}
```

Exercise 5-18. Make `dcl` recover from input errors. □

Exercise 5-19. Modify `undcl` so that it does not add redundant parentheses to declarations. □

Exercise 5-20. Expand `dcl` to handle declarations with function argument types, qualifiers like `const`, and so on. □

CHAPTER 6: **Structures**

A structure is a collection of one or more variables, possibly of different types, grouped together under a single name for convenient handling. (Structures are called "records" in some languages, notably Pascal.) Structures help to organize complicated data, particularly in large programs, because they permit a group of related variables to be treated as a unit instead of as separate entities.

One traditional example of a structure is the payroll record: an employee is described by a set of attributes such as name, address, social security number, salary, etc. Some of these in turn could be structures: a name has several components, as does an address and even a salary. Another example, more typical for C, comes from graphics: a point is a pair of coordinates, a rectangle is a pair of points, and so on.

The main change made by the ANSI standard is to define structure assignment—structures may be copied and assigned to, passed to functions, and returned by functions. This has been supported by most compilers for many years, but the properties are now precisely defined. Automatic structures and arrays may now also be initialized.

6.1 Basics of Structures

Let us create a few structures suitable for graphics. The basic object is a point, which we will assume has an x coordinate and a y coordinate, both integers.

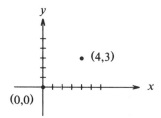

The two components can be placed in a structure declared like this:

```
struct point {
    int x;
    int y;
};
```

The keyword `struct` introduces a structure declaration, which is a list of declarations enclosed in braces. An optional name called a *structure tag* may follow the word `struct` (as with `point` here). The tag names this kind of structure, and can be used subsequently as a shorthand for the part of the declaration in braces.

The variables named in a structure are called *members*. A structure member or tag and an ordinary (i.e., non-member) variable can have the same name without conflict, since they can always be distinguished by context. Furthermore, the same member names may occur in different structures, although as a matter of style one would normally use the same names only for closely related objects.

A `struct` declaration defines a type. The right brace that terminates the list of members may be followed by a list of variables, just as for any basic type. That is,

```
struct { ... } x, y, z;
```

is syntactically analogous to

```
int x, y, z;
```

in the sense that each statement declares `x`, `y` and `z` to be variables of the named type and causes space to be set aside for them.

A structure declaration that is not followed by a list of variables reserves no storage; it merely describes a template or the shape of a structure. If the declaration is tagged, however, the tag can be used later in definitions of instances of the structure. For example, given the declaration of `point` above,

```
struct point pt;
```

defines a variable `pt` which is a structure of type `struct point`. A structure can be initialized by following its definition with a list of initializers, each a constant expression, for the members:

```
struct point maxpt = { 320, 200 };
```

An automatic structure may also be initialized by assignment or by calling a function that returns a structure of the right type.

A member of a particular structure is referred to in an expression by a construction of the form

structure-name . member

The structure member operator "`.`" connects the structure name and the member name. To print the coordinates of the point `pt`, for instance,

```
    printf("%d,%d", pt.x, pt.y);
```

or to compute the distance from the origin (0,0) to `pt`,

```
    double dist, sqrt(double);

    dist = sqrt((double)pt.x * pt.x + (double)pt.y * pt.y);
```

Structures can be nested. One representation of a rectangle is a pair of points that denote the diagonally opposite corners:

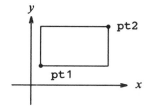

```
    struct rect {
        struct point pt1;
        struct point pt2;
    };
```

The `rect` structure contains two `point` structures. If we declare `screen` as

```
    struct rect screen;
```

then

```
    screen.pt1.x
```

refers to the *x* coordinate of the `pt1` member of `screen`.

6.2 Structures and Functions

The only legal operations on a structure are copying it or assigning to it as a unit, taking its address with &, and accessing its members. Copy and assignment include passing arguments to functions and returning values from functions as well. Structures may not be compared. A structure may be initialized by a list of constant member values; an automatic structure may also be initialized by an assignment.

Let us investigate structures by writing some functions to manipulate points and rectangles. There are at least three possible approaches: pass components separately, pass an entire structure, or pass a pointer to it. Each has its good points and bad points.

The first function, `makepoint`, will take two integers and return a `point` structure:

```
/* makepoint:  make a point from x and y components */
struct point makepoint(int x, int y)
{
    struct point temp;

    temp.x = x;
    temp.y = y;
    return temp;
}
```

Notice that there is no conflict between the argument name and the member with the same name; indeed the re-use of the names stresses the relationship.

`makepoint` can now be used to initialize any structure dynamically, or to provide structure arguments to a function:

```
struct rect screen;
struct point middle;
struct point makepoint(int, int);

screen.pt1 = makepoint(0, 0);
screen.pt2 = makepoint(XMAX, YMAX);
middle = makepoint((screen.pt1.x + screen.pt2.x)/2,
                   (screen.pt1.y + screen.pt2.y)/2);
```

The next step is a set of functions to do arithmetic on points. For instance,

```
/* addpoint:  add two points */
struct point addpoint(struct point p1, struct point p2)
{
    p1.x += p2.x;
    p1.y += p2.y;
    return p1;
}
```

Here both the arguments and the return value are structures. We incremented the components in `p1` rather than using an explicit temporary variable to emphasize that structure parameters are passed by value like any others.

As another example, the function `ptinrect` tests whether a point is inside a rectangle, where we have adopted the convention that a rectangle includes its left and bottom sides but not its top and right sides:

```
/* ptinrect:  return 1 if p in r, 0 if not */
int ptinrect(struct point p, struct rect r)
{
    return p.x >= r.pt1.x && p.x < r.pt2.x
        && p.y >= r.pt1.y && p.y < r.pt2.y;
}
```

This assumes that the rectangle is represented in a standard form where the `pt1` coordinates are less than the `pt2` coordinates. The following function returns a rectangle guaranteed to be in canonical form:

```
#define min(a, b) ((a) < (b) ? (a) : (b))
#define max(a, b) ((a) > (b) ? (a) : (b))

/* canonrect:  canonicalize coordinates of rectangle */
struct rect canonrect(struct rect r)
{
    struct rect temp;

    temp.pt1.x = min(r.pt1.x, r.pt2.x);
    temp.pt1.y = min(r.pt1.y, r.pt2.y);
    temp.pt2.x = max(r.pt1.x, r.pt2.x);
    temp.pt2.y = max(r.pt1.y, r.pt2.y);
    return temp;
}
```

If a large structure is to be passed to a function, it is generally more efficient to pass a pointer than to copy the whole structure. Structure pointers are just like pointers to ordinary variables. The declaration

```
struct point *pp;
```

says that pp is a pointer to a structure of type struct point. If pp points to a point structure, *pp is the structure, and (*pp).x and (*pp).y are the members. To use pp, we might write, for example,

```
struct point origin, *pp;

pp = &origin;
printf("origin is (%d,%d)\n", (*pp).x, (*pp).y);
```

The parentheses are necessary in (*pp).x because the precedence of the structure member operator . is higher than *. The expression *pp.x means *(pp.x), which is illegal here because x is not a pointer.

Pointers to structures are so frequently used that an alternative notation is provided as a shorthand. If p is a pointer to a structure, then

p->*member-of-structure*

refers to the particular member. (The operator -> is a minus sign immediately followed by >.) So we could write instead

```
printf("origin is (%d,%d)\n", pp->x, pp->y);
```

Both . and -> associate from left to right, so if we have

```
struct rect r, *rp = &r;
```

then these four expressions are equivalent:

```
r.pt1.x
rp->pt1.x
(r.pt1).x
(rp->pt1).x
```

The structure operators . and ->, together with ( ) for function calls and [ ] for subscripts, are at the top of the precedence hierarchy and thus bind very tightly. For example, given the declaration

```
struct {
    int len;
    char *str;
} *p;
```

then

```
++p->len
```

increments `len`, not `p`, because the implied parenthesization is `++(p->len)`. Parentheses can be used to alter the binding: `(++p)->len` increments `p` before accessing `len`, and `(p++)->len` increments `p` afterward. (This last set of parentheses is unnecessary.)

In the same way, `*p->str` fetches whatever `str` points to; `*p->str++` increments `str` after accessing whatever it points to (just like `*s++`); `(*p->str)++` increments whatever `str` points to; and `*p++->str` increments `p` after accessing whatever `str` points to.

6.3 Arrays of Structures

Consider writing a program to count the occurrences of each C keyword. We need an array of character strings to hold the names, and an array of integers for the counts. One possibility is to use two parallel arrays, `keyword` and `keycount`, as in

```
char *keyword[NKEYS];
int keycount[NKEYS];
```

But the very fact that the arrays are parallel suggests a different organization, an array of structures. Each keyword entry is a pair:

```
char *word;
int count;
```

and there is an array of pairs. The structure declaration

```
struct key {
    char *word;
    int count;
} keytab[NKEYS];
```

declares a structure type `key`, defines an array `keytab` of structures of this type, and sets aside storage for them. Each element of the array is a structure. This could also be written

```
struct key {
    char *word;
    int count;
};

struct key keytab[NKEYS];
```

Since the structure `keytab` contains a constant set of names, it is easiest to make it an external variable and initialize it once and for all when it is defined. The structure initialization is analogous to earlier ones—the definition is followed by a list of initializers enclosed in braces:

```
struct key {
    char *word;
    int count;
} keytab[] = {
    "auto", 0,
    "break", 0,
    "case", 0,
    "char", 0,
    "const", 0,
    "continue", 0,
    "default", 0,
    /* ... */
    "unsigned", 0,
    "void", 0,
    "volatile", 0,
    "while", 0
};
```

The initializers are listed in pairs corresponding to the structure members. It would be more precise to enclose initializers for each "row" or structure in braces, as in

```
    { "auto", 0 },
    { "break", 0 },
    { "case", 0 },
    ...
```

but the inner braces are not necessary when the initializers are simple variables or character strings, and when all are present. As usual, the number of entries in the array `keytab` will be computed if initializers are present and the [ ] is left empty.

The keyword-counting program begins with the definition of `keytab`. The main routine reads the input by repeatedly calling a function `getword` that fetches one word at a time. Each word is looked up in `keytab` with a version of the binary search function that we wrote in Chapter 3. The list of keywords must be sorted in increasing order in the table.

```
#include <stdio.h>
#include <ctype.h>
#include <string.h>

#define MAXWORD 100

int getword(char *, int);
int binsearch(char *, struct key *, int);

/* count C keywords */
main()
{
    int n;
    char word[MAXWORD];

    while (getword(word, MAXWORD) != EOF)
        if (isalpha(word[0]))
            if ((n = binsearch(word, keytab, NKEYS)) >= 0)
                keytab[n].count++;
    for (n = 0; n < NKEYS; n++)
        if (keytab[n].count > 0)
            printf("%4d %s\n",
                keytab[n].count, keytab[n].word);
    return 0;
}

/* binsearch:  find word in tab[0]...tab[n-1] */
int binsearch(char *word, struct key tab[], int n)
{
    int cond;
    int low, high, mid;

    low = 0;
    high = n - 1;
    while (low <= high) {
        mid = (low+high) / 2;
        if ((cond = strcmp(word, tab[mid].word)) < 0)
            high = mid - 1;
        else if (cond > 0)
            low = mid + 1;
        else
            return mid;
    }
    return -1;
}
```

We will show the function getword in a moment; for now it suffices to say that each call to getword finds a word, which is copied into the array named as its first argument.

The quantity NKEYS is the number of keywords in keytab. Although we could count this by hand, it's a lot easier and safer to do it by machine, especially if the list is subject to change. One possibility would be to terminate the list of initializers with a null pointer, then loop along `keytab` until the end is found.

But this is more than is needed, since the size of the array is completely determined at compile time. The size of the array is the size of one entry times the number of entries, so the number of entries is just

> *size of* `keytab` / *size of* `struct key`

C provides a compile-time unary operator called `sizeof` that can be used to compute the size of any object. The expressions

> `sizeof` *object*

and

> `sizeof(`*type name*`)`

yield an integer equal to the size of the specified object or type in bytes. (Strictly, `sizeof` produces an unsigned integer value whose type, `size_t`, is defined in the header `<stddef.h>`.) An object can be a variable or array or structure. A type name can be the name of a basic type like `int` or `double`, or a derived type like a structure or a pointer.

In our case, the number of keywords is the size of the array divided by the size of one element. This computation is used in a `#define` statement to set the value of NKEYS:

> `#define  NKEYS  (sizeof keytab / sizeof(struct key))`

Another way to write this is to divide the array size by the size of a specific element:

> `#define  NKEYS  (sizeof keytab / sizeof keytab[0])`

This has the advantage that it does not need to be changed if the type changes.

A `sizeof` can not be used in a `#if` line, because the preprocessor does not parse type names. But the expression in the `#define` is not evaluated by the preprocessor, so the code here is legal.

Now for the function `getword`. We have written a more general `getword` than is necessary for this program, but it is not complicated. `getword` fetches the next "word" from the input, where a word is either a string of letters and digits beginning with a letter, or a single non-white space character. The function value is the first character of the word, or EOF for end of file, or the character itself if it is not alphabetic.

```
/* getword:  get next word or character from input */
int getword(char *word, int lim)
{
    int c, getch(void);
    void ungetch(int);
    char *w = word;

    while (isspace(c = getch()))
        ;
    if (c != EOF)
        *w++ = c;
    if (!isalpha(c)) {
        *w = '\0';
        return c;
    }
    for ( ; --lim > 0; w++)
        if (!isalnum(*w = getch())) {
            ungetch(*w);
            break;
        }
    *w = '\0';
    return word[0];
}
```

getword uses the getch and ungetch that we wrote in Chapter 4. When
the collection of an alphanumeric token stops, getword has gone one character
too far. The call to ungetch pushes that character back on the input for the
next call. getword also uses isspace to skip white space, isalpha to identify letters, and isalnum to identify letters and digits; all are from the standard header <ctype.h>.

Exercise 6-1. Our version of getword does not properly handle underscores,
string constants, comments, or preprocessor control lines. Write a better version. □

6.4 Pointers to Structures

To illustrate some of the considerations involved with pointers to and arrays
of structures, let us write the keyword-counting program again, this time using
pointers instead of array indices.

The external declaration of keytab need not change, but main and
binsearch do need modification.

```
#include <stdio.h>
#include <ctype.h>
#include <string.h>
#define MAXWORD 100

int getword(char *, int);
struct key *binsearch(char *, struct key *, int);

/* count C keywords; pointer version */
main()
{
    char word[MAXWORD];
    struct key *p;

    while (getword(word, MAXWORD) != EOF)
        if (isalpha(word[0]))
            if ((p=binsearch(word, keytab, NKEYS)) != NULL)
                p->count++;
    for (p = keytab; p < keytab + NKEYS; p++)
        if (p->count > 0)
            printf("%4d %s\n", p->count, p->word);
    return 0;
}

/* binsearch:  find word in tab[0]...tab[n-1] */
struct key *binsearch(char *word, struct key *tab, int n)
{
    int cond;
    struct key *low = &tab[0];
    struct key *high = &tab[n];
    struct key *mid;

    while (low < high) {
        mid = low + (high-low) / 2;
        if ((cond = strcmp(word, mid->word)) < 0)
            high = mid;
        else if (cond > 0)
            low = mid + 1;
        else
            return mid;
    }
    return NULL;
}
```

There are several things worthy of note here. First, the declaration of binsearch must indicate that it returns a pointer to struct key instead of an integer; this is declared both in the function prototype and in binsearch. If binsearch finds the word, it returns a pointer to it; if it fails, it returns NULL.

Second, the elements of keytab are now accessed by pointers. This requires significant changes in binsearch.

The initializers for low and high are now pointers to the beginning and just past the end of the table.

The computation of the middle element can no longer be simply

```
mid = (low+high) / 2    /* WRONG */
```

because the addition of two pointers is illegal. Subtraction is legal, however, so high-low is the number of elements, and thus

```
mid = low + (high-low) / 2
```

sets mid to point to the element halfway between low and high.

The most important change is to adjust the algorithm to make sure that it does not generate an illegal pointer or attempt to access an element outside the array. The problem is that &tab[-1] and &tab[n] are both outside the limits of the array tab. The former is strictly illegal, and it is illegal to dereference the latter. The language definition does guarantee, however, that pointer arithmetic that involves the first element beyond the end of an array (that is, &tab[n]) will work correctly.

In main we wrote

```
for (p = keytab; p < keytab + NKEYS; p++)
```

If p is a pointer to a structure, arithmetic on p takes into account the size of the structure, so p++ increments p by the correct amount to get the next element of the array of structures, and the test stops the loop at the right time.

Don't assume, however, that the size of a structure is the sum of the sizes of its members. Because of alignment requirements for different objects, there may be unnamed "holes" in a structure. Thus, for instance, if a char is one byte and an int four bytes, the structure

```
struct {
    char c;
    int i;
};
```

might well require eight bytes, not five. The sizeof operator returns the proper value.

Finally, an aside on program format: when a function returns a complicated type like a structure pointer, as in

```
struct key *binsearch(char *word, struct key *tab, int n)
```

the function name can be hard to see, and to find with a text editor. Accordingly an alternate style is sometimes used:

```
struct key *
binsearch(char *word, struct key *tab, int n)
```

This is a matter of personal taste; pick the form you like and hold to it.

6.5 Self-referential Structures

Suppose we want to handle the more general problem of counting the occurrences of *all* the words in some input. Since the list of words isn't known in advance, we can't conveniently sort it and use a binary search. Yet we can't do a linear search for each word as it arrives, to see if it's already been seen; the program would take too long. (More precisely, its running time is likely to grow quadratically with the number of input words.) How can we organize the data to cope efficiently with a list of arbitrary words?

One solution is to keep the set of words seen so far sorted at all times, by placing each word into its proper position in the order as it arrives. This shouldn't be done by shifting words in a linear array, though—that also takes too long. Instead we will use a data structure called a *binary tree*.

The tree contains one "node" per distinct word; each node contains

> a pointer to the text of the word
> a count of the number of occurrences
> a pointer to the left child node
> a pointer to the right child node

No node may have more than two children; it might have only zero or one.

The nodes are maintained so that at any node the left subtree contains only words that are lexicographically less than the word at the node, and the right subtree contains only words that are greater. This is the tree for the sentence "now is the time for all good men to come to the aid of their party", as built by inserting each word as it is encountered:

```
                       now
                      /   \
                  is       the
                 /  \      /  \
             for     men of    time
            /   \        \    /   \
         all     good   party their  to
        /  \
     aid    come
```

To find out whether a new word is already in the tree, start at the root and compare the new word to the word stored at that node. If they match, the question is answered affirmatively. If the new word is less than the tree word, continue searching at the left child, otherwise at the right child. If there is no child in the required direction, the new word is not in the tree, and in fact the empty slot is the proper place to add the new word. This process is recursive, since the search from any node uses a search from one of its children. Accordingly, recursive routines for insertion and printing will be most natural.

Going back to the description of a node, it is conveniently represented as a structure with four components:

```
struct tnode {          /* the tree node: */
    char *word;             /* points to the text */
    int count;              /* number of occurrences */
    struct tnode *left;     /* left child */
    struct tnode *right;    /* right child */
};
```

This recursive declaration of a node might look chancy, but it's correct. It is illegal for a structure to contain an instance of itself, but

```
struct tnode *left;
```

declares `left` to be a pointer to a `tnode`, not a `tnode` itself.

Occasionally, one needs a variation of self-referential structures: two structures that refer to each other. The way to handle this is:

```
struct t {
    ...
    struct s *p;    /* p points to an s */
};
struct s {
    ...
    struct t *q;    /* q points to a t */
};
```

The code for the whole program is surprisingly small, given a handful of supporting routines like `getword` that we have already written. The main routine reads words with `getword` and installs them in the tree with `addtree`.

```
#include <stdio.h>
#include <ctype.h>
#include <string.h>

#define MAXWORD 100
struct tnode *addtree(struct tnode *, char *);
void treeprint(struct tnode *);
int getword(char *, int);

/* word frequency count */
main()
{
    struct tnode *root;
    char word[MAXWORD];

    root = NULL;
    while (getword(word, MAXWORD) != EOF)
        if (isalpha(word[0]))
            root = addtree(root, word);
    treeprint(root);
    return 0;
}
```

The function `addtree` is recursive. A word is presented by `main` to the top level (the root) of the tree. At each stage, that word is compared to the word already stored at the node, and is percolated down to either the left or right subtree by a recursive call to `addtree`. Eventually the word either matches something already in the tree (in which case the count is incremented), or a null pointer is encountered, indicating that a node must be created and added to the tree. If a new node is created, `addtree` returns a pointer to it, which is installed in the parent node.

```
struct tnode *talloc(void);
char *strdup(char *);

/* addtree:  add a node with w, at or below p */
struct tnode *addtree(struct tnode *p, char *w)
{
    int cond;

    if (p == NULL) {     /* a new word has arrived */
        p = talloc();    /* make a new node */
        p->word = strdup(w);
        p->count = 1;
        p->left = p->right = NULL;
    } else if ((cond = strcmp(w, p->word)) == 0)
        p->count++;      /* repeated word */
    else if (cond < 0)   /* less than into left subtree */
        p->left = addtree(p->left, w);
    else                 /* greater than into right subtree */
        p->right = addtree(p->right, w);
    return p;
}
```

Storage for the new node is fetched by a routine `talloc`, which returns a pointer to a free space suitable for holding a tree node, and the new word is copied to a hidden place by `strdup`. (We will discuss these routines in a moment.) The count is initialized, and the two children are made null. This part of the code is executed only at the leaves of the tree, when a new node is being added. We have (unwisely) omitted error checking on the values returned by `strdup` and `talloc`.

`treeprint` prints the tree in sorted order; at each node, it prints the left subtree (all the words less than this word), then the word itself, then the right subtree (all the words greater). If you feel shaky about how recursion works, simulate `treeprint` as it operates on the tree shown above.

```
/* treeprint:  in-order print of tree p */
void treeprint(struct tnode *p)
{
    if (p != NULL) {
        treeprint(p->left);
        printf("%4d %s\n", p->count, p->word);
        treeprint(p->right);
    }
}
```

A practical note: if the tree becomes "unbalanced" because the words don't arrive in random order, the running time of the program can grow too much. As a worst case, if the words are already in order, this program does an expensive simulation of linear search. There are generalizations of the binary tree that do not suffer from this worst-case behavior, but we will not describe them here.

Before we leave this example, it is also worth a brief digression on a problem related to storage allocators. Clearly it's desirable that there be only one storage allocator in a program, even though it allocates different kinds of objects. But if one allocator is to process requests for, say, pointers to chars and pointers to struct tnodes, two questions arise. First, how does it meet the requirement of most real machines that objects of certain types must satisfy alignment restrictions (for example, integers often must be located at even addresses)? Second, what declarations can cope with the fact that an allocator must necessarily return different kinds of pointers?

Alignment requirements can generally be satisfied easily, at the cost of some wasted space, by ensuring that the allocator always returns a pointer that meets *all* alignment restrictions. The alloc of Chapter 5 does not guarantee any particular alignment, so we will use the standard library function malloc, which does. In Chapter 8 we will show one way to implement malloc.

The question of the type declaration for a function like malloc is a vexing one for any language that takes its type-checking seriously. In C, the proper method is to declare that malloc returns a pointer to void, then explicitly coerce the pointer into the desired type with a cast. malloc and related routines are declared in the standard header <stdlib.h>. Thus talloc can be written as

```
#include <stdlib.h>

/* talloc:  make a tnode */
struct tnode *talloc(void)
{
    return (struct tnode *) malloc(sizeof(struct tnode));
}
```

strdup merely copies the string given by its argument into a safe place, obtained by a call on malloc:

```
char *strdup(char *s)    /* make a duplicate of s */
{
    char *p;

    p = (char *) malloc(strlen(s)+1);  /* +1 for '\0' */
    if (p != NULL)
        strcpy(p, s);
    return p;
}
```

`malloc` returns `NULL` if no space is available; `strdup` passes that value on, leaving error-handling to its caller.

Storage obtained by calling `malloc` may be freed for re-use by calling `free`; see Chapters 7 and 8.

Exercise 6-2. Write a program that reads a C program and prints in alphabetical order each group of variable names that are identical in the first 6 characters, but different somewhere thereafter. Don't count words within strings and comments. Make 6 a parameter that can be set from the command line. □

Exercise 6-3. Write a cross-referencer that prints a list of all words in a document, and, for each word, a list of the line numbers on which it occurs. Remove noise words like "the," "and," and so on. □

Exercise 6-4. Write a program that prints the distinct words in its input sorted into decreasing order of frequency of occurrence. Precede each word by its count. □

6.6 Table Lookup

In this section we will write the innards of a table-lookup package, to illustrate more aspects of structures. This code is typical of what might be found in the symbol table management routines of a macro processor or a compiler. For example, consider the `#define` statement. When a line like

```
#define  IN   1
```

is encountered, the name `IN` and the replacement text 1 are stored in a table. Later, when the name `IN` appears in a statement like

```
state = IN;
```

it must be replaced by 1.

There are two routines that manipulate the names and replacement texts. `install(s,t)` records the name s and the replacement text t in a table; s and t are just character strings. `lookup(s)` searches for s in the table, and returns a pointer to the place where it was found, or `NULL` if it wasn't there.

The algorithm is a hash search—the incoming name is converted into a small non-negative integer, which is then used to index into an array of pointers. An array element points to the beginning of a linked list of blocks describing names that have that hash value. It is NULL if no names have hashed to that value.

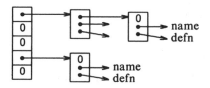

A block in the list is a structure containing pointers to the name, the replacement text, and the next block in the list. A null next-pointer marks the end of the list.

```
struct nlist {          /* table entry: */
    struct nlist *next;    /* next entry in chain */
    char *name;            /* defined name */
    char *defn;            /* replacement text */
};
```

The pointer array is just

```
#define HASHSIZE 101

static struct nlist *hashtab[HASHSIZE]; /* pointer table */
```

The hashing function, which is used by both `lookup` and `install`, adds each character value in the string to a scrambled combination of the previous ones and returns the remainder modulo the array size. This is not the best possible hash function, but it is short and effective.

```
/* hash:  form hash value for string s */
unsigned hash(char *s)
{
    unsigned hashval;

    for (hashval = 0; *s != '\0'; s++)
        hashval = *s + 31 * hashval;
    return hashval % HASHSIZE;
}
```

Unsigned arithmetic ensures that the hash value is non-negative.

The hashing process produces a starting index in the array `hashtab`; if the string is to be found anywhere, it will be in the list of blocks beginning there. The search is performed by `lookup`. If `lookup` finds the entry already present, it returns a pointer to it; if not, it returns NULL.

```
/* lookup:  look for s in hashtab */
struct nlist *lookup(char *s)
{
    struct nlist *np;

    for (np = hashtab[hash(s)]; np != NULL; np = np->next)
        if (strcmp(s, np->name) == 0)
            return np;  /* found */
    return NULL;         /* not found */
}
```

The for loop in lookup is the standard idiom for walking along a linked list:

```
for (ptr = head; ptr != NULL; ptr = ptr->next)
    ...
```

install uses lookup to determine whether the name being installed is already present; if so, the new definition will supersede the old one. Otherwise, a new entry is created. install returns NULL if for any reason there is no room for a new entry.

```
struct nlist *lookup(char *);
char *strdup(char *);

/* install:  put (name, defn) in hashtab */
struct nlist *install(char *name, char *defn)
{
    struct nlist *np;
    unsigned hashval;

    if ((np = lookup(name)) == NULL) {  /* not found */
        np = (struct nlist *) malloc(sizeof(*np));
        if (np == NULL || (np->name = strdup(name)) == NULL)
            return NULL;
        hashval = hash(name);
        np->next = hashtab[hashval];
        hashtab[hashval] = np;
    } else      /* already there */
        free((void *) np->defn);  /* free previous defn */
    if ((np->defn = strdup(defn)) == NULL)
        return NULL;
    return np;
}
```

Exercise 6-5. Write a function undef that will remove a name and definition from the table maintained by lookup and install. □

Exercise 6-6. Implement a simple version of the #define processor (i.e., no arguments) suitable for use with C programs, based on the routines of this section. You may also find getch and ungetch helpful. □

6.7 Typedef

C provides a facility called `typedef` for creating new data type names. For example, the declaration

```
typedef int Length;
```

makes the name `Length` a synonym for `int`. The type `Length` can be used in declarations, casts, etc., in exactly the same ways that the type `int` can be:

```
Length  len, maxlen;
Length  *lengths[];
```

Similarly, the declaration

```
typedef char *String;
```

makes `String` a synonym for `char *` or character pointer, which may then be used in declarations and casts:

```
String p, lineptr[MAXLINES], alloc(int);
int strcmp(String, String);
p = (String) malloc(100);
```

Notice that the type being declared in a `typedef` appears in the position of a variable name, not right after the word `typedef`. Syntactically, `typedef` is like the storage classes `extern`, `static`, etc. We have used capitalized names for `typedef`s, to make them stand out.

As a more complicated example, we could make `typedef`s for the tree nodes shown earlier in this chapter:

```
typedef struct tnode *Treeptr;

typedef struct tnode {    /* the tree node: */
    char *word;               /* points to the text */
    int count;                /* number of occurrences */
    Treeptr left;             /* left child */
    Treeptr right;            /* right child */
} Treenode;
```

This creates two new type keywords called `Treenode` (a structure) and `Treeptr` (a pointer to the structure). Then the routine `talloc` could become

```
Treeptr talloc(void)
{
    return (Treeptr) malloc(sizeof(Treenode));
}
```

It must be emphasized that a `typedef` declaration does not create a new type in any sense; it merely adds a new name for some existing type. Nor are there any new semantics: variables declared this way have exactly the same properties as variables whose declarations are spelled out explicitly. In effect, `typedef` is like `#define`, except that since it is interpreted by the compiler, it can cope with textual substitutions that are beyond the capabilities of the preprocessor. For example,

```
typedef int (*PFI)(char *, char *);
```

creates the type `PFI`, for "pointer to function (of two `char *` arguments) returning `int`," which can be used in contexts like

```
PFI strcmp, numcmp;
```

in the sort program of Chapter 5.

Besides purely aesthetic issues, there are two main reasons for using `typedefs`. The first is to parameterize a program against portability problems. If `typedefs` are used for data types that may be machine-dependent, only the `typedefs` need change when the program is moved. One common situation is to use `typedef` names for various integer quantities, then make an appropriate set of choices of `short`, `int`, and `long` for each host machine. Types like `size_t` and `ptrdiff_t` from the standard library are examples.

The second purpose of `typedefs` is to provide better documentation for a program—a type called `Treeptr` may be easier to understand than one declared only as a pointer to a complicated structure.

6.8 Unions

A *union* is a variable that may hold (at different times) objects of different types and sizes, with the compiler keeping track of size and alignment requirements. Unions provide a way to manipulate different kinds of data in a single area of storage, without embedding any machine-dependent information in the program. They are analogous to variant records in Pascal.

As an example such as might be found in a compiler symbol table manager, suppose that a constant may be an `int`, a `float`, or a character pointer. The value of a particular constant must be stored in a variable of the proper type, yet it is most convenient for table management if the value occupies the same amount of storage and is stored in the same place regardless of its type. This is the purpose of a union—a single variable that can legitimately hold any one of several types. The syntax is based on structures:

```
union u_tag {
    int ival;
    float fval;
    char *sval;
} u;
```

The variable u will be large enough to hold the largest of the three types; the specific size is implementation-dependent. Any one of these types may be assigned to u and then used in expressions, so long as the usage is consistent: the type retrieved must be the type most recently stored. It is the programmer's responsibility to keep track of which type is currently stored in a union; the results are implementation-dependent if something is stored as one type and extracted as another.

Syntactically, members of a union are accessed as

union-name . member

or

union-pointer -> member

just as for structures. If the variable `utype` is used to keep track of the current type stored in `u`, then one might see code such as

```
if (utype == INT)
    printf("%d\n", u.ival);
else if (utype == FLOAT)
    printf("%f\n", u.fval);
else if (utype == STRING)
    printf("%s\n", u.sval);
else
    printf("bad type %d in utype\n", utype);
```

Unions may occur within structures and arrays, and vice versa. The notation for accessing a member of a union in a structure (or vice versa) is identical to that for nested structures. For example, in the structure array defined by

```
struct {
    char *name;
    int flags;
    int utype;
    union {
        int ival;
        float fval;
        char *sval;
    } u;
} symtab[NSYM];
```

the member `ival` is referred to as

```
symtab[i].u.ival
```

and the first character of the string `sval` by either of

```
*symtab[i].u.sval
symtab[i].u.sval[0]
```

In effect, a union is a structure in which all members have offset zero from the base, the structure is big enough to hold the "widest" member, and the alignment is appropriate for all of the types in the union. The same operations are permitted on unions as on structures: assignment to or copying as a unit, taking the address, and accessing a member.

A union may only be initialized with a value of the type of its first member;

thus the union u described above can only be initialized with an integer value.

The storage allocator in Chapter 8 shows how a union can be used to force a variable to be aligned on a particular kind of storage boundary.

6.9   Bit-fields

When storage space is at a premium, it may be necessary to pack several objects into a single machine word; one common use is a set of single-bit flags in applications like compiler symbol tables. Externally-imposed data formats, such as interfaces to hardware devices, also often require the ability to get at pieces of a word.

Imagine a fragment of a compiler that manipulates a symbol table. Each identifier in a program has certain information associated with it, for example, whether or not it is a keyword, whether or not it is external and/or static, and so on. The most compact way to encode such information is a set of one-bit flags in a single `char` or `int`.

The usual way this is done is to define a set of "masks" corresponding to the relevant bit positions, as in

```
#define KEYWORD  01
#define EXTERNAL 02
#define STATIC   04
```

or

```
enum { KEYWORD = 01, EXTERNAL = 02, STATIC = 04 };
```

The numbers must be powers of two. Then accessing the bits becomes a matter of "bit-fiddling" with the shifting, masking, and complementing operators that were described in Chapter 2.

Certain idioms appear frequently:

```
flags |= EXTERNAL | STATIC;
```

turns on the EXTERNAL and STATIC bits in `flags`, while

```
flags &= ~(EXTERNAL | STATIC);
```

turns them off, and

```
if ((flags & (EXTERNAL | STATIC)) == 0) ...
```

is true if both bits are off.

Although these idioms are readily mastered, as an alternative C offers the capability of defining and accessing fields within a word directly rather than by bitwise logical operators. A *bit-field*, or *field* for short, is a set of adjacent bits within a single implementation-defined storage unit that we will call a "word." The syntax of field definition and access is based on structures. For example, the symbol table #defines above could be replaced by the definition of three fields:

```
struct {
    unsigned int is_keyword : 1;
    unsigned int is_extern  : 1;
    unsigned int is_static  : 1;
} flags;
```

This defines a variable called `flags` that contains three 1-bit fields. The number following the colon represents the field width in bits. The fields are declared `unsigned int` to ensure that they are unsigned quantities.

Individual fields are referenced in the same way as other structure members: `flags.is_keyword`, `flags.is_extern`, etc. Fields behave like small integers, and may participate in arithmetic expressions just like other integers. Thus the previous examples may be written more naturally as

```
flags.is_extern = flags.is_static = 1;
```

to turn the bits on;

```
flags.is_extern = flags.is_static = 0;
```

to turn them off; and

```
if (flags.is_extern == 0 && flags.is_static == 0)
    ...
```

to test them.

Almost everything about fields is implementation-dependent. Whether a field may overlap a word boundary is implementation-defined. Fields need not be named; unnamed fields (a colon and width only) are used for padding. The special width 0 may be used to force alignment at the next word boundary.

Fields are assigned left to right on some machines and right to left on others. This means that although fields are useful for maintaining internally-defined data structures, the question of which end comes first has to be carefully considered when picking apart externally-defined data; programs that depend on such things are not portable. Fields may be declared only as `int`s; for portability, specify `signed` or `unsigned` explicitly. They are not arrays, and they do not have addresses, so the & operator cannot be applied to them.

CHAPTER 7: **Input and Output**

Input and output facilities are not part of the C language itself, so we have not emphasized them in our presentation thus far. Nonetheless, programs interact with their environment in much more complicated ways than those we have shown before. In this chapter we will describe the standard library, a set of functions that provide input and output, string handling, storage management, mathematical routines, and a variety of other services for C programs. We will concentrate on input and output.

The ANSI standard defines these library functions precisely, so that they can exist in compatible form on any system where C exists. Programs that confine their system interactions to facilities provided by the standard library can be moved from one system to another without change.

The properties of library functions are specified in more than a dozen headers; we have already seen several of these, including `<stdio.h>`, `<string.h>`, and `<ctype.h>`. We will not present the entire library here, since we are more interested in writing C programs that use it. The library is described in detail in Appendix B.

7.1 Standard Input and Output

As we said in Chapter 1, the library implements a simple model of text input and output. A text stream consists of a sequence of lines; each line ends with a newline character. If the system doesn't operate that way, the library does whatever is necessary to make it appear as if it does. For instance, the library might convert carriage return and linefeed to newline on input and back again on output.

The simplest input mechanism is to read one character at a time from the *standard input*, normally the keyboard, with `getchar`:

```
int getchar(void)
```

`getchar` returns the next input character each time it is called, or EOF when it encounters end of file. The symbolic constant EOF is defined in `<stdio.h>`.

151

The value is typically -1, but tests should be written in terms of EOF so as to be independent of the specific value.

In many environments, a file may be substituted for the keyboard by using the < convention for input redirection: if a program `prog` uses `getchar`, then the command line

```
prog <infile
```

causes `prog` to read characters from `infile` instead. The switching of the input is done in such a way that `prog` itself is oblivious to the change; in particular, the string "`<infile`" is not included in the command-line arguments in `argv`. Input switching is also invisible if the input comes from another program via a pipe mechanism: on some systems, the command line

```
otherprog | prog
```

runs the two programs `otherprog` and `prog`, and pipes the standard output of `otherprog` into the standard input for `prog`.

The function

```
int putchar(int)
```

is used for output: `putchar(c)` puts the character c on the *standard output*, which is by default the screen. `putchar` returns the character written, or EOF if an error occurs. Again, output can usually be directed to a file with >*filename*: if `prog` uses `putchar`,

```
prog >outfile
```

will write the standard output to `outfile` instead. If pipes are supported,

```
prog | anotherprog
```

puts the standard output of `prog` into the standard input of `anotherprog`.

Output produced by `printf` also finds its way to the standard output. Calls to `putchar` and `printf` may be interleaved—output appears in the order in which the calls were made.

Each source file that refers to an input/output library function must contain the line

```
#include <stdio.h>
```

before the first reference. When the name is bracketed by < and > a search is made for the header in a standard set of places (for example, on UNIX systems, typically in the directory `/usr/include`).

Many programs read only one input stream and write only one output stream; for such programs, input and output with `getchar`, `putchar`, and `printf` may be entirely adequate, and is certainly enough to get started. This is particularly true if redirection is used to connect the output of one program to the input of the next. For example, consider the program `lower`, which converts its input to lower case:

```
#include <stdio.h>
#include <ctype.h>

main()  /* lower: convert input to lower case */
{
    int c;

    while ((c = getchar()) != EOF)
        putchar(tolower(c));
    return 0;
}
```

The function `tolower` is defined in `<ctype.h>`; it converts an upper case letter to lower case, and returns other characters untouched. As we mentioned earlier, "functions" like `getchar` and `putchar` in `<stdio.h>` and `tolower` in `<ctype.h>` are often macros, thus avoiding the overhead of a function call per character. We will show how this is done in Section 8.5. Regardless of how the `<ctype.h>` functions are implemented on a given machine, programs that use them are shielded from knowledge of the character set.

Exercise 7-1. Write a program that converts upper case to lower or lower case to upper, depending on the name it is invoked with, as found in `argv[0]`. □

7.2 Formatted Output—Printf

The output function `printf` translates internal values to characters. We have used `printf` informally in previous chapters. The description here covers most typical uses but is not complete; for the full story, see Appendix B.

```
int printf(char *format, arg₁, arg₂, ...)
```

`printf` converts, formats, and prints its arguments on the standard output under control of the `format`. It returns the number of characters printed.

The format string contains two types of objects: ordinary characters, which are copied to the output stream, and conversion specifications, each of which causes conversion and printing of the next successive argument to `printf`. Each conversion specification begins with a % and ends with a conversion character. Between the % and the conversion character there may be, in order:

- A minus sign, which specifies left adjustment of the converted argument.
- A number that specifies the minimum field width. The converted argument will be printed in a field at least this wide. If necessary it will be padded on the left (or right, if left adjustment is called for) to make up the field width.
- A period, which separates the field width from the precision.
- A number, the precision, that specifies the maximum number of characters to be printed from a string, or the number of digits after the decimal point of a floating-point value, or the minimum number of digits for an integer.

- An h if the integer is to be printed as a short, or 1 (letter ell) if as a long.

Conversion characters are shown in Table 7-1. If the character after the % is not a conversion specification, the behavior is undefined.

TABLE 7-1. BASIC PRINTF CONVERSIONS

CHARACTER	ARGUMENT TYPE; PRINTED AS
d, i	int; decimal number.
o	int; unsigned octal number (without a leading zero).
x, X	int; unsigned hexadecimal number (without a leading 0x or 0X), using abcdef or ABCDEF for 10, ..., 15.
u	int; unsigned decimal number.
c	int; single character.
s	char *; print characters from the string until a '\0' or the number of characters given by the precision.
f	double; [−]m.dddddd, where the number of *d*'s is given by the precision (default 6).
e, E	double; [−]m.dddddd e±xx or [−]m.dddddd E±xx, where the number of *d*'s is given by the precision (default 6).
g, G	double; use %e or %E if the exponent is less than −4 or greater than or equal to the precision; otherwise use %f. Trailing zeros and a trailing decimal point are not printed.
p	void *; pointer (implementation-dependent representation).
%	no argument is converted; print a %.

A width or precision may be specified as *, in which case the value is computed by converting the next argument (which must be an int). For example, to print at most max characters from a string s,

```
printf("%.*s", max, s);
```

Most of the format conversions have been illustrated in earlier chapters. One exception is precision as it relates to strings. The following table shows the effect of a variety of specifications in printing "hello, world" (12 characters). We have put colons around each field so you can see its extent.

```
:%s:            :hello, world:
:%10s:          :hello, world:
:%.10s:         :hello, wor:
:%-10s:         :hello, world:
:%.15s:         :hello, world:
:%-15s:         :hello, world    :
:%15.10s:       :      hello, wor:
:%-15.10s:      :hello, wor      :
```

A warning: printf uses its first argument to decide how many arguments follow and what their types are. It will get confused, and you will get wrong answers, if there are not enough arguments or if they are the wrong type. You should also be aware of the difference between these two calls:

```
printf(s);          /* FAILS if s contains % */
printf("%s", s);    /* SAFE */
```

The function `sprintf` does the same conversions as `printf` does, but stores the output in a string:

```
int sprintf(char *string, char *format, arg₁, arg₂, ...)
```

sprintf formats the arguments in arg_1, arg_2, etc., according to `format` as before, but places the result in `string` instead of on the standard output; `string` must be big enough to receive the result.

Exercise 7-2. Write a program that will print arbitrary input in a sensible way. As a minimum, it should print non-graphic characters in octal or hexadecimal according to local custom, and break long text lines. □

7.3   Variable-length Argument Lists

This section contains an implementation of a minimal version of `printf`, to show how to write a function that processes a variable-length argument list in a portable way. Since we are mainly interested in the argument processing, `minprintf` will process the format string and arguments but will call the real `printf` to do the format conversions.

The proper declaration for `printf` is

```
int printf(char *fmt, ...)
```

where the declaration `...` means that the number and types of these arguments may vary. The declaration `...` can only appear at the end of an argument list. Our `minprintf` is declared as

```
void minprintf(char *fmt, ...)
```

since we will not return the character count that `printf` does.

The tricky bit is how `minprintf` walks along the argument list when the list doesn't even have a name. The standard header `<stdarg.h>` contains a set of macro definitions that define how to step through an argument list. The implementation of this header will vary from machine to machine, but the interface it presents is uniform.

The type `va_list` is used to declare a variable that will refer to each argument in turn; in `minprintf`, this variable is called `ap`, for "argument pointer." The macro `va_start` initializes `ap` to point to the first unnamed argument. It must be called once before `ap` is used. There must be at least one named argument; the final named argument is used by `va_start` to get started.

Each call of `va_arg` returns one argument and steps `ap` to the next; `va_arg` uses a type name to determine what type to return and how big a step to take. Finally, `va_end` does whatever cleanup is necessary. It must be called before the function returns.

These properties form the basis of our simplified `printf`:

```
#include <stdarg.h>

/* minprintf:  minimal printf with variable argument list */
void minprintf(char *fmt, ...)
{
    va_list ap;    /* points to each unnamed arg in turn */
    char *p, *sval;
    int ival;
    double dval;

    va_start(ap, fmt); /* make ap point to 1st unnamed arg */
    for (p = fmt; *p; p++) {
        if (*p != '%') {
            putchar(*p);
            continue;
        }
        switch (*++p) {
        case 'd':
            ival = va_arg(ap, int);
            printf("%d", ival);
            break;
        case 'f':
            dval = va_arg(ap, double);
            printf("%f", dval);
            break;
        case 's':
            for (sval = va_arg(ap, char *); *sval; sval++)
                putchar(*sval);
            break;
        default:
            putchar(*p);
            break;
        }
    }
    va_end(ap);    /* clean up when done */
}
```

Exercise 7-3. Revise `minprintf` to handle more of the other facilities of `printf`. □

7.4 Formatted Input—Scanf

The function `scanf` is the input analog of `printf`, providing many of the same conversion facilities in the opposite direction.

```
int scanf(char *format, ...)
```

`scanf` reads characters from the standard input, interprets them according to the specification in `format`, and stores the results through the remaining arguments. The format argument is described below; the other arguments, *each of which must be a pointer*, indicate where the corresponding converted input should be stored. As with `printf`, this section is a summary of the most useful features, not an exhaustive list.

`scanf` stops when it exhausts its format string, or when some input fails to match the control specification. It returns as its value the number of successfully matched and assigned input items. This can be used to decide how many items were found. On end of file, `EOF` is returned; note that this is different from 0, which means that the next input character does not match the first specification in the format string. The next call to `scanf` resumes searching immediately after the last character already converted.

There is also a function `sscanf` that reads from a string instead of the standard input:

```
int sscanf(char *string, char *format, arg₁, arg₂, ...)
```

It scans the `string` according to the format in `format`, and stores the resulting values through arg_1, arg_2, etc. These arguments must be pointers.

The format string usually contains conversion specifications, which are used to control conversion of input. The format string may contain:

- Blanks or tabs, which are ignored.

- Ordinary characters (not %), which are expected to match the next non-white space character of the input stream.

- Conversion specifications, consisting of the character %, an optional assignment suppression character *, an optional number specifying a maximum field width, an optional h, l, or L indicating the width of the target, and a conversion character.

A conversion specification directs the conversion of the next input field. Normally the result is placed in the variable pointed to by the corresponding argument. If assignment suppression is indicated by the * character, however, the input field is skipped; no assignment is made. An input field is defined as a string of non-white space characters; it extends either to the next white space character or until the field width, if specified, is exhausted. This implies that `scanf` will read across line boundaries to find its input, since newlines are white space. (White space characters are blank, tab, newline, carriage return, vertical tab, and formfeed.)

The conversion character indicates the interpretation of the input field. The corresponding argument must be a pointer, as required by the call-by-value semantics of C. Conversion characters are shown in Table 7-2.

TABLE 7-2. BASIC SCANF CONVERSIONS

CHARACTER	INPUT DATA; ARGUMENT TYPE
d	decimal integer; `int *`.
i	integer; `int *`. The integer may be in octal (leading 0) or hexadecimal (leading `0x` or `0X`).
o	octal integer (with or without leading zero); `int *`.
u	unsigned decimal integer; `unsigned int *`.
x	hexadecimal integer (with or without leading `0x` or `0X`); `int *`.
c	characters; `char *`. The next input characters (default 1) are placed at the indicated spot. The normal skip over white space is suppressed; to read the next non-white space character, use `%1s`.
s	character string (not quoted); `char *`, pointing to an array of characters large enough for the string and a terminating `'\0'` that will be added.
e, f, g	floating-point number with optional sign, optional decimal point and optional exponent; `float *`.
%	literal `%`; no assignment is made.

The conversion characters d, i, o, u, and x may be preceded by h to indicate that a pointer to `short` rather than `int` appears in the argument list, or by l (letter ell) to indicate that a pointer to `long` appears in the argument list. Similarly, the conversion characters e, f, and g may be preceded by l to indicate that a pointer to `double` rather than `float` is in the argument list.

As a first example, the rudimentary calculator of Chapter 4 can be written with scanf to do the input conversion:

```
#include     <stdio.h>

main()  /* rudimentary calculator */
{
    double sum, v;

    sum = 0;
    while (scanf("%lf", &v) == 1)
        printf("\t%.2f\n", sum += v);
    return 0;
}
```

Suppose we want to read input lines that contain dates of the form

```
25 Dec 1988
```

The scanf statement is

```
int day, year;
char monthname[20];

scanf("%d %s %d", &day, monthname, &year);
```

No & is used with `monthname`, since an array name is a pointer.

Literal characters can appear in the `scanf` format string; they must match the same characters in the input. So we could read dates of the form mm/dd/yy with this `scanf` statement:

```
int day, month, year;

scanf("%d/%d/%d", &month, &day, &year);
```

`scanf` ignores blanks and tabs in its format string. Furthermore, it skips over white space (blanks, tabs, newlines, etc.) as it looks for input values. To read input whose format is not fixed, it is often best to read a line at a time, then pick it apart with `sscanf`. For example, suppose we want to read lines that might contain a date in either of the forms above. Then we could write

```
while (getline(line, sizeof(line)) > 0) {
    if (sscanf(line, "%d %s %d", &day, monthname, &year) == 3)
        printf("valid: %s\n", line);    /* 25 Dec 1988 form */
    else if (sscanf(line, "%d/%d/%d", &month, &day, &year) == 3)
        printf("valid: %s\n", line);    /* mm/dd/yy form */
    else
        printf("invalid: %s\n", line);  /* invalid form */
}
```

Calls to `scanf` can be mixed with calls to other input functions. The next call to any input function will begin by reading the first character not read by `scanf`.

A final warning: the arguments to `scanf` and `sscanf` *must* be pointers. By far the most common error is writing

```
scanf("%d", n);
```

instead of

```
scanf("%d", &n);
```

This error is not generally detected at compile time.

Exercise 7-4. Write a private version of `scanf` analogous to `minprintf` from the previous section. □

Exercise 7-5. Rewrite the postfix calculator of Chapter 4 to use `scanf` and/or `sscanf` to do the input and number conversion. □

7.5 File Access

The examples so far have all read the standard input and written the standard output, which are automatically defined for a program by the local operating system.

The next step is to write a program that accesses a file that is *not* already connected to the program. One program that illustrates the need for such operations is `cat`, which concatenates a set of named files onto the standard output. `cat` is used for printing files on the screen, and as a general-purpose input collector for programs that do not have the capability of accessing files by name. For example, the command

```
cat x.c y.c
```

prints the contents of the files `x.c` and `y.c` (and nothing else) on the standard output.

The question is how to arrange for the named files to be read—that is, how to connect the external names that a user thinks of to the statements that read the data.

The rules are simple. Before it can be read or written, a file has to be *opened* by the library function `fopen`. `fopen` takes an external name like `x.c` or `y.c`, does some housekeeping and negotiation with the operating system (details of which needn't concern us), and returns a pointer to be used in subsequent reads or writes of the file.

This pointer, called the *file pointer*, points to a structure that contains information about the file, such as the location of a buffer, the current character position in the buffer, whether the file is being read or written, and whether errors or end of file have occurred. Users don't need to know the details, because the definitions obtained from `<stdio.h>` include a structure declaration called `FILE`. The only declaration needed for a file pointer is exemplified by

```
FILE *fp;
FILE *fopen(char *name, char *mode);
```

This says that `fp` is a pointer to a `FILE`, and `fopen` returns a pointer to a `FILE`. Notice that `FILE` is a type name, like `int`, not a structure tag; it is defined with a `typedef`. (Details of how `fopen` can be implemented on the UNIX system are given in Section 8.5.)

The call to `fopen` in a program is

```
fp = fopen(name, mode);
```

The first argument of `fopen` is a character string containing the name of the file. The second argument is the *mode*, also a character string, which indicates how one intends to use the file. Allowable modes include read (`"r"`), write (`"w"`), and append (`"a"`). Some systems distinguish between text and binary files; for the latter, a `"b"` must be appended to the mode string.

If a file that does not exist is opened for writing or appending, it is created if possible. Opening an existing file for writing causes the old contents to be discarded, while opening for appending preserves them. Trying to read a file that does not exist is an error, and there may be other causes of error as well, like trying to read a file when you don't have permission. If there is any error, fopen will return NULL. (The error can be identified more precisely; see the discussion of error-handling functions at the end of Section 1 in Appendix B.)

The next thing needed is a way to read or write the file once it is open. There are several possibilities, of which getc and putc are the simplest. getc returns the next character from a file; it needs the file pointer to tell it which file.

```
int getc(FILE *fp)
```

getc returns the next character from the stream referred to by fp; it returns EOF for end of file or error.

putc is an output function:

```
int putc(int c, FILE *fp)
```

putc writes the character c to the file fp and returns the character written, or EOF if an error occurs. Like getchar and putchar, getc and putc may be macros instead of functions.

When a C program is started, the operating system environment is responsible for opening three files and providing file pointers for them. These files are the standard input, the standard output, and the standard error; the corresponding file pointers are called stdin, stdout, and stderr, and are declared in <stdio.h>. Normally stdin is connected to the keyboard and stdout and stderr are connected to the screen, but stdin and stdout may be redirected to files or pipes as described in Section 7.1.

getchar and putchar can be defined in terms of getc, putc, stdin, and stdout as follows:

```
#define getchar()    getc(stdin)
#define putchar(c)   putc((c), stdout)
```

For formatted input or output of files, the functions fscanf and fprintf may be used. These are identical to scanf and printf, except that the first argument is a file pointer that specifies the file to be read or written; the format string is the second argument.

```
int fscanf(FILE *fp, char *format, ...)
int fprintf(FILE *fp, char *format, ...)
```

With these preliminaries out of the way, we are now in a position to write the program cat to concatenate files. The design is one that has been found convenient for many programs. If there are command-line arguments, they are interpreted as filenames, and processed in order. If there are no arguments, the standard input is processed.

```
#include <stdio.h>

/* cat:  concatenate files, version 1 */
main(int argc, char *argv[])
{
    FILE *fp;
    void filecopy(FILE *, FILE *);

    if (argc == 1)  /* no args; copy standard input */
        filecopy(stdin, stdout);
    else
        while (--argc > 0)
            if ((fp = fopen(*++argv, "r")) == NULL) {
                printf("cat: can't open %s\n", *argv);
                return 1;
            } else {
                filecopy(fp, stdout);
                fclose(fp);
            }
    return 0;
}



/* filecopy:  copy file ifp to file ofp */
void filecopy(FILE *ifp, FILE *ofp)
{
    int c;

    while ((c = getc(ifp)) != EOF)
        putc(c, ofp);
}
```

The file pointers `stdin` and `stdout` are objects of type `FILE *`. They are constants, however, *not* variables, so it is not possible to assign to them.

The function

```
int fclose(FILE *fp)
```

is the inverse of `fopen`; it breaks the connection between the file pointer and the external name that was established by `fopen`, freeing the file pointer for another file. Since most operating systems have some limit on the number of files that a program may have open simultaneously, it's a good idea to free file pointers when they are no longer needed, as we did in `cat`. There is also another reason for `fclose` on an output file—it flushes the buffer in which `putc` is collecting output. `fclose` is called automatically for each open file when a program terminates normally. (You can close `stdin` and `stdout` if they are not needed. They can also be reassigned by the library function `freopen`.)

7.6   Error Handling—Stderr and Exit

The treatment of errors in `cat` is not ideal. The trouble is that if one of the files can't be accessed for some reason, the diagnostic is printed at the end of the concatenated output. That might be acceptable if the output is going to a screen, but not if it's going into a file or into another program via a pipeline.

To handle this situation better, a second output stream, called `stderr`, is assigned to a program in the same way that `stdin` and `stdout` are. Output written on `stderr` normally appears on the screen even if the standard output is redirected.

Let us revise `cat` to write its error messages on the standard error.

```
#include <stdio.h>

/* cat:  concatenate files, version 2 */
main(int argc, char *argv[])
{
    FILE *fp;
    void filecopy(FILE *, FILE *);
    char *prog = argv[0];    /* program name for errors */

    if (argc == 1)  /* no args; copy standard input */
        filecopy(stdin, stdout);
    else
        while (--argc > 0)
            if ((fp = fopen(*++argv, "r")) == NULL) {
                fprintf(stderr, "%s: can't open %s\n",
                    prog, *argv);
                exit(1);
            } else {
                filecopy(fp, stdout);
                fclose(fp);
            }
    if (ferror(stdout)) {
        fprintf(stderr, "%s: error writing stdout\n", prog);
        exit(2);
    }
    exit(0);
}
```

The program signals errors two ways. First, the diagnostic output produced by `fprintf` goes onto `stderr`, so it finds its way to the screen instead of disappearing down a pipeline or into an output file. We included the program name, from `argv[0]`, in the message, so if this program is used with others, the source of an error is identified.

Second, the program uses the standard library function `exit`, which terminates program execution when it is called. The argument of `exit` is available to whatever process called this one, so the success or failure of the program can be tested by another program that uses this one as a sub-process.

Conventionally, a return value of 0 signals that all is well; non-zero values usually signal abnormal situations. `exit` calls `fclose` for each open output file, to flush out any buffered output.

Within `main`, `return` *expr* is equivalent to `exit(`*expr*`)`. `exit` has the advantage that it can be called from other functions, and that calls to it can be found with a pattern-searching program like those in Chapter 5.

The function `ferror` returns non-zero if an error occurred on the stream `fp`.

```
int ferror(FILE *fp)
```

Although output errors are rare, they do occur (for example, if a disk fills up), so a production program should check this as well.

The function `feof(FILE *)` is analogous to `ferror`; it returns non-zero if end of file has occurred on the specified file.

```
int feof(FILE *fp)
```

We have generally not worried about exit status in our small illustrative programs, but any serious program should take care to return sensible, useful status values.

7.7 Line Input and Output

The standard library provides an input routine `fgets` that is similar to the `getline` function that we have used in earlier chapters:

```
char *fgets(char *line, int maxline, FILE *fp)
```

`fgets` reads the next input line (including the newline) from file `fp` into the character array `line`; at most `maxline-1` characters will be read. The resulting line is terminated with `'\0'`. Normally `fgets` returns `line`; on end of file or error it returns `NULL`. (Our `getline` returns the line length, which is a more useful value; zero means end of file.)

For output, the function `fputs` writes a string (which need not contain a newline) to a file:

```
int fputs(char *line, FILE *fp)
```

It returns `EOF` if an error occurs, and zero otherwise.

The library functions `gets` and `puts` are similar to `fgets` and `fputs`, but operate on `stdin` and `stdout`. Confusingly, `gets` deletes the terminal `'\n'`, and `puts` adds it.

To show that there is nothing special about functions like `fgets` and `fputs`, here they are, copied from the standard library on our system:

```
/* fgets:  get at most n chars from iop */
char *fgets(char *s, int n, FILE *iop)
{
    register int c;
    register char *cs;

    cs = s;
    while (--n > 0 && (c = getc(iop)) != EOF)
        if ((*cs++ = c) == '\n')
            break;
    *cs = '\0';
    return (c == EOF && cs == s) ? NULL : s;
}


/* fputs:  put string s on file iop */
int fputs(char *s, FILE *iop)
{
    int c;

    while (c = *s++)
        putc(c, iop);
    return ferror(iop) ? EOF : 0;
}
```

The standard specifies that `ferror` returns non-zero for error; `fputs` returns
EOF for error and a non-negative value otherwise.

It is easy to implement our `getline` from `fgets`:

```
/* getline:  read a line, return length */
int getline(char *line, int max)
{
    if (fgets(line, max, stdin) == NULL)
        return 0;
    else
        return strlen(line);
}
```

Exercise 7-6. Write a program to compare two files, printing the first line
where they differ. □

Exercise 7-7. Modify the pattern finding program of Chapter 5 to take its input
from a set of named files or, if no files are named as arguments, from the standard input. Should the file name be printed when a matching line is found? □

Exercise 7-8. Write a program to print a set of files, starting each new one on a
new page, with a title and a running page count for each file. □

7.8 Miscellaneous Functions

The standard library provides a wide variety of functions. This section is a brief synopsis of the most useful. More details and many other functions can be found in Appendix B.

7.8.1 String Operations

We have already mentioned the string functions `strlen`, `strcpy`, `strcat`, and `strcmp`, found in `<string.h>`. In the following, s and t are `char *`'s, and c and n are `int`s.

`strcat(s,t)`	concatenate t to end of s
`strncat(s,t,n)`	concatenate n characters of t to end of s
`strcmp(s,t)`	return negative, zero, or positive for
	s < t, s == t, or s > t
`strncmp(s,t,n)`	same as `strcmp` but only in first n characters
`strcpy(s,t)`	copy t to s
`strncpy(s,t,n)`	copy at most n characters of t to s
`strlen(s)`	return length of s
`strchr(s,c)`	return pointer to first c in s, or NULL if not present
`strrchr(s,c)`	return pointer to last c in s, or NULL if not present

7.8.2 Character Class Testing and Conversion

Several functions from `<ctype.h>` perform character tests and conversions. In the following, c is an `int` that can be represented as an `unsigned char`, or EOF. The functions return `int`.

`isalpha(c)`	non-zero if c is alphabetic, 0 if not
`isupper(c)`	non-zero if c is upper case, 0 if not
`islower(c)`	non-zero if c is lower case, 0 if not
`isdigit(c)`	non-zero if c is digit, 0 if not
`isalnum(c)`	non-zero if `isalpha(c)` or `isdigit(c)`, 0 if not
`isspace(c)`	non-zero if c is blank, tab, newline, return, formfeed, vertical tab
`toupper(c)`	return c converted to upper case
`tolower(c)`	return c converted to lower case

7.8.3 Ungetc

The standard library provides a rather restricted version of the function ungetch that we wrote in Chapter 4; it is called `ungetc`.

```
int ungetc(int c, FILE *fp)
```

pushes the character c back onto file `fp`, and returns either c, or EOF for an error. Only one character of pushback is guaranteed per file. `ungetc` may be used with any of the input functions like `scanf`, `getc`, or `getchar`.

7.8.4 Command Execution

The function `system(char *s)` executes the command contained in the character string `s`, then resumes execution of the current program. The contents of `s` depend strongly on the local operating system. As a trivial example, on UNIX systems, the statement

```
system("date");
```

causes the program `date` to be run; it prints the date and time of day on the standard output. `system` returns a system-dependent integer status from the command executed. In the UNIX system, the status return is the value returned by `exit`.

7.8.5 Storage Management

The functions `malloc` and `calloc` obtain blocks of memory dynamically.

```
void *malloc(size_t n)
```

returns a pointer to n bytes of uninitialized storage, or `NULL` if the request cannot be satisfied.

```
void *calloc(size_t n, size_t size)
```

returns a pointer to enough space for an array of n objects of the specified size, or `NULL` if the request cannot be satisfied. The storage is initialized to zero.

The pointer returned by `malloc` or `calloc` has the proper alignment for the object in question, but it must be cast into the appropriate type, as in

```
int *ip;

ip = (int *) calloc(n, sizeof(int));
```

`free(p)` frees the space pointed to by `p`, where `p` was originally obtained by a call to `malloc` or `calloc`. There are no restrictions on the order in which space is freed, but it is a ghastly error to free something not obtained by calling `calloc` or `malloc`.

It is also an error to use something after it has been freed. A typical but incorrect piece of code is this loop that frees items from a list:

```
for (p = head; p != NULL; p = p->next)    /* WRONG */
    free(p);
```

The right way is to save whatever is needed before freeing:

```
for (p = head; p != NULL; p = q) {
    q = p->next;
    free(p);
}
```

Section 8.7 shows the implementation of a storage allocator like `malloc`, in which allocated blocks may be freed in any order.

7.8.6 Mathematical Functions

There are more than twenty mathematical functions declared in `<math.h>`; here are some of the more frequently used. Each takes one or two `double` arguments and returns a `double`.

`sin(x)`	sine of x, x in radians
`cos(x)`	cosine of x, x in radians
`atan2(y,x)`	arctangent of y/x, in radians
`exp(x)`	exponential function e^x
`log(x)`	natural (base e) logarithm of x $(x>0)$
`log10(x)`	common (base 10) logarithm of x $(x>0)$
`pow(x,y)`	x^y
`sqrt(x)`	square root of x $(x \geqslant 0)$
`fabs(x)`	absolute value of x

7.8.7 Random Number Generation

The function `rand()` computes a sequence of pseudo-random integers in the range zero to `RAND_MAX`, which is defined in `<stdlib.h>`. One way to produce random floating-point numbers greater than or equal to zero but less than one is

```
#define frand() ((double) rand() / (RAND_MAX+1.0))
```

(If your library already provides a function for floating-point random numbers, it is likely to have better statistical properties than this one.)

The function `srand(unsigned)` sets the seed for `rand`. The portable implementation of `rand` and `srand` suggested by the standard appears in Section 2.7.

Exercise 7-9. Functions like `isupper` can be implemented to save space or to save time. Explore both possibilities. □

CHAPTER 8: The UNIX System Interface

The UNIX operating system provides its services through a set of *system calls*, which are in effect functions within the operating system that may be called by user programs. This chapter describes how to use some of the most important system calls from C programs. If you use UNIX, this should be directly helpful, for it is sometimes necessary to employ system calls for maximum efficiency, or to access some facility that is not in the library. Even if you use C on a different operating system, however, you should be able to glean insight into C programming from studying these examples; although details vary, similar code will be found on any system. Since the ANSI C library is in many cases modeled on UNIX facilities, this code may help your understanding of the library as well.

The chapter is divided into three major parts: input/output, file system, and storage allocation. The first two parts assume a modest familiarity with the external characteristics of UNIX systems.

Chapter 7 was concerned with an input/output interface that is uniform across operating systems. On any particular system the routines of the standard library have to be written in terms of the facilities provided by the host system. In the next few sections we will describe the UNIX system calls for input and output, and show how parts of the standard library can be implemented with them.

8.1 File Descriptors

In the UNIX operating system, all input and output is done by reading or writing files, because all peripheral devices, even keyboard and screen, are files in the file system. This means that a single homogeneous interface handles all communication between a program and peripheral devices.

In the most general case, before you read or write a file, you must inform the system of your intent to do so, a process called *opening* the file. If you are going to write on a file it may also be necessary to create it or to discard its previous contents. The system checks your right to do so (Does the file exist? Do you have permission to access it?), and if all is well, returns to the program a small non-negative integer called a *file descriptor*. Whenever input or output is to be done on the file, the file descriptor is used instead of the name to identify the file. (A file descriptor is analogous to the file pointer used by the standard library, or to the file handle of MS-DOS.) All information about an open file is maintained by the system; the user program refers to the file only by the file descriptor.

Since input and output involving keyboard and screen is so common, special arrangements exist to make this convenient. When the command interpreter (the "shell") runs a program, three files are open, with file descriptors 0, 1, and 2, called the standard input, the standard output, and the standard error. If a program reads 0 and writes 1 and 2, it can do input and output without worrying about opening files.

The user of a program can redirect I/O to and from files with < and >:

```
prog <infile >outfile
```

In this case, the shell changes the default assignments for file descriptors 0 and 1 to the named files. Normally file descriptor 2 remains attached to the screen, so error messages can go there. Similar observations hold for input or output associated with a pipe. In all cases, the file assignments are changed by the shell, not by the program. The program does not know where its input comes from nor where its output goes, so long as it uses file 0 for input and 1 and 2 for output.

8.2 Low Level I/O—Read and Write

Input and output uses the `read` and `write` system calls, which are accessed from C programs through two functions called `read` and `write`. For both, the first argument is a file descriptor. The second argument is a character array in your program where the data is to go to or come from. The third argument is the number of bytes to be transferred.

```
int n_read = read(int fd, char *buf, int n);
int n_written = write(int fd, char *buf, int n);
```

Each call returns a count of the number of bytes transferred. On reading, the number of bytes returned may be less than the number requested. A return value of zero bytes implies end of file, and – 1 indicates an error of some sort. For writing, the return value is the number of bytes written; an error has occurred if this isn't equal to the number requested.

Any number of bytes can be read or written in one call. The most common values are 1, which means one character at a time ("unbuffered"), and a number like 1024 or 4096 that corresponds to a physical block size on a peripheral device. Larger sizes will be more efficient because fewer system calls will be made.

Putting these facts together, we can write a simple program to copy its input to its output, the equivalent of the file copying program written for Chapter 1. This program will copy anything to anything, since the input and output can be redirected to any file or device.

```
#include "syscalls.h"

main()  /* copy input to output */
{
    char buf[BUFSIZ];
    int n;

    while ((n = read(0, buf, BUFSIZ)) > 0)
        write(1, buf, n);
    return 0;
}
```

We have collected function prototypes for the system calls into a file called `syscalls.h` so we can include it in the programs of this chapter. This name is not standard, however.

The parameter `BUFSIZ` is also defined in `syscalls.h`; its value is a good size for the local system. If the file size is not a multiple of `BUFSIZ`, some `read` will return a smaller number of bytes to be written by `write`; the next call to `read` after that will return zero.

It is instructive to see how `read` and `write` can be used to construct higher-level routines like `getchar`, `putchar`, etc. For example, here is a version of `getchar` that does unbuffered input, by reading the standard input one character at a time.

```
#include "syscalls.h"

/* getchar:  unbuffered single character input */
int getchar(void)
{
    char c;

    return (read(0, &c, 1) == 1) ? (unsigned char) c : EOF;
}
```

`c` must be a `char`, because `read` needs a character pointer. Casting `c` to `unsigned char` in the return statement eliminates any problem of sign extension.

The second version of `getchar` does input in big chunks, and hands out the characters one at a time.

```
#include "syscalls.h"

/* getchar:  simple buffered version */
int getchar(void)
{
    static char buf[BUFSIZ];
    static char *bufp = buf;
    static int n = 0;

    if (n == 0) {   /* buffer is empty */
        n = read(0, buf, sizeof buf);
        bufp = buf;
    }
    return (--n >= 0) ? (unsigned char) *bufp++ : EOF;
}
```

If these versions of getchar were to be compiled with <stdio.h> included, it
would be necessary to #undef the name getchar in case it is implemented as
a macro.

8.3 Open, Creat, Close, Unlink

Other than the default standard input, output and error, you must explicitly
open files in order to read or write them. There are two system calls for this,
open and creat [sic].

open is rather like the fopen discussed in Chapter 7, except that instead of
returning a file pointer, it returns a file descriptor, which is just an int. open
returns -1 if any error occurs.

```
#include <fcntl.h>

int fd;
int open(char *name, int flags, int perms);

fd = open(name, flags, perms);
```

As with fopen, the name argument is a character string containing the
filename. The second argument, flags, is an int that specifies how the file is
to be opened; the main values are

```
O_RDONLY    open for reading only
O_WRONLY    open for writing only
O_RDWR      open for both reading and writing
```

These constants are defined in <fcntl.h> on System V UNIX systems, and in
<sys/file.h> on Berkeley (BSD) versions.

To open an existing file for reading,

```
fd = open(name, O_RDONLY, 0);
```

The `perms` argument is always zero for the uses of `open` that we will discuss.

It is an error to try to `open` a file that does not exist. The system call `creat` is provided to create new files, or to re-write old ones.

```
int creat(char *name, int perms);

fd = creat(name, perms);
```

returns a file descriptor if it was able to create the file, and -1 if not. If the file already exists, `creat` will truncate it to zero length, thereby discarding its previous contents; it is not an error to `creat` a file that already exists.

If the file does not already exist, `creat` creates it with the permissions specified by the `perms` argument. In the UNIX file system, there are nine bits of permission information associated with a file that control read, write and execute access for the owner of the file, for the owner's group, and for all others. Thus a three-digit octal number is convenient for specifying the permissions. For example, 0755 specifies read, write and execute permission for the owner, and read and execute permission for the group and everyone else.

To illustrate, here is a simplified version of the UNIX program cp, which copies one file to another. Our version copies only one file, it does not permit the second argument to be a directory, and it invents permissions instead of copying them.

```
#include <stdio.h>
#include <fcntl.h>
#include "syscalls.h"
#define PERMS 0666    /* RW for owner, group, others */

void error(char *, ...);

/* cp: copy f1 to f2 */
main(int argc, char *argv[])
{
    int f1, f2, n;
    char buf[BUFSIZ];

    if (argc != 3)
        error("Usage: cp from to");
    if ((f1 = open(argv[1], O_RDONLY, 0)) == -1)
        error("cp: can't open %s", argv[1]);
    if ((f2 = creat(argv[2], PERMS)) == -1)
        error("cp: can't create %s, mode %03o",
            argv[2], PERMS);
    while ((n = read(f1, buf, BUFSIZ)) > 0)
        if (write(f2, buf, n) != n)
            error("cp: write error on file %s", argv[2]);
    return 0;
}
```

This program creates the output file with fixed permissions of 0666. With the `stat` system call, described in Section 8.6, we can determine the mode of an existing file and thus give the same mode to the copy.

Notice that the function `error` is called with variable argument lists much like `printf`. The implementation of `error` illustrates how to use another member of the `printf` family. The standard library function `vprintf` is like `printf` except that the variable argument list is replaced by a single argument that has been initialized by calling the `va_start` macro. Similarly, `vfprintf` and `vsprintf` match `fprintf` and `sprintf`.

```
#include <stdio.h>
#include <stdarg.h>

/* error:  print an error message and die */
void error(char *fmt, ...)
{
    va_list args;

    va_start(args, fmt);
    fprintf(stderr, "error: ");
    vfprintf(stderr, fmt, args);
    fprintf(stderr, "\n");
    va_end(args);
    exit(1);
}
```

There is a limit (often about 20) on the number of files that a program may have open simultaneously. Accordingly, any program that intends to process many files must be prepared to re-use file descriptors. The function `close(int fd)` breaks the connection between a file descriptor and an open file, and frees the file descriptor for use with some other file; it corresponds to `fclose` in the standard library except that there is no buffer to flush. Termination of a program via `exit` or return from the main program closes all open files.

The function `unlink(char *name)` removes the file `name` from the file system. It corresponds to the standard library function `remove`.

Exercise 8-1. Rewrite the program `cat` from Chapter 7 using `read`, `write`, `open` and `close` instead of their standard library equivalents. Perform experiments to determine the relative speeds of the two versions. □

8.4 Random Access—Lseek

Input and output are normally sequential: each `read` or `write` takes place at a position in the file right after the previous one. When necessary, however, a file can be read or written in any arbitrary order. The system call `lseek` provides a way to move around in a file without reading or writing any data:

```
long lseek(int fd, long offset, int origin);
```

sets the current position in the file whose descriptor is `fd` to `offset`, which is taken relative to the location specified by `origin`. Subsequent reading or writing will begin at that position. `origin` can be 0, 1, or 2 to specify that `offset` is to be measured from the beginning, from the current position, or from the end of the file respectively. For example, to append to a file (the redirection >> in the UNIX shell, or "a" for `fopen`), seek to the end before writing:

```
lseek(fd, 0L, 2);
```

To get back to the beginning ("rewind"),

```
lseek(fd, 0L, 0);
```

Notice the `0L` argument; it could also be written as `(long) 0` or just as `0` if `lseek` is properly declared.

With `lseek`, it is possible to treat files more or less like large arrays, at the price of slower access. For example, the following function reads any number of bytes from any arbitrary place in a file. It returns the number read, or −1 on error.

```
#include "syscalls.h"

/* get:  read n bytes from position pos */
int get(int fd, long pos, char *buf, int n)
{
    if (lseek(fd, pos, 0) >= 0)  /* get to pos */
        return read(fd, buf, n);
    else
        return -1;
}
```

The return value from `lseek` is a `long` that gives the new position in the file, or −1 if an error occurs. The standard library function `fseek` is similar to `lseek` except that the first argument is a `FILE *` and the return is non-zero if an error occurred.

8.5 Example—An Implementation of Fopen and Getc

Let us illustrate how some of these pieces fit together by showing an implementation of the standard library routines `fopen` and `getc`.

Recall that files in the standard library are described by file pointers rather than file descriptors. A file pointer is a pointer to a structure that contains several pieces of information about the file: a pointer to a buffer, so the file can be read in large chunks; a count of the number of characters left in the buffer; a pointer to the next character position in the buffer; the file descriptor; and flags describing read/write mode, error status, etc.

The data structure that describes a file is contained in <stdio.h>, which must be included (by #include) in any source file that uses routines from the standard input/output library. It is also included by functions in that library. In the following excerpt from a typical <stdio.h>, names that are intended for use only by functions of the library begin with an underscore so they are less likely to collide with names in a user's program. This convention is used by all standard library routines.

```
#define NULL      0
#define EOF       (-1)
#define BUFSIZ    1024
#define OPEN_MAX  20   /* max #files open at once */

typedef struct _iobuf {
    int  cnt;          /* characters left */
    char *ptr;         /* next character position */
    char *base;        /* location of buffer */
    int  flag;         /* mode of file access */
    int  fd;           /* file descriptor */
} FILE;
extern FILE _iob[OPEN_MAX];

#define stdin   (&_iob[0])
#define stdout  (&_iob[1])
#define stderr  (&_iob[2])

enum _flags {
    _READ   = 01,      /* file open for reading */
    _WRITE  = 02,      /* file open for writing */
    _UNBUF  = 04,      /* file is unbuffered */
    _EOF    = 010,     /* EOF has occurred on this file */
    _ERR    = 020      /* error occurred on this file */
};

int _fillbuf(FILE *);
int _flushbuf(int, FILE *);

#define feof(p)     (((p)->flag & _EOF) != 0)
#define ferror(p)   (((p)->flag & _ERR) != 0)
#define fileno(p)   ((p)->fd)

#define getc(p)    (--(p)->cnt >= 0 \
                ? (unsigned char) *(p)->ptr++ : _fillbuf(p))
#define putc(x,p)  (--(p)->cnt >= 0 \
                ? *(p)->ptr++ = (x) : _flushbuf((x),p))

#define getchar()  getc(stdin)
#define putchar(x) putc((x), stdout)
```

The getc macro normally decrements the count, advances the pointer, and returns the character. (Recall that a long #define is continued with a backslash.) If the count goes negative, however, getc calls the function _fillbuf to replenish the buffer, re-initialize the structure contents, and return a character. The characters are returned unsigned, which ensures that all characters will be positive.

Although we will not discuss any details, we have included the definition of putc to show that it operates in much the same way as getc, calling a function _flushbuf when its buffer is full. We have also included macros for accessing the error and end-of-file status and the file descriptor.

The function fopen can now be written. Most of fopen is concerned with getting the file opened and positioned at the right place, and setting the flag bits to indicate the proper state. fopen does not allocate any buffer space; this is done by _fillbuf when the file is first read.

```c
#include <fcntl.h>
#include "syscalls.h"
#define PERMS 0666    /* RW for owner, group, others */

/* fopen:  open file, return file ptr */
FILE *fopen(char *name, char *mode)
{
    int fd;
    FILE *fp;

    if (*mode != 'r' && *mode != 'w' && *mode != 'a')
        return NULL;
    for (fp = _iob; fp < _iob + OPEN_MAX; fp++)
        if ((fp->flag & (_READ | _WRITE)) == 0)
            break;              /* found free slot */
    if (fp >= _iob + OPEN_MAX)      /* no free slots */
        return NULL;

    if (*mode == 'w')
        fd = creat(name, PERMS);
    else if (*mode == 'a') {
        if ((fd = open(name, O_WRONLY, 0)) == -1)
            fd = creat(name, PERMS);
        lseek(fd, 0L, 2);
    } else
        fd = open(name, O_RDONLY, 0);
    if (fd == -1)               /* couldn't access name */
        return NULL;
    fp->fd = fd;
    fp->cnt = 0;
    fp->base = NULL;
    fp->flag = (*mode == 'r') ? _READ : _WRITE;
    return fp;
}
```

This version of fopen does not handle all of the access mode possibilities of the standard, though adding them would not take much code. In particular, our fopen does not recognize the "b" that signals binary access, since that is meaningless on UNIX systems, nor the "+" that permits both reading and writing.

The first call to getc for a particular file finds a count of zero, which forces a call of _fillbuf. If _fillbuf finds that the file is not open for reading, it returns EOF immediately. Otherwise, it tries to allocate a buffer (if reading is to be buffered).

Once the buffer is established, _fillbuf calls read to fill it, sets the count and pointers, and returns the character at the beginning of the buffer. Subsequent calls to _fillbuf will find a buffer allocated.

```
#include "syscalls.h"

/* _fillbuf:  allocate and fill input buffer */
int _fillbuf(FILE *fp)
{
    int bufsize;

    if ((fp->flag&(_READ|_EOF|_ERR)) != _READ)
        return EOF;
    bufsize = (fp->flag & _UNBUF) ? 1 : BUFSIZ;
    if (fp->base == NULL)      /* no buffer yet */
        if ((fp->base = (char *) malloc(bufsize)) == NULL)
            return EOF;        /* can't get buffer */
    fp->ptr = fp->base;
    fp->cnt = read(fp->fd, fp->ptr, bufsize);
    if (--fp->cnt < 0) {
        if (fp->cnt == -1)
            fp->flag |= _EOF;
        else
            fp->flag |= _ERR;
        fp->cnt = 0;
        return EOF;
    }
    return (unsigned char) *fp->ptr++;
}
```

The only remaining loose end is how everything gets started. The array _iob must be defined and initialized for stdin, stdout and stderr:

```
FILE _iob[OPEN_MAX] = {      /* stdin, stdout, stderr: */
    { 0, (char *) 0, (char *) 0, _READ, 0 },
    { 0, (char *) 0, (char *) 0, _WRITE, 1 },
    { 0, (char *) 0, (char *) 0, _WRITE | _UNBUF, 2 }
};
```

The initialization of the flag part of the structure shows that stdin is to be read, stdout is to be written, and stderr is to be written unbuffered.

Exercise 8-2. Rewrite fopen and _fillbuf with fields instead of explicit bit operations. Compare code size and execution speed. □

Exercise 8-3. Design and write `_flushbuf`, `fflush`, and `fclose`. □

Exercise 8-4. The standard library function

```
int fseek(FILE *fp, long offset, int origin)
```

is identical to `lseek` except that `fp` is a file pointer instead of a file descriptor
and the return value is an `int` status, not a position. Write `fseek`. Make sure
that your `fseek` coordinates properly with the buffering done for the other
functions of the library. □

8.6 Example—Listing Directories

A different kind of file system interaction is sometimes called for—
determining information *about* a file, not what it contains. A directory-listing
program such as the UNIX command `ls` is an example—it prints the names of
files in a directory, and, optionally, other information, such as sizes, permissions,
and so on. The MS-DOS `dir` command is analogous.

Since a UNIX directory is just a file, `ls` need only read it to retrieve the
filenames. But it is necessary to use a system call to access other information
about a file, such as its size. On other systems, a system call may be needed
even to access filenames; this is the case on MS-DOS, for instance. What we
want is provide access to the information in a relatively system-independent
way, even though the implementation may be highly system-dependent.

We will illustrate some of this by writing a program called `fsize`. `fsize`
is a special form of `ls` that prints the sizes of all files named in its command-
line argument list. If one of the files is a directory, `fsize` applies itself recursively to that directory. If there are no arguments at all, it processes the
current directory.

Let us begin with a short review of UNIX file system structure. A *directory*
is a file that contains a list of filenames and some indication of where they are
located. The "location" is an index into another table called the "inode list."
The *inode* for a file is where all information about a file except its name is kept.
A directory entry generally consists of only two items, the filename and an
inode number.

Regrettably, the format and precise contents of a directory are not the same
on all versions of the system. So we will divide the task into two pieces to try to
isolate the non-portable parts. The outer level defines a structure called a
`Dirent` and three routines `opendir`, `readdir`, and `closedir` to provide
system-independent access to the name and inode number in a directory entry.
We will write `fsize` with this interface. Then we will show how to implement
these on systems that use the same directory structure as Version 7 and System
V UNIX; variants are left as exercises.

The `Dirent` structure contains the inode number and the name. The maximum length of a filename component is `NAME_MAX`, which is a system-dependent value. `opendir` returns a pointer to a structure called `DIR`, analogous to `FILE`, which is used by `readdir` and `closedir`. This information is collected into a file called `dirent.h`.

```
#define NAME_MAX  14  /* longest filename component; */
                      /* system-dependent */

typedef struct {      /* portable directory entry: */
    long ino;                  /* inode number */
    char name[NAME_MAX+1];     /* name + '\0' terminator */
} Dirent;

typedef struct {      /* minimal DIR: no buffering, etc. */
    int fd;                    /* file descriptor for directory */
    Dirent d;                  /* the directory entry */
} DIR;

DIR *opendir(char *dirname);
Dirent *readdir(DIR *dfd);
void closedir(DIR *dfd);
```

The system call `stat` takes a filename and returns all of the information in the inode for that file, or –1 if there is an error. That is,

```
char *name;
struct stat stbuf;
int stat(char *, struct stat *);

stat(name, &stbuf);
```

fills the structure `stbuf` with the inode information for the file `name`. The structure describing the value returned by `stat` is in `<sys/stat.h>`, and typically looks like this:

```
struct stat      /* inode information returned by stat */
{
    dev_t   st_dev;    /* device of inode */
    ino_t   st_ino;    /* inode number */
    short   st_mode;   /* mode bits */
    short   st_nlink;  /* number of links to file */
    short   st_uid;    /* owner's user id */
    short   st_gid;    /* owner's group id */
    dev_t   st_rdev;   /* for special files */
    off_t   st_size;   /* file size in characters */
    time_t  st_atime;  /* time last accessed */
    time_t  st_mtime;  /* time last modified */
    time_t  st_ctime;  /* time inode last changed */
};
```

Most of these values are explained by the comment fields. The types like dev_t and ino_t are defined in <sys/types.h>, which must be included too.

The st_mode entry contains a set of flags describing the file. The flag definitions are also included in <sys/stat.h>; we need only the part that deals with file type:

```
#define   S_IFMT 0160000    /* type of file: */
#define   S_IFDIR  0040000  /* directory */
#define   S_IFCHR  0020000  /* character special */
#define   S_IFBLK  0060000  /* block special */
#define   S_IFREG  0100000  /* regular */

/* ... */
```

Now we are ready to write the program fsize. If the mode obtained from stat indicates that a file is not a directory, then the size is at hand and can be printed directly. If the file is a directory, however, then we have to process that directory one file at a time; it may in turn contain sub-directories, so the process is recursive.

The main routine deals with command-line arguments; it hands each argument to the function fsize.

```
#include <stdio.h>
#include <string.h>
#include "syscalls.h"
#include <fcntl.h>          /* flags for read and write */
#include <sys/types.h>      /* typedefs */
#include <sys/stat.h>       /* structure returned by stat */
#include "dirent.h"

void fsize(char *);

/* print file sizes */
main(int argc, char **argv)
{
    if (argc == 1)          /* default: current directory */
        fsize(".");
    else
        while (--argc > 0)
            fsize(*++argv);
    return 0;
}
```

The function fsize prints the size of the file. If the file is a directory, however, fsize first calls dirwalk to handle all the files in it. Note how the flag names S_IFMT and S_IFDIR from <sys/stat.h> are used to decide if the file is a directory. Parenthesization matters, because the precedence of & is lower than that of ==.

```
int stat(char *, struct stat *);
void dirwalk(char *, void (*fcn)(char *));

/* fsize:  print size of file "name" */
void fsize(char *name)
{
    struct stat stbuf;

    if (stat(name, &stbuf) == -1) {
        fprintf(stderr, "fsize: can't access %s\n", name);
        return;
    }
    if ((stbuf.st_mode & S_IFMT) == S_IFDIR)
        dirwalk(name, fsize);
    printf("%8ld %s\n", stbuf.st_size, name);
}
```

The function `dirwalk` is a general routine that applies a function to each
file in a directory. It opens the directory, loops through the files in it, calling
the function on each, then closes the directory and returns. Since `fsize` calls
`dirwalk` on each directory, the two functions call each other recursively.

```
#define MAX_PATH 1024

/* dirwalk:  apply fcn to all files in dir */
void dirwalk(char *dir, void (*fcn)(char *))
{
    char name[MAX_PATH];
    Dirent *dp;
    DIR *dfd;

    if ((dfd = opendir(dir)) == NULL) {
        fprintf(stderr, "dirwalk: can't open %s\n", dir);
        return;
    }
    while ((dp = readdir(dfd)) != NULL) {
        if (strcmp(dp->name, ".") == 0
          || strcmp(dp->name, "..") == 0)
            continue;    /* skip self and parent */
        if (strlen(dir)+strlen(dp->name)+2 > sizeof(name))
            fprintf(stderr, "dirwalk: name %s/%s too long\n",
                dir, dp->name);
        else {
            sprintf(name, "%s/%s", dir, dp->name);
            (*fcn)(name);
        }
    }
    closedir(dfd);
}
```

Each call to `readdir` returns a pointer to information for the next file, or

NULL when there are no files left. Each directory always contains entries for itself, called " . ", and its parent, " .. "; these must be skipped, or the program will loop forever.

Down to this level, the code is independent of how directories are formatted. The next step is to present minimal versions of opendir, readdir, and closedir for a specific system. The following routines are for Version 7 and System V UNIX systems; they use the directory information in the header <sys/dir.h>, which looks like this:

```
#ifndef DIRSIZ
#define DIRSIZ   14
#endif
struct direct    /* directory entry */
{
    ino_t d_ino;              /* inode number */
    char  d_name[DIRSIZ]; /* long name does not have '\0' */
};
```

Some versions of the system permit much longer names and have a more complicated directory structure.

The type ino_t is a typedef that describes the index into the inode list. It happens to be unsigned short on the system we use regularly, but this is not the sort of information to embed in a program; it might be different on a different system, so the typedef is better. A complete set of "system" types is found in <sys/types.h>.

opendir opens the directory, verifies that the file is a directory (this time by the system call fstat, which is like stat except that it applies to a file descriptor), allocates a directory structure, and records the information:

```
int fstat(int fd, struct stat *);

/* opendir:  open a directory for readdir calls */
DIR *opendir(char *dirname)
{
    int fd;
    struct stat stbuf;
    DIR *dp;

    if ((fd = open(dirname, O_RDONLY, 0)) == -1
     || fstat(fd, &stbuf) == -1
     || (stbuf.st_mode & S_IFMT) != S_IFDIR
     || (dp = (DIR *) malloc(sizeof(DIR))) == NULL)
        return NULL;
    dp->fd = fd;
    return dp;
}
```

closedir closes the directory file and frees the space:

```
/* closedir:  close directory opened by opendir */
void closedir(DIR *dp)
{
    if (dp) {
        close(dp->fd);
        free(dp);
    }
}
```

Finally, `readdir` uses `read` to read each directory entry. If a directory
slot is not currently in use (because a file has been removed), the inode number
is zero, and this position is skipped. Otherwise, the inode number and name are
placed in a `static` structure and a pointer to that is returned to the user.
Each call overwrites the information from the previous one.

```
#include <sys/dir.h>    /* local directory structure */

/* readdir:  read directory entries in sequence */
Dirent *readdir(DIR *dp)
{
    struct direct dirbuf; /* local directory structure */
    static Dirent d;       /* return: portable structure */

    while (read(dp->fd, (char *) &dirbuf, sizeof(dirbuf))
                    == sizeof(dirbuf)) {
        if (dirbuf.d_ino == 0)    /* slot not in use */
            continue;
        d.ino = dirbuf.d_ino;
        strncpy(d.name, dirbuf.d_name, DIRSIZ);
        d.name[DIRSIZ] = '\0';  /* ensure termination */
        return &d;
    }
    return NULL;
}
```

Although the `fsize` program is rather specialized, it does illustrate a couple
of important ideas. First, many programs are not "system programs"; they
merely use information that is maintained by the operating system. For such
programs, it is crucial that the representation of the information appear only in
standard headers, and that programs include those files instead of embedding
the declarations in themselves. The second observation is that with care it is
possible to create an interface to system-dependent objects that is itself relatively system-independent. The functions of the standard library are good
examples.

Exercise 8-5. Modify the `fsize` program to print the other information contained in the inode entry. □

8.7 Example—A Storage Allocator

In Chapter 5, we presented a very limited stack-oriented storage allocator. The version that we will now write is unrestricted. Calls to `malloc` and `free` may occur in any order; `malloc` calls upon the operating system to obtain more memory as necessary. These routines illustrate some of the considerations involved in writing machine-dependent code in a relatively machine-independent way, and also show a real-life application of structures, unions and `typedef`.

Rather than allocating from a compiled-in fixed-sized array, `malloc` will request space from the operating system as needed. Since other activities in the program may also request space without calling this allocator, the space that `malloc` manages may not be contiguous. Thus its free storage is kept as a list of free blocks. Each block contains a size, a pointer to the next block, and the space itself. The blocks are kept in order of increasing storage address, and the last block (highest address) points to the first.

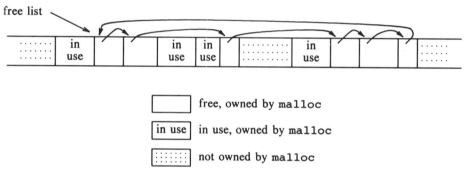

free, owned by `malloc`

in use, owned by `malloc`

not owned by `malloc`

When a request is made, the free list is scanned until a big-enough block is found. This algorithm is called "first fit," by contrast with "best fit," which looks for the smallest block that will satisfy the request. If the block is exactly the size requested it is unlinked from the list and returned to the user. If the block is too big, it is split, and the proper amount is returned to the user while the residue remains on the free list. If no big-enough block is found, another large chunk is obtained from the operating system and linked into the free list.

Freeing also causes a search of the free list, to find the proper place to insert the block being freed. If the block being freed is adjacent to a free block on either side, it is coalesced with it into a single bigger block, so storage does not become too fragmented. Determining adjacency is easy because the free list is maintained in order of increasing address.

One problem, which we alluded to in Chapter 5, is to ensure that the storage returned by `malloc` is aligned properly for the objects that will be stored in it. Although machines vary, for each machine there is a most restrictive type: if the most restrictive type can be stored at a particular address, all other types may be also. On some machines, the most restrictive type is a `double`; on others, `int` or `long` suffices.

A free block contains a pointer to the next block in the chain, a record of the size of the block, and then the free space itself; the control information at the beginning is called the "header." To simplify alignment, all blocks are multiples of the header size, and the header is aligned properly. This is achieved by a union that contains the desired header structure and an instance of the most restrictive alignment type, which we have arbitrarily made a `long`:

```
typedef long Align;   /* for alignment to long boundary */

union header {        /* block header: */
    struct {
        union header *ptr; /* next block if on free list */
        unsigned size;     /* size of this block */
    } s;
    Align x;          /* force alignment of blocks */
};

typedef union header Header;
```

The `Align` field is never used; it just forces each header to be aligned on a worst-case boundary.

In `malloc`, the requested size in characters is rounded up to the proper number of header-sized units; the block that will be allocated contains one more unit, for the header itself, and this is the value recorded in the `size` field of the header. The pointer returned by `malloc` points at the free space, not at the header itself. The user can do anything with the space requested, but if anything is written outside of the allocated space the list is likely to be scrambled.

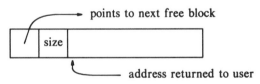

A block returned by `malloc`

The size field is necessary because the blocks controlled by `malloc` need not be contiguous—it is not possible to compute sizes by pointer arithmetic.

The variable `base` is used to get started. If `freep` is `NULL`, as it is at the first call of `malloc`, then a degenerate free list is created; it contains one block of size zero, and points to itself. In any case, the free list is then searched. The search for a free block of adequate size begins at the point (`freep`) where the last block was found; this strategy helps keep the list homogeneous. If a too-big block is found, the tail end is returned to the user; in this way the header of the original needs only to have its size adjusted. In all cases, the pointer returned to the user points to the free space within the block, which begins one unit beyond the header.

```
    static Header base;          /* empty list to get started */
    static Header *freep = NULL;      /* start of free list */

    /* malloc:  general-purpose storage allocator */
    void *malloc(unsigned nbytes)
    {
        Header *p, *prevp;
        Header *morecore(unsigned);
        unsigned nunits;

        nunits = (nbytes+sizeof(Header)-1)/sizeof(Header) + 1;
        if ((prevp = freep) == NULL) {  /* no free list yet */
            base.s.ptr = freep = prevp = &base;
            base.s.size = 0;
        }
        for (p = prevp->s.ptr; ; prevp = p, p = p->s.ptr) {
            if (p->s.size >= nunits) {     /* big enough */
                if (p->s.size == nunits)      /* exactly */
                    prevp->s.ptr = p->s.ptr;
                else {               /* allocate tail end */
                    p->s.size -= nunits;
                    p += p->s.size;
                    p->s.size = nunits;
                }
                freep = prevp;
                return (void *)(p+1);
            }
            if (p == freep)  /* wrapped around free list */
                if ((p = morecore(nunits)) == NULL)
                    return NULL;   /* none left */
        }
    }
```

The function `morecore` obtains storage from the operating system. The details of how it does this vary from system to system. Since asking the system for memory is a comparatively expensive operation, we don't want to do that on every call to `malloc`, so `morecore` requests at least NALLOC units; this larger block will be chopped up as needed. After setting the size field, `morecore` inserts the additional memory into the arena by calling `free`.

The UNIX system call `sbrk(n)` returns a pointer to n more bytes of storage. `sbrk` returns -1 if there was no space, even though NULL would have been a better design. The -1 must be cast to char * so it can be compared with the return value. Again, casts make the function relatively immune to the details of pointer representation on different machines. There is still one assumption, however, that pointers to different blocks returned by `sbrk` can be meaningfully compared. This is not guaranteed by the standard, which permits pointer comparisons only within an array. Thus this version of `malloc` is portable only among machines for which general pointer comparison is meaningful.

```
#define NALLOC  1024     /* minimum #units to request */

/* morecore:  ask system for more memory */
static Header *morecore(unsigned nu)
{
    char *cp, *sbrk(int);
    Header *up;

    if (nu < NALLOC)
        nu = NALLOC;
    cp = sbrk(nu * sizeof(Header));
    if (cp == (char *) -1)   /* no space at all */
        return NULL;
    up = (Header *) cp;
    up->s.size = nu;
    free((void *)(up+1));
    return freep;
}
```

free itself is the last thing. It scans the free list, starting at `freep`, look-ing for the place to insert the free block. This is either between two existing blocks or at one end of the list. In any case, if the block being freed is adjacent to either neighbor, the adjacent blocks are combined. The only troubles are keeping the pointers pointing to the right things and the sizes correct.

```
/* free:  put block ap in free list */
void free(void *ap)
{
    Header *bp, *p;

    bp = (Header *)ap - 1;   /* point to block header */
    for (p = freep; !(bp > p && bp < p->s.ptr); p = p->s.ptr)
        if (p >= p->s.ptr && (bp > p || bp < p->s.ptr))
            break;   /* freed block at start or end of arena */

    if (bp + bp->s.size == p->s.ptr) { /* join to upper nbr */
        bp->s.size += p->s.ptr->s.size;
        bp->s.ptr = p->s.ptr->s.ptr;
    } else
        bp->s.ptr = p->s.ptr;
    if (p + p->s.size == bp) {          /* join to lower nbr */
        p->s.size += bp->s.size;
        p->s.ptr = bp->s.ptr;
    } else
        p->s.ptr = bp;
    freep = p;
}
```

Although storage allocation is intrinsically machine-dependent, the code above illustrates how the machine dependencies can be controlled and confined to a very small part of the program. The use of `typedef` and `union` handles alignment (given that `sbrk` supplies an appropriate pointer). Casts arrange that pointer conversions are made explicit, and even cope with a badly-designed system interface. Even though the details here are related to storage allocation, the general approach is applicable to other situations as well.

Exercise 8-6. The standard library function `calloc(n,size)` returns a pointer to n objects of size `size`, with the storage initialized to zero. Write `calloc`, by calling `malloc` or by modifying it. □

Exercise 8-7. `malloc` accepts a size request without checking its plausibility; `free` believes that the block it is asked to free contains a valid size field. Improve these routines so they take more pains with error checking. □

Exercise 8-8. Write a routine `bfree(p,n)` that will free an arbitrary block p of n characters into the free list maintained by `malloc` and `free`. By using `bfree`, a user can add a static or external array to the free list at any time. □

APPENDIX A: **Reference Manual**

A1. Introduction

This manual describes the C language specified by the draft submitted to ANSI on 31 October, 1988, for approval as "American National Standard for Information Systems—Programming Language C, X3.159-1989." The manual is an interpretation of the proposed standard, not the Standard itself, although care has been taken to make it a reliable guide to the language.

For the most part, this document follows the broad outline of the Standard, which in turn follows that of the first edition of this book, although the organization differs in detail. Except for renaming a few productions, and not formalizing the definitions of the lexical tokens or the preprocessor, the grammar given here for the language proper is equivalent to that of the Standard.

> Throughout this manual, commentary material is indented and written in smaller type, as this is. Most often these comments highlight ways in which ANSI Standard C differs from the language defined by the first edition of this book, or from refinements subsequently introduced in various compilers.

A2. Lexical Conventions

A program consists of one or more *translation units* stored in files. It is translated in several phases, which are described in §A12. The first phases do low-level lexical transformations, carry out directives introduced by lines beginning with the # character, and perform macro definition and expansion. When the preprocessing of §A12 is complete, the program has been reduced to a sequence of tokens.

A2.1 Tokens

There are six classes of tokens: identifiers, keywords, constants, string literals, operators, and other separators. Blanks, horizontal and vertical tabs, newlines, formfeeds, and comments as described below (collectively, "white space") are ignored except as they separate tokens. Some white space is required to separate otherwise adjacent identifiers, keywords, and constants.

191

If the input stream has been separated into tokens up to a given character, the next token is the longest string of characters that could constitute a token.

A2.2 Comments

The characters /* introduce a comment, which terminates with the characters */. Comments do not nest, and they do not occur within string or character literals.

A2.3 Identifiers

An identifier is a sequence of letters and digits. The first character must be a letter; the underscore _ counts as a letter. Upper and lower case letters are different. Identifiers may have any length, and for internal identifiers, at least the first 31 characters are significant; some implementations may make more characters significant. Internal identifiers include preprocessor macro names and all other names that do not have external linkage (§A11.2). Identifiers with external linkage are more restricted: implementations may make as few as the first six characters as significant, and may ignore case distinctions.

A2.4 Keywords

The following identifiers are reserved for use as keywords, and may not be used otherwise:

auto	double	int	struct
break	else	long	switch
case	enum	register	typedef
char	extern	return	union
const	float	short	unsigned
continue	for	signed	void
default	goto	sizeof	volatile
do	if	static	while

Some implementations also reserve the words fortran and asm.

> The keywords const, signed, and volatile are new with the ANSI standard; enum and void are new since the first edition, but in common use; entry, formerly reserved but never used, is no longer reserved.

A2.5 Constants

There are several kinds of constants. Each has a data type; §A4.2 discusses the basic types.

constant:
    integer-constant
    character-constant
    floating-constant
    enumeration-constant

A2.5.1 Integer Constants

An integer constant consisting of a sequence of digits is taken to be octal if it begins with 0 (digit zero), decimal otherwise. Octal constants do not contain the digits 8 or 9. A sequence of digits preceded by 0x or 0X (digit zero) is taken to be a hexadecimal integer. The hexadecimal digits include a or A through f or F with values 10 through 15.

An integer constant may be suffixed by the letter u or U, to specify that it is unsigned. It may also be suffixed by the letter l or L to specify that it is long.

The type of an integer constant depends on its form, value and suffix. (See §A4 for a discussion of types.) If it is unsuffixed and decimal, it has the first of these types in which its value can be represented: int, long int, unsigned long int. If it is unsuffixed octal or hexadecimal, it has the first possible of these types: int, unsigned int, long int, unsigned long int. If it is suffixed by u or U, then unsigned int, unsigned long int. If it is suffixed by l or L, then long int, unsigned long int.

> The elaboration of the types of integer constants goes considerably beyond the first edition, which merely caused large integer constants to be long. The U suffixes are new.

A2.5.2 Character Constants

A character constant is a sequence of one or more characters enclosed in single quotes, as in 'x'. The value of a character constant with only one character is the numeric value of the character in the machine's character set at execution time. The value of a multi-character constant is implementation-defined.

Character constants do not contain the ' character or newlines; in order to represent them, and certain other characters, the following escape sequences may be used.

newline	NL (LF)	\n	backslash	\	\\
horizontal tab	HT	\t	question mark	?	\?
vertical tab	VT	\v	single quote	'	\'
backspace	BS	\b	double quote	"	\"
carriage return	CR	\r	octal number	*ooo*	*ooo*
formfeed	FF	\f	hex number	*hh*	\x*hh*
audible alert	BEL	\a			

The escape *ooo* consists of the backslash followed by 1, 2, or 3 octal digits, which are taken to specify the value of the desired character. A common example of this construction is \0 (not followed by a digit), which specifies the character NUL. The escape \x*hh* consists of the backslash, followed by x, followed by hexadecimal digits, which are taken to specify the value of the desired character. There is no limit on the number of digits, but the behavior is undefined if the resulting character value exceeds that of the largest character. For either octal or hexadecimal escape characters, if the implementation treats the char type as signed, the value is sign-extended as if cast to char type. If the character following the \ is not one of those specified, the behavior is undefined.

In some implementations, there is an extended set of characters that cannot be represented in the char type. A constant in this extended set is written with a preceding L, for example L'x', and is called a wide character constant. Such a constant has type wchar_t, an integral type defined in the standard header <stddef.h>. As with ordinary character constants, octal or hexadecimal escapes may be used; the effect is undefined if the specified value exceeds that representable with `wchar_t`.

> Some of these escape sequences are new, in particular the hexadecimal character representation. Extended characters are also new. The character sets commonly used in the Americas and western Europe can be encoded to fit in the `char` type; the main intent in adding `wchar_t` was to accommodate Asian languages.

A2.5.3 Floating Constants

A floating constant consists of an integer part, a decimal point, a fraction part, an `e` or `E`, an optionally signed integer exponent and an optional type suffix, one of `f`, `F`, `l`, or `L`. The integer and fraction parts both consist of a sequence of digits. Either the integer part or the fraction part (not both) may be missing; either the decimal point or the `e` and the exponent (not both) may be missing. The type is determined by the suffix; `F` or `f` makes it `float`, `L` or `l` makes it `long double`; otherwise it is `double`.

> Suffixes on floating constants are new.

A2.5.4 Enumeration Constants

Identifiers declared as enumerators (see §A8.4) are constants of type `int`.

A2.6 String Literals

A string literal, also called a string constant, is a sequence of characters surrounded by double quotes, as in `"..."`. A string has type "array of characters" and storage class `static` (see §A4 below) and is initialized with the given characters. Whether identical string literals are distinct is implementation-defined, and the behavior of a program that attempts to alter a string literal is undefined.

Adjacent string literals are concatenated into a single string. After any concatenation, a null byte `\0` is appended to the string so that programs that scan the string can find its end. String literals do not contain newline or double-quote characters; in order to represent them, the same escape sequences as for character constants are available.

As with character constants, string literals in an extended character set are written with a preceding `L`, as in `L"..."`. Wide-character string literals have type "array of `wchar_t`." Concatenation of ordinary and wide string literals is undefined.

> The specification that string literals need not be distinct, and the prohibition against modifying them, are new in the ANSI standard, as is the concatenation of adjacent string literals. Wide-character string literals are new.

A3. Syntax Notation

In the syntax notation used in this manual, syntactic categories are indicated by *italic* type, and literal words and characters in `typewriter` style. Alternative categories are usually listed on separate lines; in a few cases, a long set of narrow alternatives is presented on one line, marked by the phrase "one of." An optional terminal or nonterminal symbol carries the subscript "*opt*," so that, for example,

{ *expression*$_{opt}$ }

means an optional expression, enclosed in braces. The syntax is summarized in §A13.

> Unlike the grammar given in the first edition of this book, the one given here
> makes precedence and associativity of expression operators explicit.

A4. Meaning of Identifiers

Identifiers, or names, refer to a variety of things: functions; tags of structures, unions, and enumerations; members of structures or unions; enumeration constants; typedef names; and objects. An object, sometimes called a variable, is a location in storage, and its interpretation depends on two main attributes: its *storage class* and its *type*. The storage class determines the lifetime of the storage associated with the identified object; the type determines the meaning of the values found in the identified object. A name also has a scope, which is the region of the program in which it is known, and a linkage, which determines whether the same name in another scope refers to the same object or function. Scope and linkage are discussed in §A11.

A4.1 Storage Class

There are two storage classes: automatic and static. Several keywords, together with the context of an object's declaration, specify its storage class. Automatic objects are local to a block (§A9.3), and are discarded on exit from the block. Declarations within a block create automatic objects if no storage class specification is mentioned, or if the `auto` specifier is used. Objects declared `register` are automatic, and are (if possible) stored in fast registers of the machine.

Static objects may be local to a block or external to all blocks, but in either case retain their values across exit from and reentry to functions and blocks. Within a block, including a block that provides the code for a function, static objects are declared with the keyword `static`. The objects declared outside all blocks, at the same level as function definitions, are always static. They may be made local to a particular translation unit by use of the `static` keyword; this gives them *internal linkage*. They become global to an entire program by omitting an explicit storage class, or by using the keyword `extern`; this gives them *external linkage*.

A4.2 Basic Types

There are several fundamental types. The standard header `<limits.h>` described in Appendix B defines the largest and smallest values of each type in the local implementation. The numbers given in Appendix B show the smallest acceptable magnitudes.

Objects declared as characters (`char`) are large enough to store any member of the execution character set. If a genuine character from that set is stored in a `char` object, its value is equivalent to the integer code for the character, and is non-negative. Other quantities may be stored into `char` variables, but the available range of values, and especially whether the value is signed, is implementation-dependent.

Unsigned characters declared `unsigned char` consume the same amount of space as plain characters, but always appear non-negative; explicitly signed characters declared `signed char` likewise take the same space as plain characters.

> unsigned char type does not appear in the first edition of this book, but is in
> common use. signed char is new.

Besides the char types, up to three sizes of integer, declared short int, int, and
long int, are available. Plain int objects have the natural size suggested by the host
machine architecture; the other sizes are provided to meet special needs. Longer
integers provide at least as much storage as shorter ones, but the implementation may
make plain integers equivalent to either short integers, or long integers. The int types
all represent signed values unless specified otherwise.

Unsigned integers, declared using the keyword unsigned, obey the laws of arithmetic modulo 2^n where n is the number of bits in the representation, and thus arithmetic
on unsigned quantities can never overflow. The set of non-negative values that can be
stored in a signed object is a subset of the values that can be stored in the corresponding
unsigned object, and the representation for the overlapping values is the same.

Any of single precision floating point (float), double precision floating point
(double), and extra precision floating point (long double) may be synonymous, but
the ones later in the list are at least as precise as those before.

> long double is new. The first edition made long float equivalent to
> double; the locution has been withdrawn.

Enumerations are unique types that have integral values; associated with each
enumeration is a set of named constants (§A8.4). Enumerations behave like integers,
but it is common for a compiler to issue a warning when an object of a particular
enumeration type is assigned something other than one of its constants, or an expression
of its type.

Because objects of these types can be interpreted as numbers, they will be referred to
as *arithmetic* types. Types char, and int of all sizes, each with or without sign, and
also enumeration types, will collectively be called *integral* types. The types float,
double, and long double will be called *floating* types.

The void type specifies an empty set of values. It is used as the type returned by
functions that generate no value.

A4.3 Derived Types

Besides the basic types, there is a conceptually infinite class of derived types constructed from the fundamental types in the following ways:

   arrays of objects of a given type;

   functions returning objects of a given type;

   pointers to objects of a given type;

   structures containing a sequence of objects of various types;

   unions capable of containing any one of several objects of various types.

In general these methods of constructing objects can be applied recursively.

A4.4 Type Qualifiers

An object's type may have additional qualifiers. Declaring an object const
announces that its value will not be changed; declaring it volatile announces that it
has special properties relevant to optimization. Neither qualifier affects the range of
values or arithmetic properties of the object. Qualifiers are discussed in §A8.2.

A5. Objects and Lvalues

An *object* is a named region of storage; an *lvalue* is an expression referring to an object. An obvious example of an lvalue expression is an identifier with suitable type and storage class. There are operators that yield lvalues: for example, if E is an expression of pointer type, then *E is an lvalue expression referring to the object to which E points. The name "lvalue" comes from the assignment expression E1 = E2 in which the left operand E1 must be an lvalue expression. The discussion of each operator specifies whether it expects lvalue operands and whether it yields an lvalue.

A6. Conversions

Some operators may, depending on their operands, cause conversion of the value of an operand from one type to another. This section explains the result to be expected from such conversions. §A6.5 summarizes the conversions demanded by most ordinary operators; it will be supplemented as required by the discussion of each operator.

A6.1 Integral Promotion

A character, a short integer, or an integer bit-field, all either signed or not, or an object of enumeration type, may be used in an expression wherever an integer may be used. If an int can represent all the values of the original type, then the value is converted to int; otherwise the value is converted to unsigned int. This process is called *integral promotion*.

A6.2 Integral Conversions

Any integer is converted to a given unsigned type by finding the smallest non-negative value that is congruent to that integer, modulo one more than the largest value that can be represented in the unsigned type. In a two's complement representation, this is equivalent to left-truncation if the bit pattern of the unsigned type is narrower, and to zero-filling unsigned values and sign-extending signed values if the unsigned type is wider.

When any integer is converted to a signed type, the value is unchanged if it can be represented in the new type and is implementation-defined otherwise.

A6.3 Integer and Floating

When a value of floating type is converted to integral type, the fractional part is discarded; if the resulting value cannot be represented in the integral type, the behavior is undefined. In particular, the result of converting negative floating values to unsigned integral types is not specified.

When a value of integral type is converted to floating, and the value is in the representable range but is not exactly representable, then the result may be either the next higher or next lower representable value. If the result is out of range, the behavior is undefined.

A6.4 Floating Types

When a less precise floating value is converted to an equally or more precise floating type, the value is unchanged. When a more precise floating value is converted to a less precise floating type, and the value is within representable range, the result may be either the next higher or the next lower representable value. If the result is out of range, the behavior is undefined.

A6.5 Arithmetic Conversions

Many operators cause conversions and yield result types in a similar way. The effect is to bring operands into a common type, which is also the type of the result. This pattern is called the *usual arithmetic conversions*.

First, if either operand is `long double`, the other is converted to `long double`.
Otherwise, if either operand is `double`, the other is converted to `double`.
Otherwise, if either operand is `float`, the other is converted to `float`.
Otherwise, the integral promotions are performed on both operands; then, if either operand is `unsigned long int`, the other is converted to `unsigned long int`.
Otherwise, if one operand is `long int` and the other is `unsigned int`, the effect depends on whether a `long int` can represent all values of an `unsigned int`; if so, the `unsigned int` operand is converted to `long int`; if not, both are converted to `unsigned long int`.
Otherwise, if one operand is `long int`, the other is converted to `long int`.
Otherwise, if either operand is `unsigned int`, the other is converted to `unsigned int`.
Otherwise, both operands have type `int`.

> There are two changes here. First, arithmetic on `float` operands may be done in single precision, rather than double; the first edition specified that all floating arithmetic was double precision. Second, shorter unsigned types, when combined with a larger signed type, do not propagate the unsigned property to the result type; in the first edition, the unsigned always dominated. The new rules are slightly more complicated, but reduce somewhat the surprises that may occur when an unsigned quantity meets signed. Unexpected results may still occur when an unsigned expression is compared to a signed expression of the same size.

A6.6 Pointers and Integers

An expression of integral type may be added to or subtracted from a pointer; in such a case the integral expression is converted as specified in the discussion of the addition operator (§A7.7).

Two pointers to objects of the same type, in the same array, may be subtracted; the result is converted to an integer as specified in the discussion of the subtraction operator (§A7.7).

An integral constant expression with value 0, or such an expression cast to type `void *`, may be converted, by a cast, by assignment, or by comparison, to a pointer of any type. This produces a null pointer that is equal to another null pointer of the same type, but unequal to any pointer to a function or object.

Certain other conversions involving pointers are permitted, but have implementation-dependent aspects. They must be specified by an explicit type-conversion operator, or cast (§§A7.5 and A8.8).

A pointer may be converted to an integral type large enough to hold it; the required size is implementation-dependent. The mapping function is also implementation-dependent.

An object of integral type may be explicitly converted to a pointer. The mapping always carries a sufficiently wide integer converted from a pointer back to the same pointer, but is otherwise implementation-dependent.

A pointer to one type may be converted to a pointer to another type. The resulting pointer may cause addressing exceptions if the subject pointer does not refer to an object suitably aligned in storage. It is guaranteed that a pointer to an object may be converted to a pointer to an object whose type requires less or equally strict storage alignment and back again without change; the notion of "alignment" is implementation-dependent, but objects of the char types have least strict alignment requirements. As described in §A6.8, a pointer may also be converted to type void * and back again without change.

A pointer may be converted to another pointer whose type is the same except for the addition or removal of qualifiers (§§A4.4, A8.2) of the object type to which the pointer refers. If qualifiers are added, the new pointer is equivalent to the old except for restrictions implied by the new qualifiers. If qualifiers are removed, operations on the underlying object remain subject to the qualifiers in its actual declaration.

Finally, a pointer to a function may be converted to a pointer to another function type. Calling the function specified by the converted pointer is implementation-dependent; however, if the converted pointer is reconverted to its original type, the result is identical to the original pointer.

A6.7 Void

The (nonexistent) value of a void object may not be used in any way, and neither explicit nor implicit conversion to any non-void type may be applied. Because a void expression denotes a nonexistent value, such an expression may be used only where the value is not required, for example as an expression statement (§A9.2) or as the left operand of a comma operator (§A7.18).

An expression may be converted to type void by a cast. For example, a void cast documents the discarding of the value of a function call used as an expression statement.

> void did not appear in the first edition of this book, but has become common since.

A6.8 Pointers to Void

Any pointer to an object may be converted to type void * without loss of information. If the result is converted back to the original pointer type, the original pointer is recovered. Unlike the pointer-to-pointer conversions discussed in §A6.6, which generally require an explicit cast, pointers may be assigned to and from pointers of type void *, and may be compared with them.

> This interpretation of void * pointers is new; previously, char * pointers played the role of generic pointer. The ANSI standard specifically blesses the meeting of void * pointers with object pointers in assignments and relationals, while requiring explicit casts for other pointer mixtures.

A7. Expressions

The precedence of expression operators is the same as the order of the major subsections of this section, highest precedence first. Thus, for example, the expressions referred to as the operands of + (§A7.7) are those expressions defined in §§A7.1-A7.6. Within each subsection, the operators have the same precedence. Left- or right-associativity is specified in each subsection for the operators discussed therein. The grammar in §A13 incorporates the precedence and associativity of the operators.

The precedence and associativity of operators is fully specified, but the order of evaluation of expressions is, with certain exceptions, undefined, even if the subexpressions involve side effects. That is, unless the definition of an operator guarantees that its operands are evaluated in a particular order, the implementation is free to evaluate operands in any order, or even to interleave their evaluation. However, each operator combines the values produced by its operands in a way compatible with the parsing of the expression in which it appears.

> This rule revokes the previous freedom to reorder expressions with operators that are mathematically commutative and associative, but can fail to be computationally associative. The change affects only floating-point computations near the limits of their accuracy, and situations where overflow is possible.

The handling of overflow, divide check, and other exceptions in expression evaluation is not defined by the language. Most existing implementations of C ignore overflow in evaluation of signed integral expressions and assignments, but this behavior is not guaranteed. Treatment of division by 0, and all floating-point exceptions, varies among implementations; sometimes it is adjustable by a non-standard library function.

A7.1 Pointer Generation

If the type of an expression or subexpression is "array of T," for some type T, then the value of the expression is a pointer to the first object in the array, and the type of the expression is altered to "pointer to T." This conversion does not take place if the expression is the operand of the unary & operator, or of ++, --, sizeof, or as the left operand of an assignment operator or the . operator. Similarly, an expression of type "function returning T," except when used as the operand of the & operator, is converted to "pointer to function returning T."

A7.2 Primary Expressions

Primary expressions are identifiers, constants, strings, or expressions in parentheses.

> *primary-expression:*
>   *identifier*
>   *constant*
>   *string*
>   (*expression*)

An identifier is a primary expression, provided it has been suitably declared as discussed below. Its type is specified by its declaration. An identifier is an lvalue if it refers to an object (§A5) and if its type is arithmetic, structure, union, or pointer.

A constant is a primary expression. Its type depends on its form as discussed in §A2.5.

A string literal is a primary expression. Its type is originally "array of char" (for wide-character strings, "array of wchar_t"), but following the rule given in §A7.1, this is usually modified to "pointer to char" (wchar_t) and the result is a pointer to the first character in the string. The conversion also does not occur in certain initializers; see §A8.7.

A parenthesized expression is a primary expression whose type and value are identical to those of the unadorned expression. The presence of parentheses does not affect whether the expression is an lvalue.

A7.3 Postfix Expressions

The operators in postfix expressions group left to right.

> *postfix-expression:*
> > *primary-expression*
> > *postfix-expression* [*expression*]
> > *postfix-expression* (*argument-expression-list$_{opt}$*)
> > *postfix-expression* . *identifier*
> > *postfix-expression* -> *identifier*
> > *postfix-expression* ++
> > *postfix-expression* --
>
> *argument-expression-list:*
> > *assignment-expression*
> > *argument-expression-list* , *assignment-expression*

A7.3.1 Array References

A postfix expression followed by an expression in square brackets is a postfix expression denoting a subscripted array reference. One of the two expressions must have type "pointer to *T*", where *T* is some type, and the other must have integral type; the type of the subscript expression is *T*. The expression E1[E2] is identical (by definition) to *((E1)+(E2)). See §A8.6.2 for further discussion.

A7.3.2 Function Calls

A function call is a postfix expression, called the function designator, followed by parentheses containing a possibly empty, comma-separated list of assignment expressions (§A7.17), which constitute the arguments to the function. If the postfix expression consists of an identifier for which no declaration exists in the current scope, the identifier is implicitly declared as if the declaration

> extern int *identifier*();

had been given in the innermost block containing the function call. The postfix expression (after possible implicit declaration and pointer generation, §A7.1) must be of type "pointer to function returning *T*," for some type *T*, and the value of the function call has type *T*.

> In the first edition, the type was restricted to "function," and an explicit * operator was required to call through pointers to functions. The ANSI standard blesses the practice of some existing compilers by permitting the same syntax for calls to functions and to functions specified by pointers. The older syntax is still usable.

The term *argument* is used for an expression passed by a function call; the term *parameter* is used for an input object (or its identifier) received by a function definition, or described in a function declaration. The terms "actual argument (parameter)" and "formal argument (parameter)" respectively are sometimes used for the same distinction.

In preparing for the call to a function, a copy is made of each argument; all argument-passing is strictly by value. A function may change the values of its parameter objects, which are copies of the argument expressions, but these changes cannot affect the values of the arguments. However, it is possible to pass a pointer on the understanding that the function may change the value of the object to which the pointer points.

There are two styles in which functions may be declared. In the new style, the types of parameters are explicit and are part of the type of the function; such a declaration is also called a function prototype. In the old style, parameter types are not specified. Function declaration is discussed in §§A8.6.3 and A10.1.

If the function declaration in scope for a call is old-style, then default argument promotion is applied to each argument as follows: integral promotion (§A6.1) is performed on each argument of integral type, and each `float` argument is converted to `double`. The effect of the call is undefined if the number of arguments disagrees with the number of parameters in the definition of the function, or if the type of an argument after promotion disagrees with that of the corresponding parameter. Type agreement depends on whether the function's definition is new-style or old-style. If it is old-style, then the comparison is between the promoted type of the argument of the call, and the promoted type of the parameter; if the definition is new-style, the promoted type of the argument must be that of the parameter itself, without promotion.

If the function declaration in scope for a call is new-style, then the arguments are converted, as if by assignment, to the types of the corresponding parameters of the function's prototype. The number of arguments must be the same as the number of explicitly described parameters, unless the declaration's parameter list ends with the ellipsis notation (, ...). In that case, the number of arguments must equal or exceed the number of parameters; trailing arguments beyond the explicitly typed parameters suffer default argument promotion as described in the preceding paragraph. If the definition of the function is old-style, then the type of each parameter in the prototype visible at the call must agree with the corresponding parameter in the definition, after the definition parameter's type has undergone argument promotion.

> These rules are especially complicated because they must cater to a mixture of old- and new-style functions. Mixtures are to be avoided if possible.

The order of evaluation of arguments is unspecified; take note that various compilers differ. However, the arguments and the function designator are completely evaluated, including all side effects, before the function is entered. Recursive calls to any function are permitted.

A7.3.3 Structure References

A postfix expression followed by a dot followed by an identifier is a postfix expression. The first operand expression must be a structure or a union, and the identifier must name a member of the structure or union. The value is the named member of the structure or union, and its type is the type of the member. The expression is an lvalue if the first expression is an lvalue, and if the type of the second expression is not an array type.

A postfix expression followed by an arrow (built from – and >) followed by an identifier is a postfix expression. The first operand expression must be a pointer to a structure or a union, and the identifier must name a member of the structure or union. The result refers to the named member of the structure or union to which the pointer expression points, and the type is the type of the member; the result is an lvalue if the type is not an array type.

Thus the expression E1->MOS is the same as (*E1).MOS. Structures and unions are discussed in §A8.3.

> In the first edition of this book, it was already the rule that a member name in such an expression had to belong to the structure or union mentioned in the postfix expression; however, a note admitted that this rule was not firmly enforced. Recent compilers, and ANSI, do enforce it.

A7.3.4 Postfix Incrementation

A postfix expression followed by a ++ or -- operator is a postfix expression. The value of the expression is the value of the operand. After the value is noted, the operand is incremented (++) or decremented (--) by 1. The operand must be an lvalue; see the discussion of additive operators (§A7.7) and assignment (§A7.17) for further constraints on the operand and details of the operation. The result is not an lvalue.

A7.4 Unary Operators

Expressions with unary operators group right-to-left.

> *unary-expression:*
>   *postfix-expression*
>   ++ *unary-expression*
>   -- *unary-expression*
>   *unary-operator cast-expression*
>   sizeof *unary-expression*
>   sizeof (*type-name*)
>
> *unary-operator:* one of
>   &   *   +   -   ~   !

A7.4.1 Prefix Incrementation Operators

A unary expression preceded by a ++ or -- operator is a unary expression. The operand is incremented (++) or decremented (--) by 1. The value of the expression is the value after the incrementation (decrementation). The operand must be an lvalue; see the discussion of additive operators (§A7.7) and assignment (§A7.17) for further constraints on the operand and details of the operation. The result is not an lvalue.

A7.4.2 Address Operator

The unary & operator takes the address of its operand. The operand must be an lvalue referring neither to a bit-field nor to an object declared as register, or must be of function type. The result is a pointer to the object or function referred to by the lvalue. If the type of the operand is T, the type of the result is "pointer to T."

A7.4.3 Indirection Operator

The unary * operator denotes indirection, and returns the object or function to which its operand points. It is an lvalue if the operand is a pointer to an object of arithmetic, structure, union, or pointer type. If the type of the expression is "pointer to T," the type of the result is T.

A7.4.4 Unary Plus Operator

The operand of the unary + operator must have arithmetic type, and the result is the value of the operand. An integral operand undergoes integral promotion. The type of the result is the type of the promoted operand.

> The unary + is new with the ANSI standard. It was added for symmetry with unary –.

A7.4.5 Unary Minus Operator

The operand of the unary – operator must have arithmetic type, and the result is the negative of its operand. An integral operand undergoes integral promotion. The negative of an unsigned quantity is computed by subtracting the promoted value from the largest value of the promoted type and adding one; but negative zero is zero. The type of the result is the type of the promoted operand.

A7.4.6 One's Complement Operator

The operand of the ~ operator must have integral type, and the result is the one's complement of its operand. The integral promotions are performed. If the operand is unsigned, the result is computed by subtracting the value from the largest value of the promoted type. If the operand is signed, the result is computed by converting the promoted operand to the corresponding unsigned type, applying ~, and converting back to the signed type. The type of the result is the type of the promoted operand.

A7.4.7 Logical Negation Operator

The operand of the ! operator must have arithmetic type or be a pointer, and the result is 1 if the value of its operand compares equal to 0, and 0 otherwise. The type of the result is int.

A7.4.8 Sizeof Operator

The sizeof operator yields the number of bytes required to store an object of the type of its operand. The operand is either an expression, which is not evaluated, or a parenthesized type name. When sizeof is applied to a char, the result is 1; when applied to an array, the result is the total number of bytes in the array. When applied to a structure or union, the result is the number of bytes in the object, including any padding required to make the object tile an array: the size of an array of n elements is n times the size of one element. The operator may not be applied to an operand of function type, or of incomplete type, or to a bit-field. The result is an unsigned integral constant; the particular type is implementation-defined. The standard header <stddef.h> (see Appendix B) defines this type as size_t.

A7.5 Casts

A unary expression preceded by the parenthesized name of a type causes conversion of the value of the expression to the named type.

>   *cast-expression:*
>   *unary-expression*
>   (*type-name*) *cast-expression*

This construction is called a *cast*. Type names are described in §A8.8. The effects of conversions are described in §A6. An expression with a cast is not an lvalue.

A7.6 Multiplicative Operators

The multiplicative operators *, /, and % group left-to-right.

>   *multiplicative-expression:*
>   *cast-expression*
>   *multiplicative-expression* * *cast-expression*
>   *multiplicative-expression* / *cast-expression*
>   *multiplicative-expression* % *cast-expression*

The operands of * and / must have arithmetic type; the operands of % must have integral type. The usual arithmetic conversions are performed on the operands, and predict the type of the result.

The binary * operator denotes multiplication.

The binary / operator yields the quotient, and the % operator the remainder, of the division of the first operand by the second; if the second operand is 0, the result is undefined. Otherwise, it is always true that (a/b)*b + a%b is equal to a. If both operands are non-negative, then the remainder is non-negative and smaller than the divisor; if not, it is guaranteed only that the absolute value of the remainder is smaller than the absolute value of the divisor.

A7.7 Additive Operators

The additive operators + and − group left-to-right. If the operands have arithmetic type, the usual arithmetic conversions are performed. There are some additional type possibilities for each operator.

>   *additive-expression:*
>   *multiplicative-expression*
>   *additive-expression* + *multiplicative-expression*
>   *additive-expression* − *multiplicative-expression*

The result of the + operator is the sum of the operands. A pointer to an object in an array and a value of any integral type may be added. The latter is converted to an address offset by multiplying it by the size of the object to which the pointer points. The sum is a pointer of the same type as the original pointer, and points to another object in the same array, appropriately offset from the original object. Thus if P is a pointer to an object in an array, the expression P+1 is a pointer to the next object in the array. If the sum pointer points outside the bounds of the array, except at the first location beyond the high end, the result is undefined.

> The provision for pointers just beyond the end of an array is new. It legitimizes a common idiom for looping over the elements of an array.

The result of the − operator is the difference of the operands. A value of any integral type may be subtracted from a pointer, and then the same conversions and conditions as for addition apply.

If two pointers to objects of the same type are subtracted, the result is a signed integral value representing the displacement between the pointed-to objects; pointers to successive objects differ by 1. The type of the result depends on the implementation, but is defined as `ptrdiff_t` in the standard header `<stddef.h>`. The value is undefined unless the pointers point to objects within the same array; however if P points to the last member of an array, then `(P+1)-P` has value 1.

A7.8 Shift Operators

The shift operators `<<` and `>>` group left-to-right. For both operators, each operand must be integral, and is subject to the integral promotions. The type of the result is that of the promoted left operand. The result is undefined if the right operand is negative, or greater than or equal to the number of bits in the left expression's type.

> *shift-expression:*
> *additive-expression*
> *shift-expression* `<<` *additive-expression*
> *shift-expression* `>>` *additive-expression*

The value of `E1<<E2` is `E1` (interpreted as a bit pattern) left-shifted `E2` bits; in the absence of overflow, this is equivalent to multiplication by 2^{E2}. The value of `E1>>E2` is `E1` right-shifted `E2` bit positions. The right shift is equivalent to division by 2^{E2} if `E1` is unsigned or if it has a non-negative value; otherwise the result is implementation-defined.

A7.9 Relational Operators

The relational operators group left-to-right, but this fact is not useful; `a<b<c` is parsed as `(a<b)<c`, and `a<b` evaluates to either 0 or 1.

> *relational-expression:*
> *shift-expression*
> *relational-expression* `<` *shift-expression*
> *relational-expression* `>` *shift-expression*
> *relational-expression* `<=` *shift-expression*
> *relational-expression* `>=` *shift-expression*

The operators `<` (less), `>` (greater), `<=` (less or equal) and `>=` (greater or equal) all yield 0 if the specified relation is false and 1 if it is true. The type of the result is `int`. The usual arithmetic conversions are performed on arithmetic operands. Pointers to objects of the same type (ignoring any qualifiers) may be compared; the result depends on the relative locations in the address space of the pointed-to objects. Pointer comparison is defined only for parts of the same object: if two pointers point to the same simple object, they compare equal; if the pointers are to members of the same structure, pointers to objects declared later in the structure compare higher; if the pointers are to members of the same union, they compare equal; if the pointers refer to members of an array, the comparison is equivalent to comparison of the corresponding subscripts. If P points to the last member of an array, then P+1 compares higher than P, even though P+1 points outside the array. Otherwise, pointer comparison is undefined.

> These rules slightly liberalize the restrictions stated in the first edition, by permitting comparison of pointers to different members of a structure or union. They also legalize comparison with a pointer just off the end of an array.

A7.10 Equality Operators

> *equality-expression:*
>   *relational-expression*
>   *equality-expression* == *relational-expression*
>   *equality-expression* != *relational-expression*

The == (equal to) and the != (not equal to) operators are analogous to the relational operators except for their lower precedence. (Thus a<b == c<d is 1 whenever a<b and c<d have the same truth-value.)

   The equality operators follow the same rules as the relational operators, but permit additional possibilities: a pointer may be compared to a constant integral expression with value 0, or to a pointer to void. See §A6.6.

A7.11 Bitwise AND Operator

> *AND-expression:*
>   *equality-expression*
>   *AND-expression* & *equality-expression*

The usual arithmetic conversions are performed; the result is the bitwise AND function of the operands. The operator applies only to integral operands.

A7.12 Bitwise Exclusive OR Operator

> *exclusive-OR-expression:*
>   *AND-expression*
>   *exclusive-OR-expression* ^ *AND-expression*

The usual arithmetic conversions are performed; the result is the bitwise exclusive OR function of the operands. The operator applies only to integral operands.

A7.13 Bitwise Inclusive OR Operator

> *inclusive-OR-expression:*
>   *exclusive-OR-expression*
>   *inclusive-OR-expression* | *exclusive-OR-expression*

The usual arithmetic conversions are performed; the result is the bitwise inclusive OR function of its operands. The operator applies only to integral operands.

A7.14 Logical AND Operator

> *logical-AND-expression:*
>   *inclusive-OR-expression*
>   *logical-AND-expression* && *inclusive-OR-expression*

The && operator groups left-to-right. It returns 1 if both its operands compare unequal to zero, 0 otherwise. Unlike &, && guarantees left-to-right evaluation: the first operand is evaluated, including all side effects; if it is equal to 0, the value of the expression is 0. Otherwise, the right operand is evaluated, and if it is equal to 0, the expression's value is 0, otherwise 1.

   The operands need not have the same type, but each must have arithmetic type or be a pointer. The result is int.

A7.15 Logical OR Operator

> *logical-OR-expression:*
>   *logical-AND-expression*
>   *logical-OR-expression* ¦¦ *logical-AND-expression*

The ¦¦ operator groups left-to-right. It returns 1 if either of its operands compares unequal to zero, and 0 otherwise. Unlike ¦, ¦¦ guarantees left-to-right evaluation: the first operand is evaluated, including all side effects; if it is unequal to 0, the value of the expression is 1. Otherwise, the right operand is evaluated, and if it is unequal to 0, the expression's value is 1, otherwise 0.

The operands need not have the same type, but each must have arithmetic type or be a pointer. The result is int.

A7.16 Conditional Operator

> *conditional-expression:*
>   *logical-OR-expression*
>   *logical-OR-expression* ? *expression* : *conditional-expression*

The first expression is evaluated, including all side effects; if it compares unequal to 0, the result is the value of the second expression, otherwise that of third expression. Only one of the second and third operands is evaluated. If the second and third operands are arithmetic, the usual arithmetic conversions are performed to bring them to a common type, and that is the type of the result. If both are void, or structures or unions of the same type, or pointers to objects of the same type, the result has the common type. If one is a pointer and the other the constant 0, the 0 is converted to the pointer type, and the result has that type. If one is a pointer to void and the other is another pointer, the other pointer is converted to a pointer to void, and that is the type of the result.

In the type comparison for pointers, any type qualifiers (§A8.2) in the type to which the pointer points are insignificant, but the result type inherits qualifiers from both arms of the conditional.

A7.17 Assignment Expressions

There are several assignment operators; all group right-to-left.

> *assignment-expression:*
>   *conditional-expression*
>   *unary-expression assignment-operator assignment-expression*

> *assignment-operator:* one of
>   = *= /= %= += -= <<= >>= &= ^= ¦=

All require an lvalue as left operand, and the lvalue must be modifiable: it must not be an array, and must not have an incomplete type, or be a function. Also, its type must not be qualified with const; if it is a structure or union, it must not have any member or, recursively, submember qualified with const. The type of an assignment expression is that of its left operand, and the value is the value stored in the left operand after the assignment has taken place.

In the simple assignment with =, the value of the expression replaces that of the object referred to by the lvalue. One of the following must be true: both operands have arithmetic type, in which case the right operand is converted to the type of the left by the assignment; or both operands are structures or unions of the same type; or one operand is a pointer and the other is a pointer to void; or the left operand is a pointer and the right operand is a constant expression with value 0; or both operands are pointers to functions or objects whose types are the same except for the possible absence of const or volatile in the right operand.

An expression of the form E1 *op* = E2 is equivalent to E1 = E1 *op* (E2) except that E1 is evaluated only once.

A7.18 Comma Operator

> *expression:*
>> *assignment-expression*
>> *expression* , *assignment-expression*

A pair of expressions separated by a comma is evaluated left-to-right, and the value of the left expression is discarded. The type and value of the result are the type and value of the right operand. All side effects from the evaluation of the left operand are completed before beginning evaluation of the right operand. In contexts where comma is given a special meaning, for example in lists of function arguments (§A7.3.2) and lists of initializers (§A8.7), the required syntactic unit is an assignment expression, so the comma operator appears only in a parenthetical grouping; for example,

```
f(a, (t=3, t+2), c)
```

has three arguments, the second of which has the value 5.

A7.19 Constant Expressions

Syntactically, a constant expression is an expression restricted to a subset of operators:

> *constant-expression:*
>> *conditional-expression*

Expressions that evaluate to a constant are required in several contexts: after case, as array bounds and bit-field lengths, as the value of an enumeration constant, in initializers, and in certain preprocessor expressions.

Constant expressions may not contain assignments, increment or decrement operators, function calls, or comma operators, except in an operand of sizeof. If the constant expression is required to be integral, its operands must consist of integer, enumeration, character, and floating constants; casts must specify an integral type, and any floating constants must be cast to an integer. This necessarily rules out arrays, indirection, address-of, and structure member operations. (However, any operand is permitted for sizeof.)

More latitude is permitted for the constant expressions of initializers; the operands may be any type of constant, and the unary & operator may be applied to external or static objects, and to external or static arrays subscripted with a constant expression. The unary & operator can also be applied implicitly by appearance of unsubscripted arrays and functions. Initializers must evaluate either to a constant or to the address of a previously declared external or static object plus or minus a constant.

Less latitude is allowed for the integral constant expressions after #if; sizeof expressions, enumeration constants, and casts are not permitted. See §A12.5.

A8. Declarations

Declarations specify the interpretation given to each identifier; they do not necessarily reserve storage associated with the identifier. Declarations that reserve storage are called *definitions*. Declarations have the form

> *declaration:*
> *declaration-specifiers init-declarator-list_{opt}* ;

The declarators in the init-declarator-list contain the identifiers being declared; the declaration-specifiers consist of a sequence of type and storage class specifiers.

> *declaration-specifiers:*
> *storage-class-specifier declaration-specifiers_{opt}*
> *type-specifier declaration-specifiers_{opt}*
> *type-qualifier declaration-specifiers_{opt}*

> *init-declarator-list:*
> *init-declarator*
> *init-declarator-list , init-declarator*

> *init-declarator:*
> *declarator*
> *declarator = initializer*

Declarators will be discussed later (§A8.5); they contain the names being declared. A declaration must have at least one declarator, or its type specifier must declare a structure tag, a union tag, or the members of an enumeration; empty declarations are not permitted.

A8.1 Storage Class Specifiers

The storage class specifiers are:

> *storage-class-specifier:*
> ```
> auto
> register
> static
> extern
> typedef
> ```

The meanings of the storage classes were discussed in §A4.

The `auto` and `register` specifiers give the declared objects automatic storage class, and may be used only within functions. Such declarations also serve as definitions and cause storage to be reserved. A `register` declaration is equivalent to an `auto` declaration, but hints that the declared objects will be accessed frequently. Only a few objects are actually placed into registers, and only certain types are eligible; the restrictions are implementation-dependent. However, if an object is declared `register`, the unary & operator may not be applied to it, explicitly or implicitly.

> The rule that it is illegal to calculate the address of an object declared `register`, but actually taken to be `auto`, is new.

The `static` specifier gives the declared objects static storage class, and may be used either inside or outside functions. Inside a function, this specifier causes storage to be allocated, and serves as a definition; for its effect outside a function, see §A11.2.

A declaration with `extern`, used inside a function, specifies that the storage for the declared objects is defined elsewhere; for its effects outside a function, see §A11.2.

The `typedef` specifier does not reserve storage and is called a storage class specifier only for syntactic convenience; it is discussed in §A8.9.

At most one storage class specifier may be given in a declaration. If none is given, these rules are used: objects declared inside a function are taken to be `auto`; functions declared within a function are taken to be `extern`; objects and functions declared outside a function are taken to be static, with external linkage. See §§A10-A11.

A8.2 Type Specifiers

The type-specifiers are

> *type-specifier:*
> > `void`
> > `char`
> > `short`
> > `int`
> > `long`
> > `float`
> > `double`
> > `signed`
> > `unsigned`
> > *struct-or-union-specifier*
> > *enum-specifier*
> > *typedef-name*

At most one of the words `long` or `short` may be specified together with `int`; the meaning is the same if `int` is not mentioned. The word `long` may be specified together with `double`. At most one of `signed` or `unsigned` may be specified together with `int` or any of its `short` or `long` varieties, or with `char`. Either may appear alone, in which case `int` is understood. The `signed` specifier is useful for forcing `char` objects to carry a sign; it is permissible but redundant with other integral types.

Otherwise, at most one type-specifier may be given in a declaration. If the type-specifier is missing from a declaration, it is taken to be `int`.

Types may also be qualified, to indicate special properties of the objects being declared.

> *type-qualifier:*
> > `const`
> > `volatile`

Type qualifiers may appear with any type specifier. A `const` object may be initialized, but not thereafter assigned to. There are no implementation-independent semantics for `volatile` objects.

> The `const` and `volatile` properties are new with the ANSI standard. The purpose of `const` is to announce objects that may be placed in read-only memory, and perhaps to increase opportunities for optimization. The purpose of `volatile` is to force an implementation to suppress optimization that could otherwise occur. For example, for a machine with memory-mapped input/output, a pointer to a device register might be declared as a pointer to `volatile`, in order to prevent the compiler from removing apparently redundant references through the pointer. Except that it should diagnose explicit attempts to change `const` objects, a compiler may ignore these qualifiers.

A8.3 Structure and Union Declarations

A structure is an object consisting of a sequence of named members of various types. A union is an object that contains, at different times, any one of several members of various types. Structure and union specifiers have the same form.

> *struct-or-union-specifier:*
> *struct-or-union identifier$_{opt}$* { *struct-declaration-list* }
> *struct-or-union identifier*
>
> *struct-or-union:*
> struct
> union

A struct-declaration-list is a sequence of declarations for the members of the structure or union:

> *struct-declaration-list:*
> *struct-declaration*
> *struct-declaration-list struct-declaration*
>
> *struct-declaration:*
> *specifier-qualifier-list struct-declarator-list* ;
>
> *specifier-qualifier-list:*
> *type-specifier specifier-qualifier-list$_{opt}$*
> *type-qualifier specifier-qualifier-list$_{opt}$*
>
> *struct-declarator-list:*
> *struct-declarator*
> *struct-declarator-list* , *struct-declarator*

Usually, a struct-declarator is just a declarator for a member of a structure or union. A structure member may also consist of a specified number of bits. Such a member is also called a *bit-field*, or merely *field*; its length is set off from the declarator for the field name by a colon.

> *struct-declarator:*
> *declarator*
> *declarator$_{opt}$* : *constant-expression*

A type specifier of the form

> *struct-or-union identifier* { *struct-declaration-list* }

declares the identifier to be the *tag* of the structure or union specified by the list. A subsequent declaration in the same or an inner scope may refer to the same type by using the tag in a specifier without the list:

> *struct-or-union identifier*

If a specifier with a tag but without a list appears when the tag is not declared, an *incomplete type* is specified. Objects with an incomplete structure or union type may be mentioned in contexts where their size is not needed, for example in declarations (not definitions), for specifying a pointer, or for creating a typedef, but not otherwise. The type becomes complete on occurrence of a subsequent specifier with that tag, and containing a declaration list. Even in specifiers with a list, the structure or union type being declared is incomplete within the list, and becomes complete only at the } terminating the specifier.

A structure may not contain a member of incomplete type. Therefore, it is impossible to declare a structure or union containing an instance of itself. However, besides giving a name to the structure or union type, tags allow definition of self-referential structures; a structure or union may contain a pointer to an instance of itself, because pointers to incomplete types may be declared.

A very special rule applies to declarations of the form

      struct-or-union identifier ;

that declare a structure or union, but have no declaration list and no declarators. Even if the identifier is a structure or union tag already declared in an outer scope (§A11.1), this declaration makes the identifier the tag of a new, incompletely-typed structure or union in the current scope.

> This recondite rule is new with ANSI. It is intended to deal with mutually-recursive structures declared in an inner scope, but whose tags might already be declared in the outer scope.

A structure or union specifier with a list but no tag creates a unique type; it can be referred to directly only in the declaration of which it is a part.

The names of members and tags do not conflict with each other or with ordinary variables. A member name may not appear twice in the same structure or union, but the same member name may be used in different structures or unions.

> In the first edition of this book, the names of structure and union members were not associated with their parent. However, this association became common in compilers well before the ANSI standard.

A non-field member of a structure or union may have any object type. A field member (which need not have a declarator and thus may be unnamed) has type `int`, `unsigned int`, or `signed int`, and is interpreted as an object of integral type of the specified length in bits; whether an `int` field is treated as signed is implementation-dependent. Adjacent field members of structures are packed into implementation-dependent storage units in an implementation-dependent direction. When a field following another field will not fit into a partially-filled storage unit, it may be split between units, or the unit may be padded. An unnamed field with width 0 forces this padding, so that the next field will begin at the edge of the next allocation unit.

> The ANSI standard makes fields even more implementation-dependent than did the first edition. It is advisable to read the language rules for storing bit-fields as "implementation-dependent" without qualification. Structures with bit-fields may be used as a portable way of attempting to reduce the storage required for a structure (with the probable cost of increasing the instruction space, and time, needed to access the fields), or as a non-portable way to describe a storage layout known at the bit level. In the second case, it is necessary to understand the rules of the local implementation.

The members of a structure have addresses increasing in the order of their declarations. A non-field member of a structure is aligned at an addressing boundary depending on its type; therefore, there may be unnamed holes in a structure. If a pointer to a structure is cast to the type of a pointer to its first member, the result refers to the first member.

A union may be thought of as a structure all of whose members begin at offset 0 and whose size is sufficient to contain any of its members. At most one of the members can be stored in a union at any time. If a pointer to a union is cast to the type of a pointer to a member, the result refers to that member.

A simple example of a structure declaration is

```
struct tnode {
    char tword[20];
    int count;
    struct tnode *left;
    struct tnode *right;
};
```

which contains an array of 20 characters, an integer, and two pointers to similar structures. Once this declaration has been given, the declaration

```
struct tnode s, *sp;
```

declares s to be a structure of the given sort and sp to be a pointer to a structure of the given sort. With these declarations, the expression

```
sp->count
```

refers to the count field of the structure to which sp points;

```
s.left
```

refers to the left subtree pointer of the structure s; and

```
s.right->tword[0]
```

refers to the first character of the tword member of the right subtree of s.

In general, a member of a union may not be inspected unless the value of the union has been assigned using that same member. However, one special guarantee simplifies the use of unions: if a union contains several structures that share a common initial sequence, and if the union currently contains one of these structures, it is permitted to refer to the common initial part of any of the contained structures. For example, the following is a legal fragment:

```
union {
    struct {
        int type;
    } n;
    struct {
        int type;
        int intnode;
    } ni;
    struct {
        int type;
        float floatnode;
    } nf;
} u;
...
u.nf.type = FLOAT;
u.nf.floatnode = 3.14;
...
if (u.n.type == FLOAT)
    ... sin(u.nf.floatnode) ...
```

A8.4 Enumerations

Enumerations are unique types with values ranging over a set of named constants called enumerators. The form of an enumeration specifier borrows from that of structures and unions.

enum-specifier:
     enum *identifier$_{opt}$* { *enumerator-list* }
     enum *identifier*

enumerator-list:
     enumerator
     enumerator-list , *enumerator*

enumerator:
     identifier
     identifier = *constant-expression*

The identifiers in an enumerator list are declared as constants of type int, and may appear wherever constants are required. If no enumerators with = appear, then the values of the corresponding constants begin at 0 and increase by 1 as the declaration is read from left to right. An enumerator with = gives the associated identifier the value specified; subsequent identifiers continue the progression from the assigned value.

Enumerator names in the same scope must all be distinct from each other and from ordinary variable names, but the values need not be distinct.

The role of the identifier in the enum-specifier is analogous to that of the structure tag in a struct-specifier; it names a particular enumeration. The rules for enum-specifiers with and without tags and lists are the same as those for structure or union specifiers, except that incomplete enumeration types do not exist; the tag of an enum-specifier without an enumerator list must refer to an in-scope specifier with a list.

> Enumerations are new since the first edition of this book, but have been part of the language for some years.

A8.5 Declarators

Declarators have the syntax:

declarator:
     pointer$_{opt}$ direct-declarator

direct-declarator:
     identifier
     (*declarator*)
     direct-declarator [*constant-expression$_{opt}$*]
     direct-declarator (*parameter-type-list*)
     direct-declarator (*identifier-list$_{opt}$*)

pointer:
     * *type-qualifier-list$_{opt}$*
     * *type-qualifier-list$_{opt}$ pointer*

type-qualifier-list:
     type-qualifier
     type-qualifier-list type-qualifier

The structure of declarators resembles that of indirection, function, and array expressions; the grouping is the same.

A8.6 Meaning of Declarators

A list of declarators appears after a sequence of type and storage class specifiers. Each declarator declares a unique main identifier, the one that appears as the first alternative of the production for *direct-declarator*. The storage class specifiers apply directly to this identifier, but its type depends on the form of its declarator. A declarator is read as an assertion that when its identifier appears in an expression of the same form as the declarator, it yields an object of the specified type.

Considering only the type parts of the declaration specifiers (§A8.2) and a particular declarator, a declaration has the form "T D," where T is a type and D is a declarator. The type attributed to the identifier in the various forms of declarator is described inductively using this notation.

In a declaration T D where D is an unadorned identifier, the type of the identifier is T.

In a declaration T D where D has the form

(D1)

then the type of the identifier in D1 is the same as that of D. The parentheses do not alter the type, but may change the binding of complex declarators.

A8.6.1 Pointer Declarators

In a declaration T D where D has the form

* *type-qualifier-list*$_{opt}$ D1

and the type of the identifier in the declaration T D1 is "*type-modifier* T," the type of the identifier of D is "*type-modifier type-qualifier-list* pointer to T." Qualifiers following * apply to pointer itself, rather than to the object to which the pointer points.

For example, consider the declaration

int *ap[];

Here ap[] plays the role of D1; a declaration "int ap[]" (below) would give ap the type "array of int," the type-qualifier list is empty, and the type-modifier is "array of." Hence the actual declaration gives ap the type "array of pointers to int."

As other examples, the declarations

int i, *pi, *const cpi = &i;
const int ci = 3, *pci;

declare an integer i and a pointer to an integer pi. The value of the constant pointer cpi may not be changed; it will always point to the same location, although the value to which it refers may be altered. The integer ci is constant, and may not be changed (though it may be initialized, as here.) The type of pci is "pointer to const int," and pci itself may be changed to point to another place, but the value to which it points may not be altered by assigning through pci.

A8.6.2 Array Declarators

In a declaration T D where D has the form

D1[*constant-expression*$_{opt}$]

and the type of the identifier in the declaration T D1 is "*type-modifier* T," the type of the identifier of D is "*type-modifier* array of T." If the constant-expression is present, it must have integral type, and value greater than 0. If the constant expression specifying the bound is missing, the array has an incomplete type.

An array may be constructed from an arithmetic type, from a pointer, from a structure or union, or from another array (to generate a multi-dimensional array). Any type from which an array is constructed must be complete; it must not be an array or structure of incomplete type. This implies that for a multi-dimensional array, only the first dimension may be missing. The type of an object of incomplete array type is completed by another, complete, declaration for the object (§A10.2), or by initializing it (§A8.7). For example,

```
        float fa[17], *afp[17];
```

declares an array of `float` numbers and an array of pointers to `float` numbers. Also,

```
        static int x3d[3][5][7];
```

declares a static three-dimensional array of integers, with rank 3×5×7. In complete detail, `x3d` is an array of three items; each item is an array of five arrays; each of the latter arrays is an array of seven integers. Any of the expressions `x3d`, `x3d[i]`, `x3d[i][j]`, `x3d[i][j][k]` may reasonably appear in an expression. The first three have type "array," the last has type `int`. More specifically, `x3d[i][j]` is an array of 7 integers, and `x3d[i]` is an array of 5 arrays of 7 integers.

The array subscripting operation is defined so that `E1[E2]` is identical to `*(E1+E2)`. Therefore, despite its asymmetric appearance, subscripting is a commutative operation. Because of the conversion rules that apply to + and to arrays (§§A6.6, A7.1, A7.7), if `E1` is an array and `E2` an integer, then `E1[E2]` refers to the E2-th member of `E1`.

In the example, `x3d[i][j][k]` is equivalent to `*(x3d[i][j] + k)`. The first subexpression `x3d[i][j]` is converted by §A7.1 to type "pointer to array of integers;" by §A7.7, the addition involves multiplication by the size of an integer. It follows from the rules that arrays are stored by rows (last subscript varies fastest) and that the first subscript in the declaration helps determine the amount of storage consumed by an array, but plays no other part in subscript calculations.

A8.6.3 Function Declarators

In a new-style function declaration T D where D has the form

> D1(*parameter-type-list*)

and the type of the identifier in the declaration T D1 is "*type-modifier* T," the type of the identifier of D is "*type-modifier* function with arguments *parameter-type-list* returning T."

The syntax of the parameters is

> *parameter-type-list:*
> > *parameter-list*
> > *parameter-list* , . . .
>
> *parameter-list:*
> > *parameter-declaration*
> > *parameter-list* , *parameter-declaration*
>
> *parameter-declaration:*
> > *declaration-specifiers declarator*
> > *declaration-specifiers abstract-declarator$_{opt}$*

In the new-style declaration, the parameter list specifies the types of the parameters. As a special case, the declarator for a new-style function with no parameters has a parameter type list consisting solely of the keyword void. If the parameter type list ends with an ellipsis ", ...", then the function may accept more arguments than the number of parameters explicitly described; see §A7.3.2.

The types of parameters that are arrays or functions are altered to pointers, in accordance with the rules for parameter conversions; see §A10.1. The only storage class specifier permitted in a parameter's declaration specifier is register, and this specifier is ignored unless the function declarator heads a function definition. Similarly, if the declarators in the parameter declarations contain identifiers and the function declarator does not head a function definition, the identifiers go out of scope immediately. Abstract declarators, which do not mention the identifiers, are discussed in §A8.8.

In an old-style function declaration T D where D has the form

      D1 (*identifier-list$_{opt}$*)

and the type of the identifier in the declaration T D1 is "*type-modifier* T," the type of the identifier of D is "*type-modifier* function of unspecified arguments returning T." The parameters (if present) have the form

      identifier-list:
          identifier
          identifier-list , identifier

In the old-style declarator, the identifier list must be absent unless the declarator is used in the head of a function definition (§A10.1). No information about the types of the parameters is supplied by the declaration.

For example, the declaration

      int f( ), *fpi( ), (*pfi)( );

declares a function f returning an integer, a function fpi returning a pointer to an integer, and a pointer pfi to a function returning an integer. In none of these are the parameter types specified; they are old-style.

In the new-style declaration

      int strcpy(char *dest, const char *source), rand(void);

strcpy is a function returning int, with two arguments, the first a character pointer, and the second a pointer to constant characters. The parameter names are effectively comments. The second function rand takes no arguments and returns int.

> Function declarators with parameter prototypes are, by far, the most important language change introduced by the ANSI standard. They offer an advantage over the "old-style" declarators of the first edition by providing error-detection and coercion of arguments across function calls, but at a cost: turmoil and confusion during their introduction, and the necessity of accommodating both forms. Some syntactic ugliness was required for the sake of compatibility, namely void as an explicit marker of new-style functions without parameters.
>
> The ellipsis notation ", ..." for variadic functions is also new, and, together with the macros in the standard header <stdarg.h>, formalizes a mechanism that was officially forbidden but unofficially condoned in the first edition.
>
> These notations were adapted from the C++ language.

A8.7 Initialization

When an object is declared, its init-declarator may specify an initial value for the identifier being declared. The initializer is preceded by =, and is either an expression, or a list of initializers nested in braces. A list may end with a comma, a nicety for neat formatting.

> *initializer:*
>> *assignment-expression*
>> { *initializer-list* }
>> { *initializer-list* , }
>
> *initializer-list:*
>> *initializer*
>> *initializer-list* , *initializer*

All the expressions in the initializer for a static object or array must be constant expressions as described in §A7.19. The expressions in the initializer for an `auto` or `register` object or array must likewise be constant expressions if the initializer is a brace-enclosed list. However, if the initializer for an automatic object is a single expression, it need not be a constant expression, but must merely have appropriate type for assignment to the object.

> The first edition did not countenance initialization of automatic structures, unions, or arrays. The ANSI standard allows it, but only by constant constructions unless the initializer can be expressed by a simple expression.

A static object not explicitly initialized is initialized as if it (or its members) were assigned the constant 0. The initial value of an automatic object not explicitly initialized is undefined.

The initializer for a pointer or an object of arithmetic type is a single expression, perhaps in braces. The expression is assigned to the object.

The initializer for a structure is either an expression of the same type, or a brace-enclosed list of initializers for its members in order. Unnamed bit-field members are ignored, and are not initialized. If there are fewer initializers in the list than members of the structure, the trailing members are initialized with 0. There may not be more initializers than members.

The initializer for an array is a brace-enclosed list of initializers for its members. If the array has unknown size, the number of initializers determines the size of the array, and its type becomes complete. If the array has fixed size, the number of initializers may not exceed the number of members of the array; if there are fewer, the trailing members are initialized with 0.

As a special case, a character array may be initialized by a string literal; successive characters of the string initialize successive members of the array. Similarly, a wide character literal (§A2.6) may initialize an array of type `wchar_t`. If the array has unknown size, the number of characters in the string, including the terminating null character, determines its size; if its size is fixed, the number of characters in the string, not counting the terminating null character, must not exceed the size of the array.

The initializer for a union is either a single expression of the same type, or a brace-enclosed initializer for the first member of the union.

> The first edition did not allow initialization of unions. The "first-member" rule is clumsy, but is hard to generalize without new syntax. Besides allowing unions to be explicitly initialized in at least a primitive way, this ANSI rule makes definite the semantics of static unions not explicitly initialized.

An *aggregate* is a structure or array. If an aggregate contains members of aggregate type, the initialization rules apply recursively. Braces may be elided in the initialization as follows: if the initializer for an aggregate's member that is itself an aggregate begins with a left brace, then the succeeding comma-separated list of initializers initializes the members of the subaggregate; it is erroneous for there to be more initializers than members. If, however, the initializer for a subaggregate does not begin with a left brace, then only enough elements from the list are taken to account for the members of the subaggregate; any remaining members are left to initialize the next member of the aggregate of which the subaggregate is a part.

For example,

```
int x[] = { 1, 3, 5 };
```

declares and initializes x as a 1-dimensional array with three members, since no size was specified and there are three initializers.

```
float y[4][3] = {
    { 1, 3, 5 },
    { 2, 4, 6 },
    { 3, 5, 7 },
};
```

is a completely-bracketed initialization: 1, 3, and 5 initialize the first row of the array y[0], namely y[0][0], y[0][1], and y[0][2]. Likewise the next two lines initialize y[1] and y[2]. The initializer ends early, and therefore the elements of y[3] are initialized with 0. Precisely the same effect could have been achieved by

```
float y[4][3] = {
    1, 3, 5, 2, 4, 6, 3, 5, 7
};
```

The initializer for y begins with a left brace, but that for y[0] does not; therefore three elements from the list are used. Likewise the next three are taken successively for y[1] and then for y[2]. Also,

```
float y[4][3] = {
    { 1 }, { 2 }, { 3 }, { 4 }
};
```

initializes the first column of y (regarded as a two-dimensional array) and leaves the rest 0.

Finally,

```
char msg[] = "Syntax error on line %s\n";
```

shows a character array whose members are initialized with a string; its size includes the terminating null character.

A8.8 Type Names

In several contexts (to specify type conversions explicitly with a cast, to declare parameter types in function declarators, and as an argument of sizeof) it is necessary to supply the name of a data type. This is accomplished using a *type name*, which is syntactically a declaration for an object of that type omitting the name of the object.

> *type-name:*
>   *specifier-qualifier-list abstract-declarator*_{opt}
>
> *abstract-declarator:*
>   *pointer*
>   *pointer*_{opt} *direct-abstract-declarator*

> *direct-abstract-declarator:*
>   (*abstract-declarator*)
>   *direct-abstract-declarator*$_{opt}$ [*constant-expression*$_{opt}$]
>   *direct-abstract-declarator*$_{opt}$ (*parameter-type-list*$_{opt}$)

It is possible to identify uniquely the location in the abstract-declarator where the identifier would appear if the construction were a declarator in a declaration. The named type is then the same as the type of the hypothetical identifier. For example,

```
int
int *
int *[3]
int (*)[]
int *()
int (*[])(void)
```

name respectively the types "integer," "pointer to integer," "array of 3 pointers to integers," "pointer to an array of an unspecified number of integers," "function of unspecified parameters returning pointer to integer," and "array, of unspecified size, of pointers to functions with no parameters each returning an integer."

A8.9 Typedef

Declarations whose storage class specifier is `typedef` do not declare objects; instead they define identifiers that name types. These identifiers are called typedef names.

> *typedef-name:*
>   *identifier*

A `typedef` declaration attributes a type to each name among its declarators in the usual way (see §8.6). Thereafter, each such typedef name is syntactically equivalent to a type specifier keyword for the associated type.

For example, after

```
typedef long Blockno, *Blockptr;
typedef struct { double r, theta; } Complex;
```

the constructions

```
Blockno b;
extern Blockptr bp;
Complex z, *zp;
```

are legal declarations. The type of b is `long`, that of bp is "pointer to `long`," and that of z is the specified structure; zp is a pointer to such a structure.

`typedef` does not introduce new types, only synonyms for types that could be specified in another way. In the example, b has the same type as any other `long` object.

Typedef names may be redeclared in an inner scope, but a non-empty set of type specifiers must be given. For example,

```
extern Blockno;
```

does not redeclare `Blockno`, but

```
extern int Blockno;
```

does.

A8.10 Type Equivalence

Two type specifier lists are equivalent if they contain the same set of type specifiers, taking into account that some specifiers can be implied by others (for example, `long` alone implies `long int`). Structures, unions, and enumerations with different tags are distinct, and a tagless union, structure, or enumeration specifies a unique type.

Two types are the same if their abstract declarators (§A8.8), after expanding any `typedef` types, and deleting any function parameter identifiers, are the same up to equivalence of type specifier lists. Array sizes and function parameter types are significant.

A9. Statements

Except as described, statements are executed in sequence. Statements are executed for their effect, and do not have values. They fall into several groups.

> *statement:*
>> *labeled-statement*
>> *expression-statement*
>> *compound-statement*
>> *selection-statement*
>> *iteration-statement*
>> *jump-statement*

A9.1 Labeled Statements

Statements may carry label prefixes.

> *labeled-statement:*
>> *identifier* : *statement*
>> `case` *constant-expression* : *statement*
>> `default` : *statement*

A label consisting of an identifier declares the identifier. The only use of an identifier label is as a target of `goto`. The scope of the identifier is the current function. Because labels have their own name space, they do not interfere with other identifiers and cannot be redeclared. See §A11.1.

Case labels and default labels are used with the `switch` statement (§A9.4). The constant expression of `case` must have integral type.

Labels in themselves do not alter the flow of control.

A9.2 Expression Statement

Most statements are expression statements, which have the form

> *expression-statement:*
>> *expression$_{opt}$* ;

Most expression statements are assignments or function calls. All side effects from the expression are completed before the next statement is executed. If the expression is missing, the construction is called a null statement; it is often used to supply an empty body to an iteration statement or to place a label.

A9.3 Compound Statement

So that several statements can be used where one is expected, the compound statement (also called "block") is provided. The body of a function definition is a compound statement.

> *compound-statement:*
>   { *declaration-list$_{opt}$ statement-list$_{opt}$* }
>
> *declaration-list:*
>   *declaration*
>   *declaration-list declaration*
>
> *statement-list:*
>   *statement*
>   *statement-list statement*

If an identifier in the declaration-list was in scope outside the block, the outer declaration is suspended within the block (see §A11.1), after which it resumes its force. An identifier may be declared only once in the same block. These rules apply to identifiers in the same name space (§A11); identifiers in different name spaces are treated as distinct.

Initialization of automatic objects is performed each time the block is entered at the top, and proceeds in the order of the declarators. If a jump into the block is executed, these initializations are not performed. Initializations of `static` objects are performed only once, before the program begins execution.

A9.4 Selection Statements

Selection statements choose one of several flows of control.

> *selection-statement:*
>   `if` (*expression*) *statement*
>   `if` (*expression*) *statement* `else` *statement*
>   `switch` (*expression*) *statement*

In both forms of the `if` statement, the expression, which must have arithmetic or pointer type, is evaluated, including all side-effects, and if it compares unequal to 0, the first substatement is executed. In the second form, the second substatement is executed if the expression is 0. The `else` ambiguity is resolved by connecting an `else` with the last encountered `else`-less `if` at the same block nesting level.

The `switch` statement causes control to be transferred to one of several statements depending on the value of an expression, which must have integral type. The substatement controlled by a `switch` is typically compound. Any statement within the substatement may be labeled with one or more `case` labels (§A9.1). The controlling expression undergoes integral promotion (§A6.1), and the case constants are converted to the promoted type. No two of the case constants associated with the same switch may have the same value after conversion. There may also be at most one `default` label associated with a switch. Switches may be nested; a `case` or `default` label is associated with the smallest switch that contains it.

When the `switch` statement is executed, its expression is evaluated, including all side effects, and compared with each case constant. If one of the case constants is equal to the value of the expression, control passes to the statement of the matched `case` label. If no case constant matches the expression, and if there is a `default` label, control passes to the labeled statement. If no case matches, and if there is no `default`, then none of the substatements of the switch is executed.

> In the first edition of this book, the controlling expression of `switch`, and the case constants, were required to have `int` type.

A9.5 Iteration Statements

Iteration statements specify looping.

> *iteration-statement:*
> > `while` (*expression*) *statement*
> > `do` *statement* `while` (*expression*) `;`
> > `for` (*expression*$_{opt}$; *expression*$_{opt}$; *expression*$_{opt}$) *statement*

In the `while` and `do` statements, the substatement is executed repeatedly so long as the value of the expression remains unequal to 0; the expression must have arithmetic or pointer type. With `while`, the test, including all side effects from the expression, occurs before each execution of the statement; with `do`, the test follows each iteration.

In the `for` statement, the first expression is evaluated once, and thus specifies initialization for the loop. There is no restriction on its type. The second expression must have arithmetic or pointer type; it is evaluated before each iteration, and if it becomes equal to 0, the `for` is terminated. The third expression is evaluated after each iteration, and thus specifies a re-initialization for the loop. There is no restriction on its type. Side-effects from each expression are completed immediately after its evaluation. If the substatement does not contain `continue`, a statement

> `for` (*expression1* ; *expression2* ; *expression3*) *statement*

is equivalent to

> *expression1* ;
> `while` (*expression2*) {
> > *statement*
> > *expression3* ;
> }

Any of the three expressions may be dropped. A missing second expression makes the implied test equivalent to testing a non-zero constant.

A9.6 Jump Statements

Jump statements transfer control unconditionally.

> *jump-statement:*
> > `goto` *identifier* `;`
> > `continue` `;`
> > `break` `;`
> > `return` *expression*$_{opt}$ `;`

In the `goto` statement, the identifier must be a label (§A9.1) located in the current function. Control transfers to the labeled statement.

A `continue` statement may appear only within an iteration statement. It causes control to pass to the loop-continuation portion of the smallest enclosing such statement. More precisely, within each of the statements

```
while (...) {          do {                  for (...) {
   ...                    ...                    ...
contin: ;              contin: ;              contin: ;
}                      } while (...);         }
```

a `continue` not contained in a smaller iteration statement is the same as `goto contin`.

A `break` statement may appear only in an iteration statement or a `switch` statement, and terminates execution of the smallest enclosing such statement; control passes to the statement following the terminated statement.

A function returns to its caller by the `return` statement. When `return` is followed by an expression, the value is returned to the caller of the function. The expression is converted, as if by assignment, to the type returned by the function in which it appears.

Flowing off the end of a function is equivalent to a return with no expression. In either case, the returned value is undefined.

A10. External Declarations

The unit of input provided to the C compiler is called a translation unit; it consists of a sequence of external declarations, which are either declarations or function definitions.

> *translation-unit:*
> > *external-declaration*
> > *translation-unit external-declaration*
>
> *external-declaration:*
> > *function-definition*
> > *declaration*

The scope of external declarations persists to the end of the translation unit in which they are declared, just as the effect of declarations within blocks persists to the end of the block. The syntax of external declarations is the same as that of all declarations, except that only at this level may the code for functions be given.

A10.1 Function Definitions

Function definitions have the form

> *function-definition:*
> > *declaration-specifiers$_{opt}$ declarator declaration-list$_{opt}$ compound-statement*

The only storage-class specifiers allowed among the declaration specifiers are `extern` or `static`; see §A11.2 for the distinction between them.

A function may return an arithmetic type, a structure, a union, a pointer, or `void`, but not a function or an array. The declarator in a function declaration must specify explicitly that the declared identifier has function type; that is, it must contain one of the forms (see §A8.6.3)

> *direct-declarator (parameter-type-list)*
> *direct-declarator (identifier-list$_{opt}$)*

where the direct-declarator is an identifier or a parenthesized identifier. In particular, it must not achieve function type by means of a `typedef`.

In the first form, the definition is a new-style function, and its parameters, together with their types, are declared in its parameter type list; the declaration-list following the function's declarator must be absent. Unless the parameter type list consists solely of `void`, showing that the function takes no parameters, each declarator in the parameter type list must contain an identifier. If the parameter type list ends with "`, ...`" then the function may be called with more arguments than parameters; the `va_arg` macro mechanism defined in the standard header `<stdarg.h>` and described in Appendix B must be used to refer to the extra arguments. Variadic functions must have at least one named parameter.

In the second form, the definition is old-style: the identifier list names the parameters, while the declaration list attributes types to them. If no declaration is given for a parameter, its type is taken to be int. The declaration list must declare only parameters named in the list, initialization is not permitted, and the only storage-class specifier possible is `register`.

In both styles of function definition, the parameters are understood to be declared just after the beginning of the compound statement constituting the function's body, and thus the same identifiers must not be redeclared there (although they may, like other identifiers, be redeclared in inner blocks). If a parameter is declared to have type "array of *type*," the declaration is adjusted to read "pointer to *type*;" similarly, if a parameter is declared to have type "function returning *type*," the declaration is adjusted to read "pointer to function returning *type*." During the call to a function, the arguments are converted as necessary and assigned to the parameters; see §A7.3.2.

> New-style function definitions are new with the ANSI standard. There is also a small change in the details of promotion; the first edition specified that the declarations of float parameters were adjusted to read double. The difference becomes noticeable when a pointer to a parameter is generated within a function.

A complete example of a new-style function definition is

```
int max(int a, int b, int c)
{
    int m;

    m = (a > b) ? a : b;
    return (m > c) ? m : c;
}
```

Here int is the declaration specifier; max(int a, int b, int c) is the function's declarator, and { ... } is the block giving the code for the function. The corresponding old-style definition would be

```
int max(a, b, c)
int a, b, c;
{
    /* ... */
}
```

where now int max(a, b, c) is the declarator, and int a, b, c; is the declaration list for the parameters.

A10.2 External Declarations

External declarations specify the characteristics of objects, functions and other identifiers. The term "external" refers to their location outside functions, and is not directly connected with the extern keyword; the storage class for an externally-declared object may be left empty, or it may be specified as extern or static.

Several external declarations for the same identifier may exist within the same translation unit if they agree in type and linkage, and if there is at most one definition for the identifier.

Two declarations for an object or function are deemed to agree in type under the rules discussed in §A8.10. In addition, if the declarations differ because one type is an incomplete structure, union, or enumeration type (§A8.3) and the other is the corresponding completed type with the same tag, the types are taken to agree. Moreover, if one type is an incomplete array type (§A8.6.2) and the other is a completed array type, the types, if otherwise identical, are also taken to agree. Finally, if one type specifies an old-style function, and the other an otherwise identical new-style function, with parameter declarations, the types are taken to agree.

If the first external declaration for a function or object includes the `static` specifier, the identifier has *internal linkage*; otherwise it has *external linkage*. Linkage is discussed in §A11.2.

An external declaration for an object is a definition if it has an initializer. An external object declaration that does not have an initializer, and does not contain the `extern` specifier, is a *tentative definition*. If a definition for an object appears in a translation unit, any tentative definitions are treated merely as redundant declarations. If no definition for the object appears in the translation unit, all its tentative definitions become a single definition with initializer 0.

Each object must have exactly one definition. For objects with internal linkage, this rule applies separately to each translation unit, because internally-linked objects are unique to a translation unit. For objects with external linkage, it applies to the entire program.

> Although the one-definition rule is formulated somewhat differently in the first edition of this book, it is in effect identical to the one stated here. Some implementations relax it by generalizing the notion of tentative definition. In the alternate formulation, which is usual in UNIX systems and recognized as a common extension by the Standard, all the tentative definitions for an externally-linked object, throughout all the translation units of a program, are considered together instead of in each translation unit separately. If a definition occurs somewhere in the program, then the tentative definitions become merely declarations, but if no definition appears, then all its tentative definitions become a definition with initializer 0.

A11. Scope and Linkage

A program need not all be compiled at one time: the source text may be kept in several files containing translation units, and precompiled routines may be loaded from libraries. Communication among the functions of a program may be carried out both through calls and through manipulation of external data.

Therefore, there are two kinds of scope to consider: first, the *lexical scope* of an identifier, which is the region of the program text within which the identifier's characteristics are understood; and second, the scope associated with objects and functions with external linkage, which determines the connections between identifiers in separately compiled translation units.

A11.1 Lexical Scope

Identifiers fall into several name spaces that do not interfere with one another; the same identifier may be used for different purposes, even in the same scope, if the uses are in different name spaces. These classes are: objects, functions, typedef names, and enum constants; labels; tags of structures, unions, and enumerations; and members of each structure or union individually.

> These rules differ in several ways from those described in the first edition of this manual. Labels did not previously have their own name space; tags of structures and unions each had a separate space, and in some implementations

enumeration tags did as well; putting different kinds of tags into the same space is a new restriction. The most important departure from the first edition is that each structure or union creates a separate name space for its members, so that the same name may appear in several different structures. This rule has been common practice for several years.

The lexical scope of an object or function identifier in an external declaration begins at the end of its declarator and persists to the end of the translation unit in which it appears. The scope of a parameter of a function definition begins at the start of the block defining the function, and persists through the function; the scope of a parameter in a function declaration ends at the end of the declarator. The scope of an identifier declared at the head of a block begins at the end of its declarator, and persists to the end of the block. The scope of a label is the whole of the function in which it appears. The scope of a structure, union, or enumeration tag, or an enumeration constant, begins at its appearance in a type specifier, and persists to the end of the translation unit (for declarations at the external level) or to the end of the block (for declarations within a function).

If an identifier is explicitly declared at the head of a block, including the block constituting a function, any declaration of the identifier outside the block is suspended until the end of the block.

A11.2 Linkage

Within a translation unit, all declarations of the same object or function identifier with internal linkage refer to the same thing, and the object or function is unique to that translation unit. All declarations for the same object or function identifier with external linkage refer to the same thing, and the object or function is shared by the entire program.

As discussed in §A10.2, the first external declaration for an identifier gives the identifier internal linkage if the `static` specifier is used, external linkage otherwise. If a declaration for an identifier within a block does not include the `extern` specifier, then the identifier has no linkage and is unique to the function. If it does include `extern`, and an external declaration for the identifier is active in the scope surrounding the block, then the identifier has the same linkage as the external declaration, and refers to the same object or function; but if no external declaration is visible, its linkage is external.

A12. Preprocessing

A preprocessor performs macro substitution, conditional compilation, and inclusion of named files. Lines beginning with #, perhaps preceded by white space, communicate with this preprocessor. The syntax of these lines is independent of the rest of the language; they may appear anywhere and have effect that lasts (independent of scope) until the end of the translation unit. Line boundaries are significant; each line is analyzed individually (but see §A12.2 for how to adjoin lines). To the preprocessor, a token is any language token, or a character sequence giving a file name as in the `#include` directive (§A12.4); in addition, any character not otherwise defined is taken as a token. However, the effect of white space characters other than space and horizontal tab is undefined within preprocessor lines.

Preprocessing itself takes place in several logically successive phases that may, in a particular implementation, be condensed.

1. First, trigraph sequences as described in §A12.1 are replaced by their equivalents. Should the operating system environment require it, newline characters are introduced between the lines of the source file.

2. Each occurrence of a backslash character \ followed by a newline is deleted, thus splicing lines (§A12.2).

3. The program is split into tokens separated by white-space characters; comments are replaced by a single space. Then preprocessing directives are obeyed, and macros (§§A12.3-A12.10) are expanded.

4. Escape sequences in character constants and string literals (§§A2.5.2, A2.6) are replaced by their equivalents; then adjacent string literals are concatenated.

5. The result is translated, then linked together with other programs and libraries, by collecting the necessary programs and data, and connecting external function and object references to their definitions.

A12.1 Trigraph Sequences

The character set of C source programs is contained within seven-bit ASCII, but is a superset of the ISO 646-1983 Invariant Code Set. In order to enable programs to be represented in the reduced set, all occurrences of the following trigraph sequences are replaced by the corresponding single character. This replacement occurs before any other processing.

??=	#	??(	[	??<	{
??/	\	??)	]	??>	}
??'	^	??!	|	??-	~

No other such replacements occur.

Trigraph sequences are new with the ANSI standard.

A12.2 Line Splicing

Lines that end with the backslash character \ are folded by deleting the backslash and the following newline character. This occurs before division into tokens.

A12.3 Macro Definition and Expansion

A control line of the form

define *identifier token-sequence*

causes the preprocessor to replace subsequent instances of the identifier with the given sequence of tokens; leading and trailing white space around the token sequence is discarded. A second #define for the same identifier is erroneous unless the second token sequence is identical to the first, where all white space separations are taken to be equivalent.

A line of the form

define *identifier(identifier-list) token-sequence*

where there is no space between the first identifier and the (, is a macro definition with parameters given by the identifier list. As with the first form, leading and trailing white space around the token sequence is discarded, and the macro may be redefined only with a definition in which the number and spelling of parameters, and the token sequence, is identical.

A control line of the form

> # undef *identifier*

causes the identifier's preprocessor definition to be forgotten. It is not erroneous to apply #undef to an unknown identifier.

When a macro has been defined in the second form, subsequent textual instances of the macro identifier followed by optional white space, and then by (, a sequence of tokens separated by commas, and a) constitute a call of the macro. The arguments of the call are the comma-separated token sequences; commas that are quoted or protected by nested parentheses do not separate arguments. During collection, arguments are not macro-expanded. The number of arguments in the call must match the number of parameters in the definition. After the arguments are isolated, leading and trailing white space is removed from them. Then the token sequence resulting from each argument is substituted for each unquoted occurrence of the corresponding parameter's identifier in the replacement token sequence of the macro. Unless the parameter in the replacement sequence is preceded by #, or preceded or followed by ##, the argument tokens are examined for macro calls, and expanded as necessary, just before insertion.

Two special operators influence the replacement process. First, if an occurrence of a parameter in the replacement token sequence is immediately preceded by #, string quotes (") are placed around the corresponding parameter, and then both the # and the parameter identifier are replaced by the quoted argument. A \ character is inserted before each " or \ character that appears surrounding, or inside, a string literal or character constant in the argument.

Second, if the definition token sequence for either kind of macro contains a ## operator, then just after replacement of the parameters, each ## is deleted, together with any white space on either side, so as to concatenate the adjacent tokens and form a new token. The effect is undefined if invalid tokens are produced, or if the result depends on the order of processing of the ## operators. Also, ## may not appear at the beginning or end of a replacement token sequence.

In both kinds of macro, the replacement token sequence is repeatedly rescanned for more defined identifiers. However, once a given identifier has been replaced in a given expansion, it is not replaced if it turns up again during rescanning; instead it is left unchanged.

Even if the final value of a macro expansion begins with #, it is not taken to be a preprocessing directive.

> The details of the macro-expansion process are described more precisely in the ANSI standard than in the first edition. The most important change is the addition of the # and ## operators, which make quotation and concatenation admissible. Some of the new rules, especially those involving concatenation, are bizarre. (See example below.)

For example, this facility may be used for "manifest constants," as in

```
#define TABSIZE 100
int table[TABSIZE];
```

The definition

```
#define ABSDIFF(a, b)  ((a)>(b) ? (a)-(b) : (b)-(a))
```

defines a macro to return the absolute value of the difference between its arguments. Unlike a function to do the same thing, the arguments and returned value may have any arithmetic type or even be pointers. Also, the arguments, which might have side effects, are evaluated twice, once for the test and once to produce the value.

Given the definition

```
#define tempfile(dir)    #dir "/%s"
```

the macro call `tempfile(/usr/tmp)` yields

```
"/usr/tmp" "/%s"
```

which will subsequently be catenated into a single string. After

```
#define cat(x, y)    x ## y
```

the call `cat(var,123)` yields `var123`. However, the call `cat(cat(1,2),3))` is undefined: the presence of `##` prevents the arguments of the outer call from being expanded. Thus it produces the token string

```
cat  (  1  ,  2  )3
```

and `)3` (the catenation of the last token of the first argument with the first token of the second) is not a legal token. If a second level of macro definition is introduced,

```
#define xcat(x,y)    cat(x,y)
```

things work more smoothly; `xcat(xcat(1, 2), 3)` does produce `123`, because the expansion of `xcat` itself does not involve the `##` operator.

Likewise, `ABSDIFF(ABSDIFF(a,b),c)` produces the expected, fully-expanded result.

A12.4 File Inclusion

A control line of the form

```
# include <filename>
```

causes the replacement of that line by the entire contents of the file *filename*. The characters in the name *filename* must not include > or newline, and the effect is undefined if it contains any of ", ', \, or /*. The named file is searched for in a sequence of implementation-dependent places.

Similarly, a control line of the form

```
# include "filename"
```

searches first in association with the original source file (a deliberately implementation-dependent phrase), and if that search fails, then as if in the first form. The effect of using ', \, or /* in the filename remains undefined, but > is permitted.

Finally, a directive of the form

```
# include token-sequence
```

not matching one of the previous forms is interpreted by expanding the token sequence as for normal text; one of the two forms with <...> or "..." must result, and it is then treated as previously described.

`#include` files may be nested.

A12.5 Conditional Compilation

Parts of a program may be compiled conditionally, according to the following schematic syntax.

preprocessor-conditional:
    *if-line text elif-parts else-part*_{opt} `#endif`

if-line:
    `# if` *constant-expression*
    `# ifdef` *identifier*
    `# ifndef` *identifier*

elif-parts:
    elif-line text
    *elif-parts*_{opt}

elif-line:
    `# elif` *constant-expression*

else-part:
    else-line text

else-line:
    `# else`

Each of the directives (if-line, elif-line, else-line, and `#endif`) appears alone on a line. The constant expressions in `#if` and subsequent `#elif` lines are evaluated in order until an expression with a non-zero value is found; text following a line with a zero value is discarded. The text following the successful directive line is treated normally. "Text" here refers to any material, including preprocessor lines, that is not part of the conditional structure; it may be empty. Once a successful `#if` or `#elif` line has been found and its text processed, succeeding `#elif` and `#else` lines, together with their text, are discarded. If all the expressions are zero, and there is an `#else`, the text following the `#else` is treated normally. Text controlled by inactive arms of the conditional is ignored except for checking the nesting of conditionals.

The constant expression in `#if` and `#elif` is subject to ordinary macro replacement. Moreover, any expressions of the form
    `defined` *identifier*
or
    `defined (` *identifier* `)`
are replaced, before scanning for macros, by `1L` if the identifier is defined in the preprocessor, and by `0L` if not. Any identifiers remaining after macro expansion are replaced by `0L`. Finally, each integer constant is considered to be suffixed with `L`, so that all arithmetic is taken to be long or unsigned long.

The resulting constant expression (§A7.19) is restricted: it must be integral, and may not contain `sizeof`, a cast, or an enumeration constant.

The control lines
    `#ifdef` *identifier*
    `#ifndef` *identifier*
are equivalent to
    `# if defined` *identifier*
    `# if ! defined` *identifier*
respectively.

> `#elif` is new since the first edition, although it has been available in some preprocessors. The `defined` preprocessor operator is also new.

A12.6 Line Control

For the benefit of other preprocessors that generate C programs, a line in one of the forms

> # line *constant* *"filename"*
> # line *constant*

causes the compiler to believe, for purposes of error diagnostics, that the line number of the next source line is given by the decimal integer constant and the current input file is named by the identifier. If the quoted filename is absent, the remembered name does not change. Macros in the line are expanded before it is interpreted.

A12.7 Error Generation

A preprocessor line of the form

> # error *token-sequence*$_{opt}$

causes the processor to write a diagnostic message that includes the token sequence.

A12.8 Pragmas

A control line of the form

> # pragma *token-sequence*$_{opt}$

causes the processor to perform an implementation-dependent action. An unrecognized pragma is ignored.

A12.9 Null Directive

A preprocessor line of the form

> #

has no effect.

A12.10 Predefined Names

Several identifiers are predefined, and expand to produce special information. They, and also the preprocessor expression operator defined, may not be undefined or redefined.

__LINE__	A decimal constant containing the current source line number.
__FILE__	A string literal containing the name of the file being compiled.
__DATE__	A string literal containing the date of compilation, in the form "Mmm dd yyyy".
__TIME__	A string literal containing the time of compilation, in the form "hh:mm:ss".
__STDC__	The constant 1. It is intended that this identifier be defined to be 1 only in standard-conforming implementations.

> #error and #pragma are new with the ANSI standard; the predefined preprocessor macros are new, but some of them have been available in some implementations.

A13. Grammar

Below is a recapitulation of the grammar that was given throughout the earlier part of this appendix. It has exactly the same content, but is in a different order.

The grammar has undefined terminal symbols *integer-constant*, *character-constant*, *floating-constant*, *identifier*, *string*, and *enumeration-constant*; the `typewriter` style words and symbols are terminals given literally. This grammar can be transformed mechanically into input acceptable to an automatic parser-generator. Besides adding whatever syntactic marking is used to indicate alternatives in productions, it is necessary to expand the "one of" constructions, and (depending on the rules of the parser-generator) to duplicate each production with an *opt* symbol, once with the symbol and once without. With one further change, namely deleting the production *typedef-name: identifier* and making *typedef-name* a terminal symbol, this grammar is acceptable to the YACC parser-generator. It has only one conflict, generated by the `if-else` ambiguity.

> *translation-unit:*
>   *external-declaration*
>   *translation-unit external-declaration*
>
> *external-declaration:*
>   *function-definition*
>   *declaration*
>
> *function-definition:*
>   *declaration-specifiers$_{opt}$ declarator declaration-list$_{opt}$ compound-statement*
>
> *declaration:*
>   *declaration-specifiers init-declarator-list$_{opt}$* ;
>
> *declaration-list:*
>   *declaration*
>   *declaration-list declaration*
>
> *declaration-specifiers:*
>   *storage-class-specifier declaration-specifiers$_{opt}$*
>   *type-specifier declaration-specifiers$_{opt}$*
>   *type-qualifier declaration-specifiers$_{opt}$*
>
> *storage-class-specifier:* one of
>   `auto   register   static   extern   typedef`
>
> *type-specifier:* one of
>   `void   char   short   int   long   float   double   signed`
>   `unsigned` *struct-or-union-specifier* `` `  `` *enum-specifier   typedef-name*
>
> *type-qualifier:* one of
>   `const   volatile`
>
> *struct-or-union-specifier:*
>   *struct-or-union identifier$_{opt}$* { *struct-declaration-list* }
>   *struct-or-union identifier*
>
> *struct-or-union:* one of
>   `struct   union`
>
> *struct-declaration-list:*
>   *struct-declaration*
>   *struct-declaration-list struct-declaration*

init-declarator-list:
    init-declarator
    init-declarator-list , init-declarator

init-declarator:
    declarator
    declarator = initializer

struct-declaration:
    specifier-qualifier-list struct-declarator-list ;

specifier-qualifier-list:
    type-specifier specifier-qualifier-list$_{opt}$
    type-qualifier specifier-qualifier-list$_{opt}$

struct-declarator-list:
    struct-declarator
    struct-declarator-list , struct-declarator

struct-declarator:
    declarator
    declarator$_{opt}$: constant-expression

enum-specifier:
    enum *identifier$_{opt}$* { *enumerator-list* }
    enum *identifier*

enumerator-list:
    enumerator
    enumerator-list , enumerator

enumerator:
    identifier
    identifier = constant-expression

declarator:
    pointer$_{opt}$ direct-declarator

direct-declarator:
    identifier
    (*declarator*)
    direct-declarator [*constant-expression$_{opt}$*]
    direct-declarator (*parameter-type-list*)
    direct-declarator (*identifier-list$_{opt}$*)

pointer:
    * *type-qualifier-list$_{opt}$*
    * *type-qualifier-list$_{opt}$ pointer*

type-qualifier-list:
    type-qualifier
    type-qualifier-list type-qualifier

parameter-type-list:
    parameter-list
    parameter-list , ...

parameter-list:
    parameter-declaration
    parameter-list , parameter-declaration

parameter-declaration:
    declaration-specifiers declarator
    declaration-specifiers abstract-declarator$_{opt}$

identifier-list:
    identifier
    identifier-list , identifier

initializer:
    assignment-expression
    { *initializer-list* }
    { *initializer-list ,* }

initializer-list:
    initializer
    initializer-list , initializer

type-name:
    specifier-qualifier-list abstract-declarator$_{opt}$

abstract-declarator:
    pointer
    pointer$_{opt}$ direct-abstract-declarator

direct-abstract-declarator:
    (*abstract-declarator*)
    direct-abstract-declarator$_{opt}$ [*constant-expression$_{opt}$*]
    direct-abstract-declarator$_{opt}$ (*parameter-type-list$_{opt}$*)

typedef-name:
    identifier

statement:
    labeled-statement
    expression-statement
    compound-statement
    selection-statement
    iteration-statement
    jump-statement

labeled-statement:
    identifier : *statement*
    case *constant-expression* : *statement*
    default : *statement*

expression-statement:
    expression$_{opt}$;

compound-statement:
    { *declaration-list$_{opt}$ statement-list$_{opt}$* }

statement-list:
    statement
    statement-list statement

selection-statement:
    if (*expression*) *statement*
    if (*expression*) *statement* else *statement*
    switch (*expression*) *statement*

iteration-statement:
    `while` (*expression*) *statement*
    `do` *statement* `while` (*expression*) ;
    `for` ($expression_{opt}$; $expression_{opt}$; $expression_{opt}$) *statement*

jump-statement:
    `goto` *identifier* ;
    `continue` ;
    `break` ;
    `return` $expression_{opt}$;

expression:
    assignment-expression
    expression , *assignment-expression*

assignment-expression:
    conditional-expression
    unary-expression assignment-operator assignment-expression

assignment-operator: one of
    =   *=   /=   %=   +=   -=   <<=   >>=   &=   ^= |=

conditional-expression:
    logical-OR-expression
    logical-OR-expression ? *expression* : *conditional-expression*

constant-expression:
    conditional-expression

logical-OR-expression:
    logical-AND-expression
    logical-OR-expression || *logical-AND-expression*

logical-AND-expression:
    inclusive-OR-expression
    logical-AND-expression && *inclusive-OR-expression*

inclusive-OR-expression:
    exclusive-OR-expression
    inclusive-OR-expression | *exclusive-OR-expression*

exclusive-OR-expression:
    AND-expression
    exclusive-OR-expression ^ *AND-expression*

AND-expression:
    equality-expression
    AND-expression & *equality-expression*

equality-expression:
    relational-expression
    equality-expression == *relational-expression*
    equality-expression != *relational-expression*

relational-expression:
    shift-expression
    relational-expression < *shift-expression*
    relational-expression > *shift-expression*
    relational-expression <= *shift-expression*
    relational-expression >= *shift-expression*

shift-expression:
    additive-expression
    shift-expression << *additive-expression*
    shift-expression >> *additive-expression*

additive-expression:
    multiplicative-expression
    additive-expression + *multiplicative-expression*
    additive-expression − *multiplicative-expression*

multiplicative-expression:
    cast-expression
    multiplicative-expression * *cast-expression*
    multiplicative-expression / *cast-expression*
    multiplicative-expression % *cast-expression*

cast-expression:
    unary-expression
    (*type-name*) *cast-expression*

unary-expression:
    postfix-expression
    ++ *unary-expression*
    −− *unary-expression*
    unary-operator cast-expression
    sizeof *unary-expression*
    sizeof (*type-name*)

unary-operator: one of
    & * + − ~ !

postfix-expression:
    primary-expression
    postfix-expression [*expression*]
    postfix-expression (*argument-expression-list*$_{opt}$)
    postfix-expression . *identifier*
    postfix-expression −> *identifier*
    postfix-expression ++
    postfix-expression −−

primary-expression:
    identifier
    constant
    string
    (*expression*)

argument-expression-list:
    assignment-expression
    argument-expression-list , *assignment-expression*

constant:
    integer-constant
    character-constant
    floating-constant
    enumeration-constant

The following grammar for the preprocessor summarizes the structure of control lines, but is not suitable for mechanized parsing. It includes the symbol *text*, which means ordinary program text, non-conditional preprocessor control lines, or complete preprocessor conditional constructions.

control-line:
    `# define` *identifier token-sequence*
    `# define` *identifier* (*identifier* , ... , *identifier*) *token-sequence*
    `# undef` *identifier*
    `# include` *<filename>*
    `# include` *"filename"*
    `# include` *token-sequence*
    `# line` *constant "filename"*
    `# line` *constant*
    `# error` *token-sequence$_{opt}$*
    `# pragma` *token-sequence$_{opt}$*
    `#`
    preprocessor-conditional

preprocessor-conditional:
    if-line text elif-parts else-part$_{opt}$ `# endif`

if-line:
    `# if` *constant-expression*
    `# ifdef` *identifier*
    `# ifndef` *identifier*

elif-parts:
    elif-line text
    elif-parts$_{opt}$

elif-line:
    `# elif` *constant-expression*

else-part:
    else-line text

else-line:
    `# else`

APPENDIX B: **Standard Library**

This appendix is a summary of the library defined by the ANSI standard. The standard library is not part of the C language proper, but an environment that supports standard C will provide the function declarations and type and macro definitions of this library. We have omitted a few functions that are of limited utility or easily synthesized from others; we have omitted multi-byte characters; and we have omitted discussion of locale issues, that is, properties that depend on local language, nationality, or culture.

The functions, types and macros of the standard library are declared in standard *headers*:

`<assert.h>`	`<float.h>`	`<math.h>`	`<stdarg.h>`	`<stdlib.h>`
`<ctype.h>`	`<limits.h>`	`<setjmp.h>`	`<stddef.h>`	`<string.h>`
`<errno.h>`	`<locale.h>`	`<signal.h>`	`<stdio.h>`	`<time.h>`

A header can be accessed by

> `#include <header>`

Headers may be included in any order and any number of times. A header must be included outside of any external declaration or definition and before any use of anything it declares. A header need not be a source file.

External identifiers that begin with an underscore are reserved for use by the library, as are all other identifiers that begin with an underscore and an upper-case letter or another underscore.

B1. Input and Output: <stdio.h>

The input and output functions, types, and macros defined in `<stdio.h>` represent nearly one third of the library.

A *stream* is a source or destination of data that may be associated with a disk or other peripheral. The library supports text streams and binary streams, although on some systems, notably UNIX, these are identical. A text stream is a sequence of lines; each line has zero or more characters and is terminated by `'\n'`. An environment may need to convert a text stream to or from some other representation (such as mapping `'\n'` to carriage return and linefeed). A binary stream is a sequence of unprocessed bytes that record internal data, with the property that if it is written, then read back on the same system, it will compare equal.

A stream is connected to a file or device by *opening* it; the connection is broken by *closing* the stream. Opening a file returns a pointer to an object of type `FILE`, which records whatever information is necessary to control the stream. We will use "file pointer" and "stream" interchangeably when there is no ambiguity.

When a program begins execution, the three streams `stdin`, `stdout`, and `stderr` are already open.

B1.1 File Operations

The following functions deal with operations on files. The type `size_t` is the unsigned integral type produced by the `sizeof` operator.

`FILE *fopen(const char *filename, const char *mode)`
> `fopen` opens the named file, and returns a stream, or `NULL` if the attempt fails. Legal values for `mode` include

> | | |
> |---|---|
> | `"r"` | open text file for reading |
> | `"w"` | create text file for writing; discard previous contents if any |
> | `"a"` | append; open or create text file for writing at end of file |
> | `"r+"` | open text file for update (i.e., reading and writing) |
> | `"w+"` | create text file for update; discard previous contents if any |
> | `"a+"` | append; open or create text file for update, writing at end |

Update mode permits reading and writing the same file; `fflush` or a file-positioning function must be called between a read and a write or vice versa. If the mode includes b after the initial letter, as in `"rb"` or `"w+b"`, that indicates a binary file. Filenames are limited to `FILENAME_MAX` characters. At most `FOPEN_MAX` files may be open at once.

`FILE *freopen(const char *filename, const char *mode,`
                    `FILE *stream)`
> `freopen` opens the file with the specified mode and associates the stream with it. It returns `stream`, or `NULL` if an error occurs. `freopen` is normally used to change the files associated with `stdin`, `stdout`, or `stderr`.

`int fflush(FILE *stream)`
> On an output stream, `fflush` causes any buffered but unwritten data to be written; on an input stream, the effect is undefined. It returns `EOF` for a write error, and zero otherwise. `fflush(NULL)` flushes all output streams.

`int fclose(FILE *stream)`
> `fclose` flushes any unwritten data for `stream`, discards any unread buffered input, frees any automatically allocated buffer, then closes the stream. It returns `EOF` if any errors occurred, and zero otherwise.

`int remove(const char *filename)`
> `remove` removes the named file, so that a subsequent attempt to open it will fail. It returns non-zero if the attempt fails.

`int rename(const char *oldname, const char *newname)`
> `rename` changes the name of a file; it returns non-zero if the attempt fails.

```
FILE *tmpfile(void)
```
tmpfile creates a temporary file of mode "wb+" that will be automatically removed when closed or when the program terminates normally. tmpfile returns a stream, or NULL if it could not create the file.

```
char *tmpnam(char s[L_tmpnam])
```
tmpnam(NULL) creates a string that is not the name of an existing file, and returns a pointer to an internal static array. tmpnam(s) stores the string in s as well as returning it as the function value; s must have room for at least L_tmpnam characters. tmpnam generates a different name each time it is called; at most TMP_MAX different names are guaranteed during execution of the program. Note that tmpnam creates a name, not a file.

```
int setvbuf(FILE *stream, char *buf, int mode, size_t size)
```
setvbuf controls buffering for the stream; it must be called before reading, writing, or any other operation. A mode of _IOFBF causes full buffering, _IOLBF line buffering of text files, and _IONBF no buffering. If buf is not NULL, it will be used as the buffer; otherwise a buffer will be allocated. size determines the buffer size. setvbuf returns non-zero for any error.

```
void setbuf(FILE *stream, char *buf)
```
If buf is NULL, buffering is turned off for the stream. Otherwise, setbuf is equivalent to (void) setvbuf(stream, buf, _IOFBF, BUFSIZ).

B1.2 Formatted Output

The printf functions provide formatted output conversion.

```
int fprintf(FILE *stream, const char *format, ...)
```
fprintf converts and writes output to stream under the control of format. The return value is the number of characters written, or negative if an error occurred.

The format string contains two types of objects: ordinary characters, which are copied to the output stream, and conversion specifications, each of which causes conversion and printing of the next successive argument to fprintf. Each conversion specification begins with the character % and ends with a conversion character. Between the % and the conversion character there may be, in order:

- Flags (in any order), which modify the specification:

  -, which specifies left adjustment of the converted argument in its field.

  +, which specifies that the number will always be printed with a sign.

  space: if the first character is not a sign, a space will be prefixed.

  0: for numeric conversions, specifies padding to the field width with leading zeros.

  #, which specifies an alternate output form. For o, the first digit will be zero. For x or X, 0x or 0X will be prefixed to a non-zero result. For e, E, f, g, and G, the output will always have a decimal point; for g and G, trailing zeros will not be removed.

- A number specifying a minimum field width. The converted argument will be printed in a field at least this wide, and wider if necessary. If the converted argument has fewer characters than the field width it will be padded on the left (or right, if left adjustment has been requested) to make up the field width. The padding character is normally space, but is 0 if the zero padding flag is present.

- A period, which separates the field width from the precision.

- A number, the precision, that specifies the maximum number of characters to be printed from a string, or the number of digits to be printed after the decimal point for e, E, or f conversions, or the number of significant digits for g or G conversion, or the minimum number of digits to be printed for an integer (leading 0s will be added to make up the necessary width).

- A length modifier h, 1 (letter ell), or L. "h" indicates that the corresponding argument is to be printed as a short or unsigned short; "1" indicates that the argument is a long or unsigned long; "L" indicates that the argument is a long double.

Width or precision or both may be specified as *, in which case the value is computed by converting the next argument(s), which must be int.

The conversion characters and their meanings are shown in Table B-1. If the character after the % is not a conversion character, the behavior is undefined.

TABLE B-1. PRINTF CONVERSIONS

CHARACTER	ARGUMENT TYPE; CONVERTED TO
d, i	int; signed decimal notation.
o	int; unsigned octal notation (without a leading zero).
x, X	int; unsigned hexadecimal notation (without a leading 0x or 0X), using abcdef for 0x or ABCDEF for 0X.
u	int; unsigned decimal notation.
c	int; single character, after conversion to unsigned char.
s	char *; characters from the string are printed until a '\0' is reached or until the number of characters indicated by the precision have been printed.
f	double; decimal notation of the form [−]mmm.ddd, where the number of d's is specified by the precision. The default precision is 6; a precision of 0 suppresses the decimal point.
e, E	double; decimal notation of the form [−]m.dddddd e±xx or [−]m.dddddd E±xx, where the number of d's is specified by the precision. The default precision is 6; a precision of 0 suppresses the decimal point.
g, G	double; %e or %E is used if the exponent is less than −4 or greater than or equal to the precision; otherwise %f is used. Trailing zeros and a trailing decimal point are not printed.
p	void *; print as a pointer (implementation-dependent representation).
n	int *; the number of characters written so far by this call to printf is *written into* the argument. No argument is converted.
%	no argument is converted; print a %.

```
int printf(const char *format, ...)
   printf(...) is equivalent to fprintf(stdout,...).
```

```
int sprintf(char *s, const char *format, ...)
```
　　sprintf is the same as printf except that the output is written into the string s, terminated with '\0'. s must be big enough to hold the result. The return count does not include the '\0'.

```
vprintf(const char *format, va_list arg)
vfprintf(FILE *stream, const char *format, va_list arg)
vsprintf(char *s, const char *format, va_list arg)
```
　　The functions vprintf, vfprintf, and vsprintf are equivalent to the corresponding printf functions, except that the variable argument list is replaced by arg, which has been initialized by the va_start macro and perhaps va_arg calls. See the discussion of <stdarg.h> in Section B7.

B1.3 Formatted Input

　　The scanf functions deal with formatted input conversion.

```
int fscanf(FILE *stream, const char *format, ...)
```
　　fscanf reads from stream under control of format, and assigns converted values through subsequent arguments, *each of which must be a pointer*. It returns when format is exhausted. fscanf returns EOF if end of file or an error occurs before any conversion; otherwise it returns the number of input items converted and assigned.

　　The format string usually contains conversion specifications, which are used to direct interpretation of input. The format string may contain:

- Blanks or tabs, which are ignored.

- Ordinary characters (not %), which are expected to match the next non-white space character of the input stream.

- Conversion specifications, consisting of a %, an optional assignment suppression character *, an optional number specifying a maximum field width, an optional h, l, or L indicating the width of the target, and a conversion character.

　　A conversion specification determines the conversion of the next input field. Normally the result is placed in the variable pointed to by the corresponding argument. If assignment suppression is indicated by *, as in %*s, however, the input field is simply skipped; no assignment is made. An input field is defined as a string of non-white space characters; it extends either to the next white space character or until the field width, if specified, is exhausted. This implies that scanf will read across line boundaries to find its input, since newlines are white space. (White space characters are blank, tab, newline, carriage return, vertical tab, and formfeed.)

　　The conversion character indicates the interpretation of the input field. The corresponding argument must be a pointer. The legal conversion characters are shown in Table B-2.

　　The conversion characters d, i, n, o, u, and x may be preceded by h if the argument is a pointer to short rather than int, or by l (letter ell) if the argument is a pointer to long. The conversion characters e, f, and g may be preceded by l if a pointer to double rather than float is in the argument list, and by L if a pointer to a long double.

Table B-2. Scanf Conversions

Character	Input Data; Argument Type
d	decimal integer; `int *`.
i	integer; `int *`. The integer may be in octal (leading 0) or hexadecimal (leading 0x or 0X).
o	octal integer (with or without leading zero); `int *`.
u	unsigned decimal integer; `unsigned int *`.
x	hexadecimal integer (with or without leading 0x or 0X); `int *`.
c	characters; `char *`. The next input characters are placed in the indicated array, up to the number given by the width field; the default is 1. No `'\0'` is added. The normal skip over white space characters is suppressed in this case: to read the next non-white space character, use %1s.
s	string of non-white space characters (not quoted); `char *`, pointing to an array of characters large enough to hold the string and a terminating `'\0'` that will be added.
e, f, g	floating-point number; `float *`. The input format for `float`'s is an optional sign, a string of numbers possibly containing a decimal point, and an optional exponent field containing an E or e followed by a possibly signed integer.
p	pointer value as printed by `printf("%p")`; `void *`.
n	writes into the argument the number of characters read so far by this call; `int *`. No input is read. The converted item count is not incremented.
[...]	matches the longest non-empty string of input characters from the set between brackets; `char *`. A `'\0'` is added. `[ ]...]` includes] in the set.
[^...]	matches the longest non-empty string of input characters *not* from the set between brackets; `char *`. A `'\0'` is added. `[^]...]` includes] in the set.
%	literal %; no assignment is made.

```
int scanf(const char *format, ...)
```
scanf(...) is identical to fscanf(stdin,...).

```
int sscanf(char *s, const char *format, ...)
```
sscanf(s,...) is equivalent to scanf(...) except that the input characters are taken from the string s.

B1.4 Character Input and Output Functions

```
int fgetc(FILE *stream)
```
fgetc returns the next character of stream as an unsigned char (converted to an int), or EOF if end of file or error occurs.

```
char *fgets(char *s, int n, FILE *stream)
```
fgets reads at most the next n-1 characters into the array s, stopping if a newline is encountered; the newline is included in the array, which is terminated by '\0'. fgets returns s, or NULL if end of file or error occurs.

```
int fputc(int c, FILE *stream)
```
fputc writes the character c (converted to an unsigned char) on stream. It returns the character written, or EOF for error.

```
int fputs(const char *s, FILE *stream)
```
fputs writes the string s (which need not contain '\n') on stream; it returns non-negative, or EOF for an error.

```
int getc(FILE *stream)
```
getc is equivalent to fgetc except that if it is a macro, it may evaluate stream more than once.

```
int getchar(void)
```
getchar is equivalent to getc(stdin).

```
char *gets(char *s)
```
gets reads the next input line into the array s; it replaces the terminating newline with '\0'. It returns s, or NULL if end of file or error occurs.

```
int putc(int c, FILE *stream)
```
putc is equivalent to fputc except that if it is a macro, it may evaluate stream more than once.

```
int putchar(int c)
```
putchar(c) is equivalent to putc(c,stdout).

```
int puts(const char *s)
```
puts writes the string s and a newline to stdout. It returns EOF if an error occurs, non-negative otherwise.

```
int ungetc(int c, FILE *stream)
```
ungetc pushes c (converted to an unsigned char) back onto stream, where it will be returned on the next read. Only one character of pushback per stream is guaranteed. EOF may not be pushed back. ungetc returns the character pushed back, or EOF for error.

B1.5 Direct Input and Output Functions

```
size_t fread(void *ptr, size_t size, size_t nobj, FILE *stream)
```
fread reads from stream into the array ptr at most nobj objects of size size. fread returns the number of objects read; this may be less than the number requested. feof and ferror must be used to determine status.

```
size_t fwrite(const void *ptr, size_t size, size_t nobj,
                      FILE *stream)
```
fwrite writes, from the array ptr, nobj objects of size size on stream. It returns the number of objects written, which is less than nobj on error.

B1.6 File Positioning Functions

`int fseek(FILE *stream, long offset, int origin)`
    `fseek` sets the file position for `stream`; a subsequent read or write will access data beginning at the new position. For a binary file, the position is set to `offset` characters from `origin`, which may be `SEEK_SET` (beginning), `SEEK_CUR` (current position), or `SEEK_END` (end of file). For a text stream, `offset` must be zero, or a value returned by `ftell` (in which case `origin` must be `SEEK_SET`). `fseek` returns non-zero on error.

`long ftell(FILE *stream)`
    `ftell` returns the current file position for `stream`, or $-1L$ on error.

`void rewind(FILE *stream)`
    `rewind(fp)` is equivalent to `fseek(fp,0L,SEEK_SET); clearerr(fp)`.

`int fgetpos(FILE *stream, fpos_t *ptr)`
    `fgetpos` records the current position in `stream` in `*ptr`, for subsequent use by `fsetpos`. The type `fpos_t` is suitable for recording such values. `fgetpos` returns non-zero on error.

`int fsetpos(FILE *stream, const fpos_t *ptr)`
    `fsetpos` positions `stream` at the position recorded by `fgetpos` in `*ptr`. `fsetpos` returns non-zero on error.

B1.7 Error Functions

Many of the functions in the library set status indicators when error or end of file occur. These indicators may be set and tested explicitly. In addition, the integer expression `errno` (declared in `<errno.h>`) may contain an error number that gives further information about the most recent error.

`void clearerr(FILE *stream)`
    `clearerr` clears the end of file and error indicators for `stream`.

`int feof(FILE *stream)`
    `feof` returns non-zero if the end of file indicator for `stream` is set.

`int ferror(FILE *stream)`
    `ferror` returns non-zero if the error indicator for `stream` is set.

`void perror(const char *s)`
    `perror(s)` prints `s` and an implementation-defined error message corresponding to the integer in `errno`, as if by

        `fprintf(stderr, "%s: %s\n", s, "error message")`

    See `strerror` in Section B3.

B2. Character Class Tests: `<ctype.h>`

The header `<ctype.h>` declares functions for testing characters. For each function, the argument is an `int`, whose value must be `EOF` or representable as an `unsigned` char, and the return value is an int. The functions return non-zero (true) if the argument c satisfies the condition described, and zero if not.

isalnum(c)	isalpha(c) or isdigit(c) is true
isalpha(c)	isupper(c) or islower(c) is true
iscntrl(c)	control character
isdigit(c)	decimal digit
isgraph(c)	printing character except space
islower(c)	lower-case letter
isprint(c)	printing character including space
ispunct(c)	printing character except space or letter or digit
isspace(c)	space, formfeed, newline, carriage return, tab, vertical tab
isupper(c)	upper-case letter
isxdigit(c)	hexadecimal digit

In the seven-bit ASCII character set, the printing characters are 0x20 (' ') to 0x7E ('~'); the control characters are 0 (NUL) to 0x1F (US), and 0x7F (DEL).

In addition, there are two functions that convert the case of letters:

int tolower(int c)	convert c to lower case
int toupper(int c)	convert c to upper case

If c is an upper-case letter, tolower(c) returns the corresponding lower-case letter; otherwise it returns c. If c is a lower-case letter, toupper(c) returns the corresponding upper-case letter; otherwise it returns c.

B3. String Functions: <string.h>

There are two groups of string functions defined in the header <string.h>. The first have names beginning with str; the second have names beginning with mem. Except for memmove, the behavior is undefined if copying takes place between overlapping objects. Comparison functions treat arguments as unsigned char arrays.

In the following table, variables s and t are of type char *; cs and ct are of type const char *; n is of type size_t; and c is an int converted to char.

char *strcpy(s,ct)	copy string ct to string s, including '\0'; return s.
char *strncpy(s,ct,n)	copy at most n characters of string ct to s; return s. Pad with '\0's if t has fewer than n characters.
char *strcat(s,ct)	concatenate string ct to end of string s; return s.
char *strncat(s,ct,n)	concatenate at most n characters of string ct to string s, terminate s with '\0'; return s.
int strcmp(cs,ct)	compare string cs to string ct; return <0 if cs<ct, 0 if cs==ct, or >0 if cs>ct.
int strncmp(cs,ct,n)	compare at most n characters of string cs to string ct; return <0 if cs<ct, 0 if cs==ct, or >0 if cs>ct.
char *strchr(cs,c)	return pointer to first occurrence of c in cs or NULL if not present.
char *strrchr(cs,c)	return pointer to last occurrence of c in cs or NULL if not present.

`size_t strspn(cs,ct)`	return length of prefix of `cs` consisting of characters in `ct`.
`size_t strcspn(cs,ct)`	return length of prefix of `cs` consisting of characters *not* in `ct`.
`char *strpbrk(cs,ct)`	return pointer to first occurrence in string `cs` of any character of string `ct`, or `NULL` if none are present.
`char *strstr(cs,ct)`	return pointer to first occurrence of string `ct` in `cs`, or `NULL` if not present.
`size_t strlen(cs)`	return length of `cs`.
`char *strerror(n)`	return pointer to implementation-defined string corresponding to error `n`.
`char *strtok(s,ct)`	`strtok` searches `s` for tokens delimited by characters from `ct`; see below.

A sequence of calls of `strtok(s,ct)` splits `s` into tokens, each delimited by a character from `ct`. The first call in a sequence has a non-`NULL` `s`. It finds the first token in `s` consisting of characters not in `ct`; it terminates that by overwriting the next character of `s` with `'\0'` and returns a pointer to the token. Each subsequent call, indicated by a `NULL` value of `s`, returns the next such token, searching from just past the end of the previous one. `strtok` returns `NULL` when no further token is found. The string `ct` may be different on each call.

The `mem...` functions are meant for manipulating objects as character arrays; the intent is an interface to efficient routines. In the following table, `s` and `t` are of type `void *`; `cs` and `ct` are of type `const void *`; `n` is of type `size_t`; and `c` is an `int` converted to an `unsigned char`.

`void *memcpy(s,ct,n)`	copy `n` characters from `ct` to `s`, and return `s`.
`void *memmove(s,ct,n)`	same as `memcpy` except that it works even if the objects overlap.
`int memcmp(cs,ct,n)`	compare the first `n` characters of `cs` with `ct`; return as with `strcmp`.
`void *memchr(cs,c,n)`	return pointer to first occurrence of character `c` in `cs`, or `NULL` if not present among the first `n` characters.
`void *memset(s,c,n)`	place character `c` into first `n` characters of `s`, return `s`.

B4. Mathematical Functions: `<math.h>`

The header `<math.h>` declares mathematical functions and macros.

The macros `EDOM` and `ERANGE` (found in `<errno.h>`) are non-zero integral constants that are used to signal domain and range errors for the functions; `HUGE_VAL` is a positive `double` value. A *domain error* occurs if an argument is outside the domain over which the function is defined. On a domain error, `errno` is set to `EDOM`; the return value is implementation-dependent. A *range error* occurs if the result of the function cannot be represented as a `double`. If the result overflows, the function returns `HUGE_VAL` with the right sign, and `errno` is set to `ERANGE`. If the result underflows, the function returns zero; whether `errno` is set to `ERANGE` is implementation-defined.

In the following table, `x` and `y` are of type `double`, `n` is an `int`, and all functions return `double`. Angles for trigonometric functions are expressed in radians.

`sin(x)`	sine of x
`cos(x)`	cosine of x
`tan(x)`	tangent of x
`asin(x)`	$\sin^{-1}(x)$ in range $[-\pi/2, \pi/2]$, $x \in [-1, 1]$.
`acos(x)`	$\cos^{-1}(x)$ in range $[0, \pi]$, $x \in [-1, 1]$.
`atan(x)`	$\tan^{-1}(x)$ in range $[-\pi/2, \pi/2]$.
`atan2(y,x)`	$\tan^{-1}(y/x)$ in range $[-\pi, \pi]$.
`sinh(x)`	hyperbolic sine of x
`cosh(x)`	hyperbolic cosine of x
`tanh(x)`	hyperbolic tangent of x
`exp(x)`	exponential function e^x
`log(x)`	natural logarithm $\ln(x)$, $x > 0$.
`log10(x)`	base 10 logarithm $\log_{10}(x)$, $x > 0$.
`pow(x,y)`	x^y. A domain error occurs if `x=0` and `y`$\leqslant$`0`, or if `x`$\leqslant$`0` and `y` is not an integer.
`sqrt(x)`	$\sqrt{x}$, $x \geqslant 0$.
`ceil(x)`	smallest integer not less than `x`, as a `double`.
`floor(x)`	largest integer not greater than `x`, as a `double`.
`fabs(x)`	absolute value $\lvert x \rvert$
`ldexp(x,n)`	$x \cdot 2^n$
`frexp(x, int *exp)`	splits `x` into a normalized fraction in the interval $[1/2, 1)$, which is returned, and a power of 2, which is stored in `*exp`. If `x` is zero, both parts of the result are zero.
`modf(x, double *ip)`	splits `x` into integral and fractional parts, each with the same sign as `x`. It stores the integral part in `*ip`, and returns the fractional part.
`fmod(x,y)`	floating-point remainder of `x/y`, with the same sign as `x`. If `y` is zero, the result is implementation-defined.

B5. Utility Functions: <stdlib.h>

The header `<stdlib.h>` declares functions for number conversion, storage allocation, and similar tasks.

`double atof(const char *s)`
   `atof` converts `s` to `double`; it is equivalent to `strtod(s, (char**)NULL)`.

`int atoi(const char *s)`
   converts `s` to `int`; it is equivalent to `(int)strtol(s, (char**)NULL, 10)`.

`long atol(const char *s)`
   converts `s` to `long`; it is equivalent to `strtol(s, (char**)NULL, 10)`.

`double strtod(const char *s, char **endp)`
   `strtod` converts the prefix of `s` to `double`, ignoring leading white space; it stores a pointer to any unconverted suffix in `*endp` unless `endp` is `NULL`. If the answer

would overflow, HUGE_VAL is returned with the proper sign; if the answer would underflow, zero is returned. In either case errno is set to ERANGE.

long strtol(const char *s, char **endp, int base)

strtol converts the prefix of s to long, ignoring leading white space; it stores a pointer to any unconverted suffix in *endp unless endp is NULL. If base is between 2 and 36, conversion is done assuming that the input is written in that base. If base is zero, the base is 8, 10, or 16; leading 0 implies octal and leading 0x or 0X hexadecimal. Letters in either case represent digits from 10 to base−1; a leading 0x or 0X is permitted in base 16. If the answer would overflow, LONG_MAX or LONG_MIN is returned, depending on the sign of the result, and errno is set to ERANGE.

unsigned long strtoul(const char *s, char **endp, int base)

strtoul is the same as strtol except that the result is unsigned long and the error value is ULONG_MAX.

int rand(void)

rand returns a pseudo-random integer in the range 0 to RAND_MAX, which is at least 32767.

void srand(unsigned int seed)

srand uses seed as the seed for a new sequence of pseudo-random numbers. The initial seed is 1.

void *calloc(size_t nobj, size_t size)

calloc returns a pointer to space for an array of nobj objects, each of size size, or NULL if the request cannot be satisfied. The space is initialized to zero bytes.

void *malloc(size_t size)

malloc returns a pointer to space for an object of size size, or NULL if the request cannot be satisfied. The space is uninitialized.

void *realloc(void *p, size_t size)

realloc changes the size of the object pointed to by p to size. The contents will be unchanged up to the minimum of the old and new sizes. If the new size is larger, the new space is uninitialized. realloc returns a pointer to the new space, or NULL if the request cannot be satisfied, in which case *p is unchanged.

void free(void *p)

free deallocates the space pointed to by p; it does nothing if p is NULL. p must be a pointer to space previously allocated by calloc, malloc, or realloc.

void abort(void)

abort causes the program to terminate abnormally, as if by raise(SIGABRT).

void exit(int status)

exit causes normal program termination. atexit functions are called in reverse order of registration, open files are flushed, open streams are closed, and control is returned to the environment. How status is returned to the environment is implementation-dependent, but zero is taken as successful termination. The values EXIT_SUCCESS and EXIT_FAILURE may also be used.

```
int atexit(void (*fcn)(void))
```
   atexit registers the function fcn to be called when the program terminates normally; it returns non-zero if the registration cannot be made.

```
int system(const char *s)
```
   system passes the string s to the environment for execution. If s is NULL, system
   returns non-zero if there is a command processor. If s is not NULL, the return value
   is implementation-dependent.

```
char *getenv(const char *name)
```
   getenv returns the environment string associated with name, or NULL if no string
   exists. Details are implementation-dependent.

```
void *bsearch(const void *key, const void *base,
     size_t n, size_t size,
     int (*cmp)(const void *keyval, const void *datum))
```
   bsearch searches base[0]...base[n-1] for an item that matches *key. The
   function cmp must return negative if its first argument (the search key) is less than
   its second (a table entry), zero if equal, and positive if greater. Items in the array
   base must be in ascending order. bsearch returns a pointer to a matching item,
   or NULL if none exists.

```
void qsort(void *base, size_t n, size_t size,
                int (*cmp)(const void *, const void *))
```
   qsort sorts into ascending order an array base[0]...base[n-1] of objects of size
   size. The comparison function cmp is as in bsearch.

```
int abs(int n)
```
   abs returns the absolute value of its int argument.

```
long labs(long n)
```
   labs returns the absolute value of its long argument.

```
div_t div(int num, int denom)
```
   div computes the quotient and remainder of num/denom. The results are stored in
   the int members quot and rem of a structure of type div_t.

```
ldiv_t ldiv(long num, long denom)
```
   div computes the quotient and remainder of num/denom. The results are stored in
   the long members quot and rem of a structure of type ldiv_t.

B6. Diagnostics: <assert.h>

   The assert macro is used to add diagnostics to programs:
```
        void assert(int expression)
```
If *expression* is zero when
```
        assert(expression)
```
is executed, the assert macro will print on stderr a message, such as
        Assertion failed: *expression*, file *filename*, line *nnn*
It then calls abort to terminate execution. The source filename and line number come

from the preprocessor macros `__FILE__` and `__LINE__`.

If `NDEBUG` is defined at the time `<assert.h>` is included, the assert macro is ignored.

B7. Variable Argument Lists: `<stdarg.h>`

The header `<stdarg.h>` provides facilities for stepping through a list of function arguments of unknown number and type.

Suppose *lastarg* is the last named parameter of a function `f` with a variable number of arguments. Then declare within `f` a variable `ap` of type `va_list` that will point to each argument in turn:

```
va_list ap;
```

`ap` must be initialized once with the macro `va_start` before any unnamed argument is accessed:

```
va_start(va_list ap, lastarg);
```

Thereafter, each execution of the macro `va_arg` will produce a value that has the type and value of the next unnamed argument, and will also modify `ap` so the next use of `va_arg` returns the next argument:

```
type va_arg(va_list ap, type);
```

The macro

```
void va_end(va_list ap);
```

must be called once after the arguments have been processed but before `f` is exited.

B8. Non-local Jumps: `<setjmp.h>`

The declarations in `<setjmp.h>` provide a way to avoid the normal function call and return sequence, typically to permit an immediate return from a deeply nested function call.

int setjmp(jmp_buf env)

The macro `setjmp` saves state information in `env` for use by `longjmp`. The return is zero from a direct call of `setjmp`, and non-zero from a subsequent call of `longjmp`. A call to `setjmp` can only occur in certain contexts, basically the test of `if`, `switch`, and loops, and only in simple relational expressions.

```
if (setjmp(env) == 0)
    /* get here on direct call */
else
    /* get here by calling longjmp */
```

void longjmp(jmp_buf env, int val)

`longjmp` restores the state saved by the most recent call to `setjmp`, using information saved in `env`, and execution resumes as if the `setjmp` function had just executed and returned the non-zero value `val`. The function containing the `setjmp` must not have terminated. Accessible objects have the values they had when `longjmp` was called, except that non-volatile automatic variables in the function calling `setjmp` become undefined if they were changed after the `setjmp` call.

B9. Signals: <signal.h>

The header `<signal.h>` provides facilities for handling exceptional conditions that arise during execution, such as an interrupt signal from an external source or an error in execution.

```
void (*signal(int sig, void (*handler)(int)))(int)
```
    `signal` determines how subsequent signals will be handled. If `handler` is `SIG_DFL`, the implementation-defined default behavior is used; if it is `SIG_IGN`, the signal is ignored; otherwise, the function pointed to by `handler` will be called, with the argument of the type of signal. Valid signals include

SIGABRT	abnormal termination, e.g., from abort
SIGFPE	arithmetic error, e.g., zero divide or overflow
SIGILL	illegal function image, e.g., illegal instruction
SIGINT	interactive attention, e.g., interrupt
SIGSEGV	illegal storage access, e.g., access outside memory limits
SIGTERM	termination request sent to this program

`signal` returns the previous value of `handler` for the specific signal, or `SIG_ERR` if an error occurs.

When a signal `sig` subsequently occurs, the signal is restored to its default behavior; then the signal-handler function is called, as if by `(*handler)(sig)`. If the handler returns, execution will resume where it was when the signal occurred.

The initial state of signals is implementation-defined.

```
int raise(int sig)
```
    `raise` sends the signal `sig` to the program; it returns non-zero if unsuccessful.

B10. Date and Time Functions: <time.h>

The header `<time.h>` declares types and functions for manipulating date and time. Some functions process *local time*, which may differ from calendar time, for example because of time zone. `clock_t` and `time_t` are arithmetic types representing times, and `struct tm` holds the components of a calendar time:

int tm_sec;	seconds after the minute (0, 61)
int tm_min;	minutes after the hour (0, 59)
int tm_hour;	hours since midnight (0, 23)
int tm_mday;	day of the month (1, 31)
int tm_mon;	months *since* January (0, 11)
int tm_year;	years since 1900
int tm_wday;	days since Sunday (0, 6)
int tm_yday;	days since January 1 (0, 365)
int tm_isdst;	Daylight Saving Time flag

`tm_isdst` is positive if Daylight Saving Time is in effect, zero if not, and negative if the information is not available.

```
clock_t clock(void)
```
    `clock` returns the processor time used by the program since the beginning of execution, or –1 if unavailable. `clock()/CLOCKS_PER_SEC` is a time in seconds.

```
time_t time(time_t *tp)
```
time returns the current calendar time or −1 if the time is not available. If tp is not NULL, the return value is also assigned to *tp.

```
double difftime(time_t time2, time_t time1)
```
difftime returns time2−time1 expressed in seconds.

```
time_t mktime(struct tm *tp)
```
mktime converts the local time in the structure *tp into calendar time in the same representation used by time. The components will have values in the ranges shown. mktime returns the calendar time or −1 if it cannot be represented.

The next four functions return pointers to static objects that may be overwritten by other calls.

```
char *asctime(const struct tm *tp)
```
asctime converts the time in the structure *tp into a string of the form

```
        Sun Jan  3 15:14:13 1988\n\0
```

```
char *ctime(const time_t *tp)
```
ctime converts the calendar time *tp to local time; it is equivalent to

```
        asctime(localtime(tp))
```

```
struct tm *gmtime(const time_t *tp)
```
gmtime converts the calendar time *tp into Coordinated Universal Time (UTC). It returns NULL if UTC is not available. The name gmtime has historical significance.

```
struct tm *localtime(const time_t *tp)
```
localtime converts the calendar time *tp into local time.

```
size_t strftime(char *s, size_t smax, const char *fmt,
                    const struct tm *tp)
```
strftime formats date and time information from *tp into s according to fmt, which is analogous to a printf format. Ordinary characters (including the terminating '\0') are copied into s. Each %c is replaced as described below, using values appropriate for the local environment. No more than smax characters are placed into s. strftime returns the number of characters, excluding the '\0', or zero if more than smax characters were produced.

%a	abbreviated weekday name.
%A	full weekday name.
%b	abbreviated month name.
%B	full month name.
%c	local date and time representation.
%d	day of the month (01-31).
%H	hour (24-hour clock) (00-23).
%I	hour (12-hour clock) (01-12).
%j	day of the year (001-366).

%m	month (01-12).
%M	minute (00-59).
%p	local equivalent of AM or PM.
%S	second (00-61).
%U	week number of the year (Sunday as 1st day of week) (00-53).
%w	weekday (0-6, Sunday is 0).
%W	week number of the year (Monday as 1st day of week) (00-53).
%x	local date representation.
%X	local time representation.
%y	year without century (00-99).
%Y	year with century.
%Z	time zone name, if any.
%%	%.

B11. Implementation-defined Limits: <limits.h> and <float.h>

The header `<limits.h>` defines constants for the sizes of integral types. The values below are acceptable minimum magnitudes; larger values may be used.

CHAR_BIT	8	bits in a char
CHAR_MAX	UCHAR_MAX *or*	
	SCHAR_MAX	maximum value of char
CHAR_MIN	0 *or* SCHAR_MIN	minimum value of char
INT_MAX	+32767	maximum value of int
INT_MIN	-32767	minimum value of int
LONG_MAX	+2147483647	maximum value of long
LONG_MIN	-2147483647	minimum value of long
SCHAR_MAX	+127	maximum value of signed char
SCHAR_MIN	-127	minimum value of signed char
SHRT_MAX	+32767	maximum value of short
SHRT_MIN	-32767	minimum value of short
UCHAR_MAX	255	maximum value of unsigned char
UINT_MAX	65535	maximum value of unsigned int
ULONG_MAX	4294967295	maximum value of unsigned long
USHRT_MAX	65535	maximum value of unsigned short

The names in the table below, a subset of `<float.h>`, are constants related to floating-point arithmetic. When a value is given, it represents the minimum magnitude for the corresponding quantity. Each implementation defines appropriate values.

FLT_RADIX	2	radix of exponent representation, e.g., 2, 16
FLT_ROUNDS		floating-point rounding mode for addition
FLT_DIG	6	decimal digits of precision
FLT_EPSILON	1E-5	smallest number x such that $1.0 + x \neq 1.0$
FLT_MANT_DIG		number of base FLT_RADIX digits in mantissa
FLT_MAX	1E+37	maximum floating-point number
FLT_MAX_EXP		maximum n such that FLT_RADIX^n-1 is representable
FLT_MIN	1E-37	minimum normalized floating-point number
FLT_MIN_EXP		minimum n such that 10^n is a normalized number

`DBL_DIG`	10	decimal digits of precision
`DBL_EPSILON`	1E-9	smallest number x such that $1.0 + x \neq 1.0$
`DBL_MANT_DIG`		number of base `FLT_RADIX` digits in mantissa
`DBL_MAX`	1E+37	maximum `double` floating-point number
`DBL_MAX_EXP`		maximum n such that $\text{FLT\_RADIX}^n - 1$ is representable
`DBL_MIN`	1E-37	minimum normalized `double` floating-point number
`DBL_MIN_EXP`		minimum n such that 10^n is a normalized number

APPENDIX C: **Summary of Changes**

Since the publication of the first edition of this book, the definition of the C language has undergone changes. Almost all were extensions of the original language, and were carefully designed to remain compatible with existing practice; some repaired ambiguities in the original description; and some represent modifications that change existing practice. Many of the new facilities were announced in the documents accompanying compilers available from AT&T, and have subsequently been adopted by other suppliers of C compilers. More recently, the ANSI committee standardizing the language incorporated most of these changes, and also introduced other significant modifications. Their report was in part anticipated by some commercial compilers even before issuance of the formal C standard.

This Appendix summarizes the differences between the language defined by the first edition of this book, and that expected to be defined by the final Standard. It treats only the language itself, not its environment and library; although these are an important part of the Standard, there is little to compare with, because the first edition did not attempt to prescribe an environment or library.

- Preprocessing is more carefully defined in the Standard than in the first edition, and is extended: it is explicitly token based; there are new operators for catenation of tokens (##), and creation of strings (#); there are new control lines like #elif and #pragma; redeclaration of macros by the same token sequence is explicitly permitted; parameters inside strings are no longer replaced. Splicing of lines by \ is permitted everywhere, not just in strings and macro definitions. See §A12.

- The minimum significance of all internal identifiers is increased to 31 characters; the smallest mandated significance of identifiers with external linkage remains 6 monocase letters. (Many implementations provide more.)

- Trigraph sequences introduced by ?? allow representation of characters lacking in some character sets. Escapes for #\^[]{}|~ are defined; see §A12.1. Observe that the introduction of trigraphs may change the meaning of strings containing the sequence ??.

- New keywords (void, const, volatile, signed, enum) are introduced. The stillborn entry keyword is withdrawn.

- New escape sequences, for use within character constants and string literals, are defined. The effect of following \ by a character not part of an approved escape sequence is undefined. See §A2.5.2.

259

- Everyone's favorite trivial change: 8 and 9 are not octal digits.

- The Standard introduces a larger set of suffixes to make the type of constants explicit: `U` or `L` for integers, `F` or `L` for floating. It also refines the rules for the type of unsuffixed constants (§A2.5).

- Adjacent string literals are concatenated.

- There is a notation for wide-character string literals and character constants; see §A2.6.

- Characters, as well as other types, may be explicitly declared to carry, or not to carry, a sign by using the keywords `signed` or `unsigned`. The locution `long float` as a synonym for `double` is withdrawn, but `long double` may be used to declare an extra-precision floating quantity.

- For some time, type `unsigned char` has been available. The standard introduces the `signed` keyword to make signedness explicit for `char` and other integral objects.

- The `void` type has been available in most implementations for some years. The Standard introduces the use of the `void *` type as a generic pointer type; previously `char *` played this role. At the same time, explicit rules are enacted against mixing pointers and integers, and pointers of different type, without the use of casts.

- The Standard places explicit minima on the ranges of the arithmetic types, and mandates headers (`<limits.h>` and `<float.h>`) giving the characteristics of each particular implementation.

- Enumerations are new since the first edition of this book.

- The Standard adopts from C++ the notion of type qualifier, for example `const` (§A8.2).

- Strings are no longer modifiable, and so may be placed in read-only memory.

- The "usual arithmetic conversions" are changed, essentially from "for integers, `unsigned` always wins; for floating point, always use `double`" to "promote to the smallest capacious-enough type." See §A6.5.

- The old assignment operators like `=+` are truly gone. Also, assignment operators are now single tokens; in the first edition, they were pairs, and could be separated by white space.

- A compiler's license to treat mathematically associative operators as computationally associative is revoked.

- A unary `+` operator is introduced for symmetry with unary `-`.

- A pointer to a function may be used as a function designator without an explicit `*` operator. See §A7.3.2.

- Structures may be assigned, passed to functions, and returned by functions.

- Applying the address-of operator to arrays is permitted, and the result is a pointer to the array.

- The `sizeof` operator, in the first edition, yielded type `int`; subsequently, many implementations made it `unsigned`. The Standard makes its type explicitly implementation-dependent, but requires the type, `size_t`, to be defined in a standard header (<stddef.h>). A similar change occurs in the type (ptrdiff_t) of the difference between pointers. See §A7.4.8 and §A7.7.

- The address-of operator & may not be applied to an object declared register, even if the implementation chooses not to keep the object in a register.

- The type of a shift expression is that of the left operand; the right operand can't promote the result. See §A7.8.

- The Standard legalizes the creation of a pointer just beyond the end of an array, and allows arithmetic and relations on it; see §A7.7.

- The Standard introduces (borrowing from C++) the notion of a function prototype declaration that incorporates the types of the parameters, and includes an explicit recognition of variadic functions together with an approved way of dealing with them. See §§A7.3.2, A8.6.3, B7. The older style is still accepted, with restrictions.

- Empty declarations, which have no declarators and don't declare at least a structure, union, or enumeration, are forbidden by the Standard. On the other hand, a declaration with just a structure or union tag redeclares that tag even if it was declared in an outer scope.

- External data declarations without any specifiers or qualifiers (just a naked declarator) are forbidden.

- Some implementations, when presented with an extern declaration in an inner block, would export the declaration to the rest of the file. The Standard makes it clear that the scope of such a declaration is just the block.

- The scope of parameters is injected into a function's compound statement, so that variable declarations at the top level of the function cannot hide the parameters.

- The name spaces of identifiers are somewhat different. The Standard puts all tags in a single name space, and also introduces a separate name space for labels; see §A11.1. Also, member names are associated with the structure or union of which they are a part. (This has been common practice from some time.)

- Unions may be initialized; the initializer refers to the first member.

- Automatic structures, unions, and arrays may be initialized, albeit in a restricted way.

- Character arrays with an explicit size may be initialized by a string literal with exactly that many characters (the \0 is quietly squeezed out).

- The controlling expression, and the case labels, of a switch may have any integral type.

Index

263